Management Ethics

Ethics has become big business. But have businesses become ethical? This is a central question for today's managers.

Large scale corporate collapses, dishonest business dealings, corruption, and worker exploitation all engender heated debates. Managing ethics is critical in an era characterized by unprecedented corporate power and myriad competing ethical traditions. In such a complex context, the purpose of this book is to develop some insight into ethics as it relates to contemporary managerial practice.

Management Ethics presents differing critiques of ethics in the context of today's management challenges including:

- globalization
- sustainability
- consumerism
- neo-liberalism
- corporate collapses
- leadership
- corporate regulation

Bringing together analyses from the fields of sociology, philosophy, management, organization studies, public administration, socio-legal studies and education, this book demonstrates how the moral imperative of management is a core issue facing businesses in practice. It shows that it is the depth and sensitivity with which moral dilemmas are addressed which constitutes management ethics capable of addressing today's business challenges.

Stewart R. Clegg is Professor of Management at the University of Technology Sydney.
Carl Rhodes is Associate Professor of Management at the University of Technology Sydney.

Management Ethics

Contemporary contexts

Edited by
Stewart R. Clegg and
Carl Rhodes

LONDON AND NEW YORK

First published 2006
by Routledge
2 Park Square, Milton Park, Abingdon, Oxon OX14 4RN

Simultaneously published in the USA and Canada
by Routledge
270 Madison Ave, New York, NY 10016

Routledge is an imprint of the Taylor & Francis Group, an informa business

This book is a special project of the Academy of the Social Sciences,
funded by the Australian Research Council.

Typeset in Sabon and Bell Gothic by
HWA Text and Data Management, Tunbridge Wells
Printed and bound in Great Britain by
MPG Books Ltd, Bodmin

British Library Cataloguing in Publication Data
A catalogue record for this book is available from the British Library

Library of Congress Cataloging-in-Publication Data
Management ethics : contemporary contexts / edited by Stewart R. Clegg
and Carl Rhodes.
     p. cm.
   Includes bibliographical references and index.
   1. Business ethics. 2. Social responsibility of business.
   3. Management – Moral and ethical aspects. 4. Corporate
   governance – Moral and ethical aspects. I. Clegg, Stewart. II.
   Rhodes, Carl, 1967–
HF5387.M3343 2006
174'.4–dc22   2005034763

ISBN10: 0–415–39335–3 ISBN13: 978–0–415–39333–5 (hbk)
ISBN10: 0–415–39336–1 ISBN13: 978–0–415–39336–2 (pbk)

Contents

Contributors

Subhabrata Bobby Banerjee is Professor of Strategic Management and Director of Research at the International Graduate School of Management, University of South Australia, Adelaide. He has taught at the University of Massachusetts where he received his PhD, at the University of Wollongong where he headed the doctoral program, and at RMIT University where he was Director of the Doctor of Business Administration program. His research interests are in the areas of sustainable development, corporate environmentalism, socio-cultural aspects of globalization, postcolonial theories, and indigenous ecology. His work has appeared in many international journals including *Journal of Marketing*, *Organization Studies*, *Journal of Management Studies*, *Organization*, *Social Semiotics* and *Journal of Corporate Citizenship*.

Stewart R. Clegg is Professor at the University of Technology, Sydney, and Director of ICAN Research (Innovative Collaborations, Alliances and Networks Research), a Key University Research Centre. He also holds a Professorial position at Aston Business School UK, is a Visiting Professor at Maastricht University Business Faculty, and is an International Fellow in Discourse and Management Theory in the Centre of Comparative Social Studies, Free University of Amsterdam. He has recently published *Managing and Organizations: an introduction to theory and practice* (London: Sage, 2004, with Martin Kornberger and Tyrone Pitsis).

Stephen Cohen is founder and director of the graduate programs in professional ethics at the University of New South Wales. He is also Associate Professor of Philosophy. He has published widely in the areas of applied ethics, business and professional ethics, corporate governance, moral reasoning, and the philosophy of law. He was recently named in *Journal of Business Ethics* (2002), as the most productive business ethics scholar in Australia, and among the most productive in the world. His publications include *A Theory of Moral Reasoning: The Framework and Activities of Ethical Deliberation, Argument, and Decision-Making* (2004) and the *Business Ethics: Problems and Cases* (2005), now in its third edition. He is a frequent panellist and interviewee on radio, television, and in the print media on matters concerning ethics.

Eduardo Ibarra-Colado is Professor of Organization Studies at the Autonomous Metropolitan University, Campus Cuajimalpa (UAM-C). He is also a National Researcher of the National System of Researchers, and regular member of the Mexican Academy of Sciences. He is co-editor (with S. R. Clegg and L. Bueno) of *Global Management: Universal Theories and Local Realities* (Sage 1999). His latest book is *La universidad en México hoy: gubernamentalidad y modernización* (*The Mexican University Today: Governmentality and Modernization*) (UNAM 2001). Professor Ibarra-Colado is currently working on a research Project on *Corporate Ethics, Corruption and Governance* giving special attention to the case of transnational corporations in Mexico.

Michael Muetzelfeldt is Professor of Management at Victoria University, Melbourne. His research, consultancy and teaching focuses on strategic management and governance, particularly in the public sector and the non-government organization sector. He has published widely on the organizational and social consequences of new public management. His current major research focus is on collaborative management in distributed organizations and in networks of organizations. His work locates knowledge and professionalism within social and cultural contexts that extend beyond formal organizational boundaries.

Carl Rhodes is Associate Professor in the School of Management at the University of Technology Sydney (UTS). He has researched and written widely on issues related to knowledge, language, culture and learning in organizations. His current research is related to identity at work, management ethics, and organizations in popular culture. Carl is the author of *Writing Organization: (Re) presentation and Control in Narratives at Work* (Benjamins, 2001), co-author of *Reconstructing the Lifelong Learner* (Routledge, 2003) and co-editor of *Research and Knowledge at Work* (Routledge, 2000). His work has also been published in leading journals such as *Organization, Organization Studies, The Leadership Quarterly, The Journal of Business Ethics* and *The Journal of Management Education.*

George Ritzer is Distinguished University Professor at the University of Maryland. He has served as Chair of two Sections of the American Sociological Association – Organizations and Occupations and Theoretical Sociology. In 2004 he received an honorary doctorate (*Honoris Causa*) from La Trobe University, Melbourne, Australia. In addition to *The McDonaldization of Society* (1993, 1996, 2000, 2004; translated into a dozen languages), his other efforts to apply social theory to the everyday realms of the economy and consumption include *Expressing America: A Critique of the Global Credit Card Society* (1995), *The McDonaldization Thesis: Explorations and Extensions* (1998), *Enchanting a Disenchanted*

World: Revolutionizing the Means of Consumption (1999; 2005), *McDonaldization: The Reader* (2002), and *The Globalization of Nothing* (2004). Professor Ritzer is widely regarded as one of the world's most accomplished and respected sociologists.

René ten Bos is Professor of Organization and Philosophy at the University of Nijmegen. He has published numerous books and articles in both English and his native Dutch. These include *Fashion and Utopia in Management Thinking* (2000), *The Hygiene Machine* (2001) and *Rational Angels* (2003). *For Business Ethics* (co-authored with Martin Parker and Campbell Jones) was published by Routledge in 2005.

Robin Usher is Professor of Research Education and Director of Research Training at RMIT University, Melbourne, Australia. His publications include *Globalization and Pedagogy: Space, Place and Identity* (Routledge/Falmer, 2000), *Situated Ethics in Educational Research* (Routledge/Falmer, 2000), *Space, Curriculum and Learning* (Information Age Publishing, 2004), and *Rhetoric and Educational Discourse: Persuasive Texts?* (Routledge/Falmer, 2004). Research interests include the impact of post-structuralism on theory and practice in education, actor-network theory, ethics in alternative forms of research, policy and discourse in higher education.

Robert van Krieken is Associate Professor of Sociology in the Department of Sociology and Social Policy at the University of Sydney. He is co-author of *Sociology: Themes and Perspectives*, 2nd edn (2000), and author of *Norbert Elias* (1998) and *Children and the State* (1992).

Foreword

Martin Parker

Once upon a time business ethicists might have imagined that they just tried to make businesses ethical. Now, of course, most of us know that neither business nor ethics are matters that can be tidied up by the application of some humanist common sense, moral philosophy or old time religion. Business and ethics are much more complex matters, inextricably related to capitalism, globalization, law, professions, culture, organization, management, community and many other big ideas. So let me try to simplify matters a little. An image that I have been puzzled by for a long time is the idea of being able to look yourself in the face in the mirror each morning. This, of course, is a metaphor for the impossibility of hiding from yourself. I imagine that some people twitch and skulk and try not to catch their own eyes, remembering all the betrayals and hypocrisy of the previous day. Others, the virtuous ones, regard themselves carefully and steadily, but not unkindly, for they are pure of heart. I have always wanted to be the second sort of person, but fear that my will is too weak and my intelligence too limited. Which are you?

Some time ago, I taught managers about business ethics – money for me, credentials for them. They almost always began by asserting, perhaps defensively, that it is not possible to be pure of heart if you are a manager. (Although they seemed to think that this purity is possible for academics, leisured idealists that we are.) Management and ethics do not mix, they said. It is as if the managers have resigned themselves to skulking in front of mirrors for the rest of their lives, making do with quiet compromises and desperate promotions. That, after all, is the 'bottom line', and it is already long past the time to put away childish things like idealism. But the more we talk in the business ethics classroom, the less this reflection makes sense. These managers are kind to kittens, worried about global warming, and understand the complexities of the human soul. They often occupy positions that require them to do unpleasant things, but they are not bad people.

I usually conclude from this that hectoring managers about Aristotle, Kant and Bentham is unlikely to be helpful for them, but do it anyway. (Which is pretty much a summary of 50 years of research on the effectiveness of business ethics teaching.) More lately, however, another possibility has begun to emerge. The frustrating – and fascinating – thing about a word like 'ethics' is that it has no clear 'definition'. That is to say, whatever someone asserts that ethics is, it is quite possible to assert the opposite without being incoherent. Ethics is about following rules. Ethics is about breaking rules. Ethics is a matter of consequences. Ethics is a matter of intentions. Ethics is the reasoning that ordinary people use to come to judgements. Ethics is the discipline that people need in order to come to proper judgements. And so on. So how could such a bag of contradictions be related to looking at oneself in the mirror in the morning?

Consider the metaphor carefully. When you look in the mirror, do you see your own soul? Are you so transparent to yourself that the good that you do shines out from your skin, or the bad clouds your eyes like cataracts? Can you judge yourself easily? For myself, the answer has to be no. Although I might have good days and bad days, the texture of my life is a tightrope suspended between quiet heroism and equally quiet evasion of responsibility. Sometimes I judge myself harshly, and sometimes I ignore the pile of stinking crap that I am complicit with, and only notice the glimmering pearl. Looking in the mirror, we forget, excuse, and explain. Mirrors might not lie, but the people who look in them do. So what's the moral(ity) of this story? If I can't judge myself with any certainty, how can I judge others? If I can't judge others, then how can I judge my managers, or my society, or business, or capitalism, or bureaucracy? And – most importantly of all – if I can't judge, then should I leave ethics alone, and just concentrate on worrying about the bottom line, about what works?

It might be attractive for some to pretend that they can do without the mirror, and that the business of business does not need to slow itself down by worrying about its reflection. The world would be tidier like that. The problem with such a position is that it does not, can not, stop judgement from happening. Philosophical relativism or sociopathic instrumentalism might be sensible responses to confusion, but neither is adequate to describe what most humans actually do. Managers, whether they like it or not, will be judged by employees, customers, auditors, shareholders, suppliers, neighbours, taxpayers, journalists, activists, politicians and business ethicists. It doesn't matter that all these judgements might be contradictory, and leave the manager in a position of not knowing what to do, because the judgements will still happen. The reflections will not stop through any act of will. This hall of mirrors certainly doesn't add up to a clear picture, but it is inevitable and – I would argue – a good thing. (Which is a lucky co-incidence.) In a general sense then, business and management are no different to any of the other practices that human beings engage in, and none of the things that managers do should be immune from the reflections in the mirror of others. It might be inconvenient, but questioning the ethics of management practice is an everyday practice. It happens every morning, and only dictators would wish it otherwise.

The chapters in this book provide a set of important contemporary reflections on management practice. They suggest a wide variety of ways of thinking about ethics, business, and management. They do not – like certain textbooks, consultants and institutes – claim to have any final answers, but instead invite the reader to look in a variety of mirrors that highlight certain issues, and leave others in the shade. It is then up to the reader to decide whether they like what they see, or want to play some part in changing it. Readers might also want to consider the fairy stories told by those selling easy versions of corporate social responsibility as a beauty contest that brings great rewards to the winners. 'Mirror, mirror on the wall ...'. But mirrors do not have to be flattering. The reflections that you find in this book might not make you prettier, or show you your soul in the mirror in the morning, but they will certainly make you think.

Acknowledgements

This book is a direct result of a research project entitled 'What is to be done with Management Ethics?'. This was a special project of the Academy of the Social Sciences in Australia (ASSA) funded by the Australia Research Council (ARC) Special Projects funding for the Learned Academies. As the directors of this project, the editors would like to thank both the ARC and ASSA for their support in enabling the work to be done that has resulted in the book. In particular, our gratitude goes to Dr John Robertson, Research Director of ASSA, for his active involvement and steadfast support of the project. For their guidance through the project we also thank the President of ASSA, Professor Sue Richardson of Flinders University, the chair of ASSA's Research Committee, Professor Stuart Macintyre of the University of Melbourne, and ASSA Fellow, Professor Peter Beilharz of La Trobe University.

We would also like to thank the University of Technology, Sydney (UTS), where we both work, for providing a professional environment that continues to support our research endeavours, especially through its support of the ICAN Research Centre, which coordinated the event that produced the book. Special thanks go to Dr Anne Ross-Smith, Head of the School of Management at UTS, for encouraging and sustaining an academic unit where research is valued and encouraged. Finally, we express our sincere appreciation to Cleo Lester for her invaluable assistance in administering the project and for organizing and preparing the final manuscript.

Chapter 1

Introduction

Questioning the ethics of management practice

Stewart R. Clegg and Carl Rhodes

In days gone by, managers might have imagined that their job was just to manage without attracting adverse attention from the principals in whose interests – as shareholders – they managed. Today, the notion of managing as agents acting on behalf only of principals located elsewhere is increasingly hard to sustain. Even if the principals do not appreciate it, there are a great many others who take a specific interest in the organization's activities: communities, citizens, and customers not to mention employees and innumerable civil society associations and organizations who see keeping a watching eye on corporate affairs as a part of their brief. Indeed, business events in recent years have clearly highlighted that the ethicality of management and organizations is something that is of significant and broad social concern. Large scale corporate collapses, the increased awareness of dishonest business dealings – such as rogue trading, insider trading, as well as ongoing issues of corruption and worker exploitation on a global scale – attract significant attention in the business world, in political arenas, and in society more generally.

In a global arena which is increasingly fragmented and in which myriad ethical traditions constantly come into contact with one another, sometimes violently so, and in which organizations of business and government are the major intermediaries between cultures, peoples, and states, simple solutions to what have been made complex ethical problems are nowhere to be found. Moreover, the notion of ethical issues having 'solutions' seems problematic as the ethical vicissitudes in which organizations find themselves seem increasingly complex and unpredictable. In such contexts the practice of management is imbued with a responsibility for moral choice that can be taken up in many ways. Increasingly, moral dilemmas admitting with no easy resolution confront managers and organizations whose ethical awareness is accelerating with the tenor of the times.

Some still pretend that a code of practice or a commitment to established moral principles might serve as a sufficient, if not necessary, cover for everyday practices that might not always correspond with the spirit of the rules contained therein. Located within the ambiguity and unpredictability of practical situations, however, such pretensions offer only a thin veil of comfort. When moral issues are pressing, problematic, and particular, ethics can no longer be regarded as the domain of universalizing principles designed to appease anxiety. How managers of organizations confront moral responsibilities amidst the importance and ambiguity of the conditions in which they find themselves is a central existential question. Through the various ways in which the managers of an organization answer the calling implicit in this existential question the moral character of an organization emerges: it is in the way that the organization deals with such complexity and the way that it takes responsibility for the actions conducted on its behalf that the sense of character and vocation of the managers charged with its management is revealed.

The twentieth century was the era of the dominance of the organization, and the organization man (Whyte 1960) but in the twenty-first century that dominance is increasingly eroded. The problems have changed, and whereas the organization man of old may have been seen as a rather grey character, today's business person is often seen as too 'colourful' by far. What makes ethical action more confusing for today's managers is that the success of the neo-liberal project has dizavowed many of the moral and ethical bases from which mercantile activity once drew sustenance. When Weber (1976) saw the success of the Protestant ethic in creating the preconditions for an economic culture of rampant capitalism he foresaw that the very thing that made it rich – an untrammelled, competitive acquisitive impulse – would be the very thing that would destroy its ethical foundations. While some CEOs might still act as if they manage 'with God on their side' (Dylan 1963), for most captains of industry there is little mileage in speaking of a deity as a stakeholder in their annual reports. God may be on their side but the shareholders want to know what his value-proposition is in terms of the bottom line.

If CEOs want to speak from the high moral ground and pass judgement on the ethical conduct of others, from a metaphorical mountain of moral clarity and certainty, they had better not do so in such a way that has an adverse effect on market indicators. For others who make no such claims, God's enlistment by the ranks of religious fundamentalism in the production of a morally charged project for individual acquisitiveness and competitiveness might seem a paradoxical basis for an ethical project. Recourse to a belief in some transcendent entity may have once enabled western managers to invoke the commandments of ancient and established religions, however mediaeval or modern they may be, but in an increasingly globalized and postmodern world, characterized by a multiplicity of fundamentally irreconcilable beliefs, we need to examine ethics in all their complexity, multiplicity and perspectivity, rather than reduce them to quasi-religious nostrums for the faithful.

In a globalized economy where cultures and rationalities are both multiple and diffuse, the warm glow of ethical certainty founded in religious beliefs is little more than a security blanket for those who seek the comforting certainty of authoritative pronouncements on right and wrong. Too many others confront one by holding implacably opposed ethical commitments. Yet others may hold that any such commitments have no place in the hardheaded world of business. Today, ethics have to engage a world beset by contradictions. Thus, the purpose of this book is to develop and elucidate some insight into ethics and organizations as they relate to organization and managerial practice in a way that acknowledges the complexity and ambiguity characterizing ethically charged organizational contexts.

The contributions that constitute the book offer a scholarly discussion and critique of ethics as they relate to key contemporary challenges and issues for organizations – these include globalization, sustainability, consumerism, neo-liberalism, corporate collapses, leadership, and corporate regulation. Underlying each of the chapters is the basic premise that ethical conduct is not comprised of a set of rules, codes or judgements that are externally imposed but is constituted by practices that are deeply embedded and daily enacted in everyday management activities. In God some may trust but we still have to place our faith in the service of real men and women.

The collective project of the book is to investigate how managerial practice is – or is not – informed by ethical considerations and to enquire what the implications of this are for business and society. On the whole we do not attempt to make judgement about organizational ethicality from singular political positions; we prefer to try and tease out the ethical complexities of organizational life so that its dilemmas might be better understood, and perhaps even better 'managed'.

The book is organized around a core question: *What are the ethics of organizing in today's institutional environment and what do they mean for the practice of management and the organization of work and business?* In responding to this question, the different contributors have examined ethics as located in the practice and discourse of management, constituted in and through actions and exercises where people and organizations make choices. In taking this approach we join a growing yet still underdeveloped interest in the challenge of studying and understanding ethics as they play out in real business settings in order to question and critique the way that ethical discourse is – and is not – located within managerial responsibility. The book will thus be concerned with how management practice and organizational action is socially constructed as 'ethical' or 'unethical' or as not related to ethics at all.

Ethics are not just as something 'added-on' to other organizational activities (Stark 1993; Jackson 2000); one does not do business first and add ethics, rather as milk to a coffee, something that lightens the darkness. On the contrary, ethics are embedded in the practices of business people, managers and employees, and in the discourses that inform that practice. In terms of practice, ethics can be considered in relation to individual actions and conduct, where people make choices rather than merely follow rules

(Ibarra 2002), and where those choices are realized through organizational norms, policies and expectations. Such ethics are played out in practical settings and are manifest in the way that everyday activities are socially constructed as 'ethical' or 'unethical' (Parker 1998), or as not related to ethics at all.

In recent years the study of business ethics has been particularly critical of the assumption that organizations can collapse ethics into systems of rules, codes or administrative procedures (e.g. Parker 2002; Desmond 1998; Munro 1998; Letiche 1998; Roberts 2003). Such thinking radically questions the condition where 'the means-end rationalization that ends in the practice now known as business ethics [...] seems to be destroying the very possibility of ethics itself' (Parker 1998: 289). The implications of this, at the very least, are that business ethics cannot be equated with codes or laws (Letiche 1998); ethics are best considered in terms of the way that organizations present themselves to their members and stakeholders as sites for ethical difficulties, dilemmas, and deliberations (Roberts 2003). Indeed, as ten Bos (1997) has argued, the ethical predicament faced by people in organizations concerns the way that they bring morality to bear on their interaction with organizational requirements; rather than being a matter of the nature of the rules and norms it is more likely to concern how people interact with these rules in constituting their own – and others' – conduct.

To understand an ethics of organizations and management that is not restricted to pre-ordained ethical structures we believe it important to consider ethics in the context of those contemporary challenges that contextualize action rather than appeal to abstract or universalizing moral principles or arguments. Indeed, it is in this 'postmodern condition' that the ethical consequences of organizing are magnified both in scale and scope and the possibility of a universalizing meta-ethics applicable to all organizations, all societies, and all cultures, at all times, is diminished to such an extent that it is both untenable and undesirable.

We follow Zygmunt Bauman, in asserting that the context in which organizations face ethical situations is one where there are 'many agencies, and many ethical standards, whose presence casts the individual in a condition of moral uncertainty from which there is no completely satisfactory, foolproof exit [...] the modern individual [is] bombarded by conflicting moral demands, options and cravings, with responsibility for actions landing back on her shoulders' (Bauman 1992: 31). The manager as such an individual is faced with situations of moral choice that can be taken up in many ways. This responsibility of individual action is, however, always confronted by the 'undecidability' (Derrida 1995) of the future without recourse to an all-encompassing moral 'meta-narrative' (Lyotard 1979). An ethics of freedom in which (managerial) subjectivity is constituted through ethical action (Foucault 1997), and where the character of that action determines an organization's ethics, seems to be increasingly unavoidable.

Ethically aware managers and organizations inhabit 'moral mazes' (Jackall 1988) where individuals are confronted with a plethora of maps through the maze, each vying for attention, none of which is able to provide monologically reliable guides to the territories that they purport to represent. When universalising moral principles are seen to be located within the ambiguity and unpredictability of practical situations, they seem designed to appease anxiety rather more than steer action and lose their attractiveness, even as ethical issues become more pressing. The issue, as we see it, is how organizations confront moral responsibility in ambiguous conditions. Indeed, one might say that the moral character of an organization emerges in the way that it deals with such complexity and the orientation adopted to those actions that are taken on its behalf by those who 'speak' for it in some way.

In suggesting such an approach to organizational ethics we recognize that older instincts are not extinguished. The modern desire to formulate rule systems to guarantee morality is still alive and well in organizations. Indeed, 78 per cent of the US top 1000 companies have a code of conduct (Nijhof *et al.* 2003). Such tendencies, although rarely assumed to guarantee that great ethical behaviour will result, still rank high as a practical 'solution' to ethical dilemmas. But do they work as their progenitors claim? We think not. In the context of an ethical moral maze, codes of conduct framed by corporate legislation and enhanced corporate governance increase the probability of organizational hypocrisy (Brunsson 1989) as words and deeds fail to align. If we were to look to the disciplinary foundations laid by Max Weber for the study of organizations as an enquiry into rational legality, it is hardly surprising that this should be the case, any more than it is surprising that Weber, with his legal training, should have laid these foundations. We have known for some time that formal rationality is no guarantee of substantive rationality.

As a premise for the investigations in this book, we suggest that pre-determined, prescriptive, and normative sets of rules or codes that should govern everyday actions and decisions are, at best, insufficient to provide organizations with an ethical framework in which to operate. At worst, such approaches might lead to what Bauman (1992) calls 'adiaphorization' – the carving out of certain practices as morally indifferent. Where a code is a substitute for ethical reasoning, ethics might just fail to be seriously considered. Such an adiaphorization can also be seen in the apparent 'moral muteness' of those businesses that locate managerial responsibility purely in terms of shareholder value and interests (Johnson and Smith 1999).

When rule makers, informed in whatever way by moral thought, formulate ethical systems into codes as '*moral* intentions and acts [which] could only be the fruit of social engineering' (Bauman 1992: 64) they are often attempting coercion – foreclosing opposition through framing one best way. Such notions of ethics come dangerously close to being conflated with practices of domination. This is a conception of morality that, as Bauman argues, is based on mistrust of the autonomous moral subject; while distrusting the ethicality of the real human subjects the organization will make them accountable in terms of principles endorsed by an authority that purports to be able to speak for 'everybody'. Such moral principles make morality something procedurally measurable by observing how closely rules were followed such that '[t]he search that starts from the disbelief in the self's moral *capacity* ends up in the denial of the self's *right* to moral judgement' (Bauman 1992: 69). In following Bauman, we thus wish to propose a view of business ethics that places moral judgements, the moral impulse, and individual responsibility, as central to and constitutive of business practice – especially when such an ethics is located in a context of power, complexity and uncertainty. It is in this sense that now, perhaps more than ever, ethics have become both more critically important and radically difficult than in the past.

Given our focus on ethics in relation to individual responsibility, it could be suggested that recent tendencies in management, informed by neo-liberalism and post-bureaucratization, might be taken as a move towards an engagement with ethical concerns. The essence is that organizational subjects should be constituted and framed by organization relations that make them responsible. The ethics present in such moves seem to hold true to an older liberal tradition where, organizationally, 'everybody is an entrepreneur and the pursuit of economic self-interest has come to characterize not only business enterprise but management as well' (Hendry 2001: 210). In some senses, such a 'post-bureaucratization' has seen a retreat – although not escape – from the advocacy of rule-governed organizational behaviour. However, this does not necessarily spell out a re-engagement with ethics on the part of organizations. Indeed, where managers are supposed to be enterprising subjects, ethics can appear less organizationally relevant (du Gay 2000).

Entrepreneurs are not noted for their ethicality: indeed, in certain circles, the appellation 'entrepreneurial' is almost an insult, suggesting behaviour that is dangerously fly-by-night. The removal – at least partially – of rules – including those purporting to be ethical – does not necessarily free up the space of an organization such that there is an outpouring of moral reasoning by responsible subjects. On the contrary, there is often confusion as the regulated world recedes. In contemporary conditions, where ethics cannot be understood adequately either as code of conduct or moralistic imperative, the flexible nature of organizations poses pressing ethical issues, which managers may or may not choose to take up in the course of practice. There is no guarantee that they will and for those who were once schooled in bureaucratic ethics, becoming the new responsible and enterprising subjects demanded by contemporary management discourses can often be plain confusing, challenging, and contested (Stokes and Clegg 2002). Such issues are crucial when, as Bauman puts it, in the past, 'the organization's answer to [the] autonomy of moral behaviour [has been] the heteronomy of instrumental and procedural rationalities ... actors are challenged to justify their conduct by reason as defined either by the approved goal or by the rules of behaviour' (Bauman 1992: 124).

Bauman claims that all social organization consists of 'neutralizing the disruptive and deregulating impact of moral impulse' (Bauman 1992: 125) and renders social action susceptible to moral *adiaphorization*. Hence 'most activities regulated by organizations are subject to adiaphorization: one performs duty not bearing moral responsibility for it' (Bauman in Cantell and Pederson 1993). Thus, that which constitutes organizational action may actually adiaphorize social action – it is herein, we suggest, that the ethical challenge for contemporary organizations can be situated. Without recourse to absolute, universal or foundational ethics, the moral imperative of managerial practice is a core issue facing businesses – one where a consideration of ethics poses significant, uncertain, complex and ambivalent challenges for practice. It is the character of such challenges that our book will seek to elucidate.

Background and outline

This book brings together an interdisciplinary team of renowned scholars. Rather than being written by business ethics 'experts' the varied backgrounds and interests of the authors enables an engagement that does not repeat well worn tracks of thought; herein, ethics will be reconsidered in a way that is both broad yet focused. The result is an examination of ethics and organization that enables them to be understood from a variety of perspectives as well as creating a scholarly dialogue that will advance their study. The book includes perspectives from the fields of sociology, philosophy, management, organization studies, public administration, socio-legal studies, and education. The focus has been on contributions that are at the forefront of theory in the social sciences, and which engage directly with case studies and illustrative examples drawn from practice.

The book emerged directly from a research project entitled 'What is to be done about management ethics?' directed by the editors. The project was funded through the Academy of Social Sciences Australia (ASSA) and the Australia Research Council (ARC) and conducted in 2004. As part of this, each of the contributors to the book was commissioned to write a research paper, examining the questions and issues outlined above, from the particular perspective of their own discipline and in relation to their own ongoing research. The papers were presented at a public symposium held at the University of Technology, Sydney in December 2004. The papers were workshopped prior to that meeting and revised substantially in light of the excellent discussion that our audience engendered on the day. The result is a theoretically diverse yet thematically unified collection that provides a unique interdisciplinary perspective on management ethics.

The book is organized into two main parts – each part contains four chapters, and each chapter is preceded by a short editorial introduction. Part I, *Global Issues for Management Ethics*, examines ethics in relation to core issues of community, globalization, social responsibility and legality. In Chapter 2 René ten Bos commences proceedings by taking on the formidable question of whether such a thing as an ethical business community is possible. In addressing this question, he both extends and disturbs, deeply, debates between communitarian and libertarian standpoints that have informed much ethical discourse. He questions the project of 'business ethics' *tout court*, by arguing for the need for a business ethics that is open to ideas from the outside, which might embrace a practice of freedom that sees business as engaging in the world – this is an ethics that, rather than trying to plan and achieve an ideal ethical organization, remains in continual exploration of the possibilities of its own ethics. Chapter 3 opens a discussion of the vexing and complex issues of ethics and globalization. Written with a specific focus on the economic and political realities of the Latin American experience, Eduardo Ibarra-Colado critiques the neo-liberal discourse that is leaching from the North into the South. Arguing that a corporatized and marketized economic world order constitute an 'attack' on ethics, Ibarra-Colado makes a case for a normative ethics based on global democracy and transparency where regulatory systems can be socially constructed so as to link global values with national civic communities, with management practices, and with individual behaviour. In Chapter 4, Subhabrata Bobby Banerjee continues the focus on global ethical issues by considering organizations in relation to corporate social responsibility (CSR). By offering a critique of contemporary debates around corporate citizenship, social responsibility and sustainability, he argues that the apparent emancipatory rhetoric of these debates only thinly masks a set of narrowly conceived business agendas that actually work against the interests of many of the stakeholders that they claim to be speaking for. Banerjee argues for a broader notion of social responsibility that is not limited by the ideological narrow mindedness that seeks to place corporate interests at the centre of stakeholder interests. In the final chapter of Part I, Robert van Krieken considers the relationship between the legal construction of the corporation as a person and the social construction of organizational subjectivity. By understanding management practice in relation to a long-term process of civilization, van Krieken locates the bases of ethical conduct in contradictions between explicit ethical and implicit structural and cultural expectations so as to identify the overall long-term trends in the civilization of management.

The second part of the book considers ethics in relation to more specific management practices – those of public management, culture management, management within organizational networks, and consumer management. In Chapter 6, Michael Muetzelfeldt examines the ethics of the professions with a specific interest in the recent development of knowledge-based professions. Focussing on professions in the public sector, he suggests a divide between professionally or organizationally sanctioned ethics and those that inform people's everyday professional practice. His point is that this bifurcation of ethics provides professionals with the possibility of enacting a role as an ethical mediator, which, in turn, provides them with a potential for enhancing professional ethics through situated action and judgement. Chapter 7, by Stephen Cohen, investigates ethics in relation to empowerment and organizational culture. Starting by explaining the difference between 'accountability' and 'responsibility', Cohen develops an understanding of ethical empowerment in organizations that provides the possibilities for managers to exercise judgement in a way that goes beyond the necessarily minimal standards that ethical rules can provide. In Chapter 8, Robin Usher deploys the theoretical resources of Actor-Network Theory (ANT) to examine the immanent and relational character of ethics, with specific reference to the collapse of the Enron Corporation in 2001. The core argument focuses on how, given the *embeddedness* of ethics, there is a requirement to foreground the practices within which ethics are 'performed' by agents dealing with the possibilities and constraints of particular situations within organizational settings. In the case of Enron, this created a situation where the line between the ethical and the unethical became blurred beyond recognition through the entrepreneurial logic of contemporary capitalism. Part II of the book closes with George Ritzer's chapter 'Management ethics and consumers'. Here, Ritzer deploys the idea of a 'postmodern ethics' to understand the social problems traceable to phenomena such as 'hyper-consumption', the 'temptation of imprudence' and 'loss amidst monumental abundance'. He argues that an ethics of 'being for the other' radically questions accepted organizational ethics, in terms of the other constituted only as being a consumer, a buyer who should beware, and a self whose sole ethical interest is in profit maximization. The ethical requirement Ritzer argues for demands a paradigm shift in business from self-interest to a concern for the consumer as *other*. The book ends with a concluding comment reflecting on some possible implications of the various contributions for the study and practice of ethics in organizations.

Part I

Global issues for management ethics

Chapter 2

The ethics of business communities

René ten Bos[1]

Editors' introduction

Is an ethical business community possible? Indeed, what would it mean to call for an enquiry into the ethical possibility of business per se rather than individual business people? Such questions are of critical importance in considering the ethical contexts in which businesses both do and can operate. In this chapter, René ten Bos considers such questions without easy recourse to rehearsing, once again, those arguments between communitarians and libertarians that are so well known, with their opposition between an ethics of the community and social justice opposed to the individual and their liberties. The temporal issue with such polarized and well-worn positions is that while the former are nostalgic for an imagined and mythical past, the latter long for and pursue a dream for an imagined future.

What ten Bos notes is that debates over community are not merely academic: they have considerable currency in recent disagreements and positions concerning the kind of community that Europe should aspire to be. Should it be a liberal market society, on what is called the Anglo-Saxon model, or a community, on what is often regarded as a French model? Torn between the two poles, of nostalgic communalism and imagined liberalism, the pivotal and radical point is that the discourse of business ethics has been addressing the wrong kind of questions. What ten Bos provocatively suggests is that we need to ask questions of business and business ethics from outside the community of practice that is constituted by both business persons and business ethicists. He closes with a provocative list of what such questions might be – questions that might invigorate the meaning and practice of business ethics.

Ethics is about the good. And because it is about the good, it is also about the absence of the good which is often referred to as 'evil' or 'bad'. It is rare, however, that ethicists address the good and the absence of good in such straightforward terms. More often they talk, among many other things, about duties, about rules, about codes of conduct, about something referred to as moral scope, that is to say, about the question for whom we should do and should not do the good. They also talk about the characteristics of the other for whom we should care, about the role of emotion in ethics or morality and hence about the difference between ethics and morality, about ethics as theory and ethics as practice, about specific kinds of ethics – such as the ethics of science, the ethics of professionals, the ethics of gender, the ethics of identity, and, indeed, the ethics of business – or even about the mind-boggling relationship between the world of ethics – '*ought*' – and the world of fact – '*is*'. And they also talk about communities.

In this chapter, I too am going to talk about communities. In line with the other chapters, which all somehow ask the question as to whether an ethics, *some* ethics, is possible in the world of business, I should be asking whether an ethical business community is possible. My answer to this question, however, is an unashamed 'no'. By this I do not mean that people in the world of business are somehow moral bastards or that business makes you a bad person. My position is that while business communities may indeed make you a bad person they do not necessarily have this effect. More precisely, I fail to understand why there should be a difference in this regard between business communities and, for example, academic communities, scientific communities, religious communities, and other kinds of community all of which *may* make you bad as well. It is here that I find myself in agreement with Bobby Bannerjee who argues, in Chapter 4 of this book, that there are no special managerial obligations. Thinking that there are such special obligations for people in the world of business is grounded on the indeed immensely popular assumption that business managers somehow form a very special kind of community. This is why there is so much talk about fiduciary relationships, responsibility, or trust.

I am going to take issue with the way in which participants in these debates conceptualize community. My argument is that we should not ask whether an ethical – virtuous, excellent, or socially responsible – business community is possible before asking what an ethics of new communal possibilities might mean. The chapter is therefore not so much about the possibility of ethics as about the *ethics of possibility*: What does it mean to talk about possible communities? What is so wrong with actual communities that we are enticed to muse about the possibility of other kinds of community? And how should we relate these other kinds of community to the world of business communities?

I will proceed in four steps. In the first section, I am going to put the craving for community that is prevalent in the discourse of business ethics in the perspective of the well-known debate between communitarians and libertarians. Business ethics is torn apart between both positions. I will argue that it should not be, because both communitarians and libertarians hold positions that are fatally flawed. In the second section, I will underscore this by rehearsing some ideas developed a long time ago by the German sociologist Alfred Tönnies. More particularly, I will enter into his renowned distinction between community – '*Gemeinschaft*' – and society – '*Gesellschaft*' – and argue that Tönnies alerts us to the dangers of a nostalgic craving for the former. This danger is totally ignored in the discourse on business ethics in which it is generally assumed that community and all that goes with it – communal feelings, a sense of safety, unequivocal norms and values, social coherence, and so on – equals good. In the third section, I will rather briefly introduce a prominent representative of recent European thought about community: Jean-Luc Nancy, a French philosopher, who has highlighted the need to develop post-nostalgic understandings of community. To do this, we have to overcome what he refers to as the 'problem of immanentism' that dominates the debate between communitarians and libertarians. Nancy does not stand alone in this debate: the community is a central preoccupation of contemporary European thinkers such as, among others, Maurice Blanchot, Peter Sloterdijk, Giorgio Agamben, Etienne Balibar, or Alain Badiou. For the sake of brevity, however, I will only indicate in very broad terms how Nancy should be positioned in this discussion which, of course, cannot be isolated from the wider political ambition to create something like a European Community. We will see that much of the ideas developed in this debate focus on the possibility of a *non-exclusive* community. One of the questions that might be raised here is whether such a community is a possibility that can somehow be organized or become a manageable project. These are, I will maintain, exactly the kind of questions that business ethics blissfully refuses to engage itself with. In the fourth and final section of the chapter, I will, in rather polemical fashion and basing myself on Nancy's musings about community, formulate some challenges for business ethics.

Between community and liberality

The widespread interest among business ethicists in communities and, related to this, virtue ethics (e.g. Solomon 1992, 1993 and 2004) is partly due to a misconception of the Aristotelian community, which is much more pervaded with conflict and dialogue than is often suggested. Indeed, it would not be wrongheaded to say that Aristotle's entire conception of ethics is based on the recognition of conflict, incompleteness, and debate. These communities are, as Yack (1999) argues, perhaps better understood as argumentative practices that provide the members of the community with a social place where words, speech, and messages can be interchanged. It is the endless debate among philosophical friends that provides the internal good that ultimately relates to these practices. Admittedly, Aristotle stresses the importance of unity and cohesion in an ethical community of friends – understandings that permeate contemporary business ethics as well – but this in no way rules out that actual life in the polis is teeming with discord. Indeed, it is the willingness to expose oneself to this discord that is what is ultimately shared by the members of the community (Nancy 1991: xxxviii).

The upsurge of a – pseudo-Aristotelian – virtue ethics in contemporary ethical discourse, which is often related to Elizabeth Anscombe's famous polemic with imperative-based ethics and the subsequent effort to redeem an ethics of virtuousness grounded in the philosophy of psychology (Anscombe 1958), has caused a widespread interest in the notion of the *community*. In the wake of Anscombe, many philosophers, most notably the so-called 'communitarians', have been beguiled by this concept and tried to use it in a polemic against liberalism. More specifically, they take issue with the primacy of the individual in liberal society and argue for a reinvigoration of small-scale communities in which there is no disagreement about the good and in which the community constitutes individual moral identity (Devisch 2003: 18). At the heart of their argument lies an understanding that desires and goods are not objects of choice, which liberalism would hold, but rather something that each of us is carrying with him or her all along. Communitarians do not believe in 'the unencumbered self' that is guided by singular preferences and emphasize that individual freedom needs a coherent social context if it is to be something valuable (Sandel 1982: 84; Kymlicka 2002: 270). The very idea of a market where individual preferences for particular moral desires and goods collide is rejected as a liberal figment that at best creates 'weakly valued goods' rather than goods that people strongly believe in (Taylor 1989: 89). The individual, it is argued, is not 'free to propose and to live by whatever conception of the good he or she pleases, derived from whatever theory or tradition he or she may adhere to ...' (MacIntyre 1988: 336). Not only does this erode any sense of a public good, but also shatters the dream of a robust identity that is firmly rooted in the community. Rather than focusing on the unencumbered individual, we had better develop a political or moral philosophy that takes into account the factual encumbrances people inherit from the traditions or cultural settings in which they learned to acquire meanings, habits, and values. Some of the communitarians even go so far as to argue that the individual in a liberal society is in essence an opaque entity that is bound to disappear if we are willing to fit it into a pattern of clearly determined relations (Sandel 1982: 172–3).

Devisch makes a useful distinction between radical and moderate communitarians. He argues that in the end the radicals are willing to set aside individual civil and political rights and to replace them by a 'teleological expression of the common good or of group rights' (2003: 19). This merely is to say that all actions of the members of the community are directed towards the realization of a common goal. Michael Sandel and Alisdair MacIntyre are classified as radicals. Not all communitarians, however, would go so far as these two thinkers, but they all agree that the prioritization of the individual at the expense of the community – tradition, framework, and so on – is an unholy attribute of liberalism because it undermines both the notion of a public good and that of a robust moral character. All that we are left with in liberal society are shards of both.

In the communitarian view, the culprits are philosophers like John Rawls, Robert Nozick, or Richard Dworkin. These 'libertarians' emphasize individual freedom *within the context of morally neutral institutions*. As Rawls puts it:

> In a well-ordered society each person understands the first principles that govern the whole scheme as it is to be carried out over many generations; and all have a settled intention to adhere to these principles in their plan of life. Thus a plan of each person is given a more ample and rich structure than it would otherwise have; it is adjusted to the plans of others by mutually acceptable principles. Everyone's more private life is so to speak a plan within a plan ... But this larger plan does not establish a dominant end, such as that of religious unity or the greatest excellence of culture, much less national power and prestige, to which the aims of all individuals and associations are subordinate ... [J]ust institutions allow for and encourage the diverse life of associations in which individuals realize their more particular aims.
>
> (Rawls 1971: 528–9; see also: 1971: 448)

In a just society, therefore, the dominant institutions do not enforce a particular vision about the good upon the individual. Their function is rather to neutralize and regulate the inevitable diversity among citizens and the best way to proceed is to assume a formality and abstraction that recognizes each individual as a legal person who exists independent from particular cultural and moral backgrounds (Devisch 2003: 20). Libertarians do not have high expectations of what the community will bring and relentlessly point to its inhering dangers – marginalization, discrimination, xenophobia, power, lack of dynamics, terror, and so on. They do not seek inspiration in the works of Aristotle, even though the Aristotelian community with all its emphasis on debate and discord is perhaps much more akin to a liberal community than communitarians might have it, but they seek support in people like Locke, Hume, and Kant. With these philosophers in mind, they argue that we do not need to fear fragmentation for we are able to cope with it thanks to our increased individual freedom. Right is more important as good, Rawls would argue, simply because in a liberal society public consensus about the good is unavailable and unnecessary (Rawls 1971: 388). Prudence in public affairs does not require, as the communitarians believe, a process during which the self eventually becomes situated in a clearly defined social and moral context, but is warranted by a widespread respect for the rights of each individual (Kymlicka 2002).

Against the communitarians, it has been argued that their position teems with a nostalgic desire for the by now lost community. This has tempted some commentators to mock the communitarian position for being unrealistic or for being simply conservative (e.g. Fisk 2001: 76). However, we ought not to forget that the communitarian doubts about the liberal-individualist society have a long and respectable standing in philosophical thinking that goes back at least to Rousseau who argued that the presence of God in an evil world is no longer in need of justification – this is the so-called theodicy-problem – but that the presence of man clearly is (Cassirer 1967: 77). The latter problem is also known as the problem of *sociodicy*: evil and suffering are explained as a consequence of worldly rather than otherworldly forces, that is to say, as consequence of free will and action. For people like Adam Smith or Karl Marx, this implied that one should *both* acknowledge that institutions – politics, organizations, markets, and so on – could bring evil into the world *and* take this evil as justifiable for it would in the end contribute to welfare or even to human progress. These thinkers alert us to the (im)possibility of a sociodicy that is in many respects analogous to Leibniz's theodicy (Murphy 1993: 184–7).

Now, the communitarians, at least the more radical ones among them, refuse to accept any justification of modern institutions, that is, they do not think that a sociodicy in modern or postmodern circumstances is desirable or possible and ask us to reconsider premodern forms of togetherness as an alternative. In other words, what they offer us, nostalgic as it may be, is nothing less than a history of decline which in some sense resembles Heidegger's *Verfallsgeschichte des Seins* (Tugendhat 1993: 210). Obviously MacIntyre (1981, 1988), who is probably the most important representative of the communitarians, is a case in point. Much of the contemporary moral predicament is due to the loss of moral robustness and clarity that MacIntyre attributes to people like Aristotle and Thomas Aquinas. What we have instead is a lack of orientation which results in moral arbitrariness and subjectivism, according to MacIntrye a dire legacy of the Enlightenment. For MacIntyre, morality is never and can never become a matter of choice.

His position, especially his belief in a redemption of Aristotelian or Thomistic practices, has been extensively discussed in the literature. Is it possible to reinvigorate these practices or not? Do communitarians like MacIntyre have something worthwhile to offer to inhabitants of late-capitalist society? While some commentators would argue that, for example, Aristotelian notions such as *phronesis* are still actual and, indeed, have a tendency to become more and more actual (e.g. Kingwell 2003: 112), others have claimed that the debate has abated somewhat, partially because the issues raised in the debate – what comes first: the individual or the community? – seem to be irresolvable, partially also because the debate is pitched against the background of liberal society. For all of their criticisms on liberal society, it would be hard to prove that communitarians radically reject the liberal project. Put otherwise, there is hardly a communitarian who would claim that freedom and individualism are not valuable. That is, sometimes the entire discussion seems to boil down to what are merely shifts of emphasis. To be sure, MacIntyre clearly opposes individualism as it is envisaged by liberalism. In his opinion, there is no self which says: 'I am what I choose to be. I can always, if I wish to, put into question what are taken to be merely the contingent social features of my existence'. This self can only accept that it is a part of a story, which is to say that it is imbedded in traditions, narratives and history (MacIntyre 1981: 201; see also Horton and Mendus 1994: 8–9). To calm down his critics, however, MacIntyre is keen to deny any deterministic consequences of this position. The self is embedded in history, but this is not to say that it cannot relate itself critically to this tradition. Indeed, it might be argued that this is exactly what MacIntyre is doing with respect to the liberal tradition.

The overall point here is that if criticism would be ruled out beforehand, traditions would have to be denied any dynamics whatsoever whereas, in fact, they rise and perish. Hence, there is, as Horton and Mendus point out (1994: 12), nothing intrinsically conservative about MacIntyre's conception of the tradition. In some sense, it might even be argued that MacIntyre borders on a position that is quintessentially Aristotelian: the American philosopher claims that a tradition is 'a socially embedded argument', an argument, he adds, that is precisely about the rights and wrongs of that tradition (MacIntyre 1981: 207). It is difficult to see how this argument can be maintained in our society if one refuses to accept that the self cannot somehow shake off the shackles of tradition.

In sum, the gap between communitarians and libertarians might be grossly overrated. It is not difficult to refer to passages in libertarian texts that stress the importance of the community, the social nature of the self, the agreement on rights and wrongs, and so on (e.g. Rawls 1971: 522–3). As is often the case in philosophical debate, participants cover themselves and try to smooth down the most radical consequences of what they have to say. In the end, the gap between them and their adversaries is not so enormous at all. This is, I suggest, exactly why business ethics can easily reconcile a communitarian position with a libertarian one that, at face value, seems to prevail in the world of business. There is no substantial debate for there is no substantial opposition between both positions. As a consequence, any substantial moral critique of the prevailing system is painfully absent in business ethics. In what follows, I will try to outline how such a critique might be formulated. Tönnies will be our first guide.

The delusory community

When Tönnies published his *Gemeinschaft und Gesellschaft* in 1887, he wanted to draw attention to a fundamentally ambivalent aspect of social life (Tönnies 2001). I think that this ambivalence is undervalued in business ethics, especially in those texts that are based on Aristotelian virtue ethics (e.g. Solomon 1993; see for extensive discussion: Parker *et al.* 2005). It is therefore important to discuss Tönnies' work in some detail, all the more because he has had a profound and until now hardly recognized influence on contemporary thinkers on sociality – Nancy being one of them.

Tönnies' ideas about our society were strongly influenced by Marx who had argued, as is well known, that there is a sharp contrast between the capitalist society and the communist society, claiming that in the former the cash nexus necessitates formal and alienated relationships between men whereas in the latter these problems were solved and relationships were more organic and warmer. We should never forget that communism is a word that signifies a desire for a communal place that is beyond social classification and stratification and that escapes techno–political dominion (see also: Nancy 1991: 1). Communism implies that such a place is still to be found. The classless society is, if anything, a society that is yet to come. Tönnies' novel idea was that we do not have to look for a utopian or transcendent future in order to find forms of sociality that are not alienating or formal. He claimed that rural communities, village life, perhaps also exotic life outside Europe, did not succumb to the temptations of plutocracy and modernity. What Marx had in mind about an ideal community in the future, was perhaps present at the fringes of the social world as we know it. The theme that is raised by Tönnies is well known and is often related to a possible criticism of capitalism that is supposed to 'threaten' or 'colonize' or 'swallow' these allegedly organic forms of sociality. After all, Tönnies himself made a famous distinction between *Gemeinschaft* – community, *communitas* – and *Gesellschaft* – society, *societas*. The obvious point to be made here – and that communitarians of various denominations were only too keen to make – is that community is always threatened by society. I hope to show, however, that this cannot be maintained on the basis of Tönnies' text. His construction of the relationship between community and society is too complicated for an easy communitarian, anti-modernistic or anti-capitalistic agenda. There is, in other words, no reason for nostalgia.

Tönnies starts with claiming that two forms of sociality are pervaded by two entirely different kind of wills. In the community, relationships between people are guided by the *Wesenswille* – the essential will; in the society, on the other hand, these relationships are governed by a *Kürwille* – a will which is simultaneously rational and capricious or opportunistic. The essential will is described by Tönnies as 'the psychological equivalent of the body' (2001/1935: 87): it is thought of as a vital principle that bestows human life with a unity the social expression of which is the community. This community is thought of as something real and organic, in other words, its essence is understood as real and organic life. It is especially the latter word – 'organic' – that is frequent in popular business textbooks – including those on business ethics – but Tönnies' understanding of the notion might puzzle the average business manager. For him, 'organic' refers to all that is real insofar as it can be conceived as being *connected* with reality as such. We will see below that this insight becomes crucial in the work of Nancy. As connection with and openness to reality, the organic cannot be made or produced for this would imply that in a community a detached position is possible in the sense that a producer of an instrument is detached from the instrument that s/he is making. However, a position of transcendence with respect to the community defies its very reality. Those who create a community cannot create it in the sense that a violin-maker makes a violin. Members of the community participate in the community in a way that a violin-maker does not with respect to the violin. The implication of this is that the community is not operative or working in the sense that an instrument or even an entire organization can be. You can only work *in* and not *with* a community. It is, in other words, ultimately impossible to create new realities with a community: it is always already its own realization.

The society – *Gesellschaft* – is governed by the *Kürwille* – rational/ capricious will – which is, much more than is the case with the essential will, connected to intellectual processes in the individual – rather than to intensities in a pre- or non-individual body. More particularly, this will resonate in the intentional deliberation characteristic of the individual: What do I want? What do I need? How can I get it? Do I want the same under different circumstances? The social expression of this calculative rationality is the 'society' which is described by Tönnies as 'ideal' and 'mechanic' (2001/1935: 88–9). This implies that the society is not real: it has a fickle ontological status in the sense that it is *not* existing as such but merely an idea. To make this idea work, it is necessary not to focus on reality as such but to produce or create particular portions of reality that may help to make the idea 'true'. In fact, this is the scientific 'fiction' underlying all kinds of 'societal' togetherness. What we are supposed to derive from this fiction is that the unity with the world can somehow be maintained in the details. What atoms are to reality, are individuals to society. As individuals, we are essentially isolated from each other – in a way that mother and child, or two lovers, and so on, are not. It is only by means of a recourse to the smaller parts, to all these isolated details as it were, that society can become what community will never be: operative, intentional, functional, and so on. So it seems that for Tönnies it is the unreal that is operative and working whereas it is the real which does not work, which does not have a goal and which does not function. Society is demiurgic in a way that community will never be. And it can only be demiurgic inasmuch as it disallows its component parts – individuals – an organic reality.

There is, however, more to Tönnies' distinction. It is true that community is characterized by one will (2001/1935: 8) and that it is therefore an unfaltering unity. It is also true that society is a sociality of essentially isolated individuals who will always experience certain tensions with others or, indeed, with the social body of which they are a part: one will only work for society if it provides certain benefits (2001/1935: 40). Compensation is therefore an essential feature of society: transaction, exchange, and contracts are more important than communal values. Tönnies explicitly relates this to the world of business. In fact, he argues, should we understand society as a construct or an *idea* for business people, for merchants, perhaps even for workers all of whom are its voluntary subjects (2001/1935: 81; see also: ten Bos and Kaulingfreks 2005)? The rational and arbitrary will that permeates society is a will that allows one to make a clear distinction between means and end. In Kantian terms, community is always an end in itself.

So, it seems that *Gemeinschaft* and *Gesellschaft* represent two different ways of understanding social reality. Tönnies, however, has always been careful to emphasize that both terms are theoretical categories rather than empirical ones. Moreover, both should be understood as relational concepts: more society entails less community, and *vice versa*. Social reality is therefore a blend of society and community. This is, Tönnies maintains, its fundamental ambivalence. But an important question rises here: how can something real – the *Gemeinschaft* – blend with something ideal – the *Gesellschaft*? The answer to this question is that community has also a very unstable ontological status. If it is real, then it is only real for its members, but these members will very likely not theorize upon it in the way that sociologists or philosophers will do that. Being in the intimacy of community defies any objectivity. As Sloterdijk (2004: 261) beautifully puts it:

> Human beings are the beings-in-common who cannot properly speak about the grounds of their commonality. Indeed, what is to-be-in-common? When nobody asks me, I know; when I have to explain it to an inquirer, I do not know.
>
> (*my translation*)

The reason is that knowledge about your own commonality – rather than other people's commonality – goes, in a very literal sense, without saying: you know what it is to be together with those who are close to you but your knowledge cannot in any way whatsoever be made explicit. You are, as Sloterdijk (ibid.) phrases it, 'blindly immersed' in the community to which you belong. If you want to see and to become a sociologist of your own community, you have to die as a member of it and to return as an observer from outside. The very idea to raise the question of the community is a question that is deemed to be exterior to the community itself. In communities, self-reflection is hardly an option. Inasmuch as sociology or, for that matter, ethics – virtue ethics, business ethics, and so on – is posing the question of the community, one might argue not only that it is simply an effort to make explicit what is implicit but also that during the process of explication the implicit will inevitably slip through your fingers. Another way of putting this is that one cannot construct or create the community instrumentally. It cannot be *organized* or *planned*.

Moreover, the community itself seems to be a construct that betrays a deep desire for those who are weighed down by the contractual regimens that characterize society. In a way that reminds one of Levinas's understanding that rationality will sooner or later develop disgust for itself, the members of the society develop disgust of whatever it is that they are members of and start to long for more amiable or congenial forms of togetherness. And it is here that the community appears as a nostalgic fantasy for those who have been unable to extricate themselves from the societal straightjacket. The community as such is not something that took place. As Nancy (1991: 11) argues:

> ... [I]f it is indeed certain that humanity has known (or still knows, outside the industrial world) social ties quite different from those familiar to us, community has never taken place along the lines of our projections of it according to these different social forms. It did not take place for the Guayaqui Indians, it did not take place in an age of huts; nor did it take place in the Hegelian 'spirit of the people' or in the Christian agape. No *Gesellschaft* has come along to help the State, industry, and capital dissolve a prior *Gemeinschaft*.

Gemeinschaft and *Gesellschaft* are therefore just *ideas* that presuppose each other. This raises all sorts of questions: what about the ontological status of the community? What can be properly called a community and what not?, Do we have identities and where do we derive them from?, and Why is it that so many people, business ethicists included, have been allured by the prospect of a better or even perfect community that substitutes society? Can such a community be planned, organized, designed, worked out? These questions become more urgent than ever. Posing them merely in terms of a distinction between communitarians and libertarians seems to be inadequate. The question of the community is a question that needs to be asked anew and this is exactly what a few contemporary European philosophers have done. It is to one of them that I will turn now.

Possible communities?

Jean-Luc Nancy (France) belongs to a generation of European thinkers who were all born in the 1940s and who have witnessed the rise of the European Community, an unprecedented social and political experiment about which they have serious doubts. This, however, is not to imply that they are simply against it. As Sloterdijk, another eminent voice in the debate, has put it, Europeans have very good reasons to be frightened for what is proper to them and it is by no means certain that the European experiment with community will be able to keep the cause of all fear at bay. To be a European, Sloterdijk (1995: 59) argues, has until now entailed that you are submerged in a theatre where high-risk experiments with 'post-Roman imperial forms' will be conducted. To keep the shadows of the past away, however, the newest European experiment, one that began in the early 1950s and that has really gained momentum in the new millennium, must break away from 'the traditional myth-engine' and somehow construct a community that is not a supra-power or an empire anymore but a 'confederation of states' or, more simply, 'a trans-imperial or post-imperial form' (1995: 60–1). Such a new form would imply an *ethical* effort to reject all forms of megalomania, arrogance, cynicism, and contempt that have so long guided the imperial pretensions of European political thought (1995: 74). Hence, many European thinkers have tried to formulate alternatives for what is 'proper' to Europe since it is the 'proper' that might indeed re-animate the shadows of the past. Nowadays, the cream of European intelligentsia are calling for a new political imagination that does not focus on the proper anymore but instead focuses on what is not proper in the proper: they try to think 'subversive traditions and courses of action which expose the strange in the familiar or the other in the same ...' (1995: 59). What Europe needs is somehow an 'alienating continuation of its own history', one that would bring the traditional myth-engines that have so plagued the continent to a standstill (1995: 59–60).

Now this agenda of European philosophy, oftentimes related to postmodernism but in some sense already present in Cartesian and Kantian traditions as well, has profound ethical implications. That is, we have to formulate an ethics which is no longer directed to what is proper to the own community but one which aims at what does not necessarily belong to the proper. What is being thought here is, in a sense, nothing else than our capacity to stretch the moral scope of our thinking and our actions. In an era that is increasingly characterized by communication and interconnection, communitarian ethics as well as individualistic ethics become obsolete and, indeed, dangerous. At the time of writing this chapter, however, many politicians in Europe, not only the conservatives among them, argue that membership of the European Union can only be an option for those who are born in one of the member states. This implies that about 13 million inhabitants of Europe are being excluded from the European Community for the simple reason that they have been born elsewhere or have ties elsewhere. Spectres from the past still haunt Europe: apartheid, racism, and discrimination are still very serious threats, not only in the daily lives of many people – in the wake of 9/11, mosques and Islamic schools have been incinerated, Jewish graves have been desecrated, and so on – but also on an institutional level – European citizenship for non-Europeans is blocked off by the Maastricht Treaty of 1992 (Balibar 2004: 43–5). Especially at times when people feel the threat of Islamic terrorism, the proclivity to go once more into one's own imperial or national shell can be sensed everywhere. Against this, some philosophers argue for new, post-communitarian and post-individual forms of ethicality or communality. We need to conceive, they argue, of an ethics that wants to lend an ear to different voices, ones that have been unheard for too long a time. The strategy is to think in terms of what is not proper to Europe. We need to think of what appears at first outside of, and strange to, Europe and locate it in the heart of Europe. In other words, the strange and the alien are not 'over there', on the other side of some imagined border but already in us. Nancy is just a voice in a much wider discussion (see, for example: Agamben 1993; Cacciari 1998; Rancière 2003; Hardt and Negri 2004; Sloterdijk 2004). These voices tell us of a new ethics, an ethics of a new communality, that is to say, an ethics that assumes as its starting point a responsibility for what is the most fragile thing in the world – the way in which people are in common. To think of this communality as a soap-bubble (Sloterdijk 2004: 260) will make you aware how fragile this new ethics might turn out to be. Rather than business ethics or any other communitarian or libertarian ethics, we need an ethics of intrusion and strangeness rather than an ethics of identity and immunity.

Nancy is exactly a philosopher of intrusion and strangeness. In 2000, he published a semi-autobiographic article in which he tries to come to terms with the heart transplantation that he underwent in the early 1990s. When a cardiologist explained to him that the palpitations that he already had for years were the sign of a very serious problem and that his heart was 'programmed' to function only 50 years, he became painfully aware that the proper can betray the self:

> My heart became a stranger to me, it intruded right at the moment when it failed me; because it was almost as if I rejected it or shitted it out. (...) From now on, it becomes increasingly weaker, and this strangeness brings me closer to myself. 'I' am, because I am ill. ('Ill' is not the right word: not 'infected' but rather: rusty, stiff, stuck.) But the other, my heart, is up the spout. My heart which from now on is an intruder and which must be thrown out.
>
> (Nancy 2002: 12–13; *my translation*)

Here, in a disturbing sense, we see what it might mean to think the stranger within each of us. Nancy concludes that right from the beginning strangers and strangeness are part of his existence, indeed, of his very identity. It is its 'own' life that is being saved by the transplantation, but what does this word 'own' mean when strangers explain to you that the heart is not a destiny but a program and that it can simply be substituted by another program? What does it mean when the 'own' can be pervaded by tubes and wires in order to help it 'survive'? Where is this 'own'? Is it clearly locatable, for example, in the organ that is, if anything, a symbol of intimacy? Is it still a symbol of intimacy? Sloterdijk (1999) wonders whether the heart, after its scientific exposure as a pump in a kind of bureaucratic system, is still able to exercise this symbolic function?

Your 'own' life, Nancy goes on to explain, is not located in an organ, even though this life is nothing without organs. He concludes that the 'own' cannot be somewhere because it is so vulnerable for various kinds of intrusion. There is never one intruder: there is always a multiplicity of intruders. In the wake of his heart transplantation, Nancy's immunity system is seriously undermined: strangers such as cancer, shingles, and viruses enter. He experiences what others have argued for philosophically, to wit, the coexistence of identity and immunity (Sloterdijk 1999; see also: Kaulingfreks and ten Bos 2002). Yet, he also experiences that in a sense both are just fantasies that presuppose each other. To put it more precisely, my identity = immunity has always been strange to me, has always been pervaded with viruses and cancers, has always been undermined. The truth of subjectivity, Nancy (2002: 24) argues, is 'its externality: its endless exposition'. Nancy concludes:

> The intruder exposes me excessively. The intruder extrudes me, exports me, expropriates me. (...) The intruder is nobody else than myself and the human being himself. Nobody else than the same who never ceases to change, who is simultaneously keen and exhausted, naked and excessively equipped, who is an intruder in the world just as he is an intruder in himself, an uncanny (*unheimlich*) advance of strangeness, the *conatus* of rampant infinity.
>
> (2002: 24–5; *my translation*)

How do these musings relate to the idea of the community? In what is probably his best-known text, Nancy (1991: 3) has defined the idea that man cannot be intruded by strangeness and that he is therefore always and necessarily immanent to himself as 'the stumbling block to a thinking of community'. As long as we are unable to conceive of the self as a being that is constantly exposed to other and not necessarily humane beings, we will be unable to think the community of all being. To put it in even more dramatic terms, the inability to think the openness of man to the world is what sooner or later bring the demons of the past to life once again. The reason is that it coerces us to think the community in terms of essences or rather, as Nancy himself puts it, to have these essences *work* in it.[2] The community, in other words, merely serves to effect our essence, to effect our goal, to protect our identity. For Nancy, this amounts to 'totalitarianism' or 'immanentism' and he thinks that in our vulnerable democratic society the desire for identity and essence is an ominous sign. Organization and politics are still under the spell of this desire. This is what one might refer to as the quintessential seduction of totalitarianism: just as we imagine ourselves to possess a body that is governed by a ghost, the proverbial captain on the ship, we also imagine ourselves to be united in a political body that works under a leader (Hardt and Negri 2004: 158). An ethics needs to be formulated that counteracts this baleful tendency. This would be an ethics that Nancy (1996: 62) has described as one that is capable of saying 'we' 'right from the moment that no boss and no God is saying it for us'. This is not a communitarian 'we', but simply the moral requirement that Nancy tries to capture in expressions such as 'coexistence' and especially in the idea of 'sharing sense'. Such an ethics is not about values or norms and other communitarian rubbish that merely serve to divide the human community; no, it is an ethics about the possibility of sense-sharing (Nancy 1997: 127). And this merely implies that this is an ethics that is firmly grounded in an ontology of the community.

This ethics thus starts with an emphasis on the openness of individual and community. All efforts to think both as capable of an existence without relations are totalitarian. Nancy's ethics circles around a categorical rejection of all interiority and immanence. In an exceptionally clear piece called *'In praise of the melee'*, he writes:

> What is a community? It is neither a macro-organism nor a big family (always assuming we know what an organism or what a family actually are ...). The *common*, having-in-common or being-in-common excludes from itself any interior unity, any subsistence and presence in itself or by itself. To be with, to be together, and even to be 'united' is precisely not to be one. Of communities that are one with themselves, there are only dead ones. These are not to be found in the cemetery, moreover, a place of dispersed space, of distinction; no, they lie in the ashes of ovens or under the oil of mass graves.
>
> (2003: 285)

All human being is, in terms of Heidegger, being-with. Being is community. And community is here understood as the 'being-ecstatic of being itself' (Nancy 1991: 6). Ecstasy should be taken here literally: each singular being 'stands out' towards other singular beings. Community takes *place* for others and through others. Community is not a collection of atomic individuals who, as libertarians have it, engage in contractual relationships. The place of the community, its *topos*, is not the place of 'egos' but a place of 'I's who are always already others – for otherwise they would be nothing at all.

Here, it is important to stress that place is hardly ever thought of, neither in communitarian nor in libertarian discussions and the reason is their ingrained immanentism. How, after all, can you think place when you have cancelled out all relations? Is place, the taking-place of community, not the refutation of interiority? Where communitarians occasionally have sometimes a rather primitive understanding of place – often couched in terms of a 'holy', 'immortal', 'unchanging', or 'perennial' soil that 'grounds' the community – libertarians are generally blissfully unaware of place. The idea of atomic individuals signing contracts that allow them to live together leaves one to ponder *where* it was that this signing session took place. The well-known idea that there was a primordial situation that was put to an end by a signing of contracts is, according to Sloterdijk (2004: 288), nothing less than a 'topological nirvana'. The libertarian assumes that human beings are capable of community insofar as they are 'groundless'. Only a pure population, uncontaminated by history, by bodies, by soil and by place, can function as 'guinea pigs in Rawlsian experimentations of justice' (2004: 289). Sloterdijk reminds us that this kind of thinking underpins immigration policies in Europe: it is assumed that migrants who aspire to become citizens are somehow able to wipe away the dust of yesterday. Rawls presupposes a humanity capable of breaking up with itself. The best philosopher of justice, Sloterdijk remarks, turns out to be a very bad sociologist.

For Nancy, the ecstasy that is community implies that one singular being – a body, my body, your body, *not* the body – is the locus of other singular beings. He uses neologisms such as 'clinamen' – leaning over – or 'compearance' – appearing together – but also ordinary concepts such as 'sharing', 'passion', 'contagion', or 'exposure' to express the openness of one singular being to the other: what is my or your own is exactly our readiness to open ourselves to whatever it is that can intrude us. A new ethics thinks community as a community of singular beings. In a crucial passage, Nancy explains why this is different from the communitarian or libertarian experiments with community. The task of the community is not a *project* that consists of activities that lead to the figuring or modelling of 'a communitarian essence in order to present it to ourselves and to celebrate it'; on the contrary, it is a matter of *thinking* community 'beyond communitarians models and remodelings' (Nancy 1991: 22). To understand this task in terms of a project, that is in terms of work that needs to be done, is to succumb to the idea that community can be technically organized (Nancy 2003: 26), indeed, that it is, in fact, nothing else than organization. Those who crave for excellent business communities fail to understand the true meaning of community and will therefore inevitably fail in their efforts. The paradox of communitarian initiatives, in the world of management and organization often carried out in the name of business ethics, is that community is thought of in terms of a subject, that is to say, in terms of what is the very denial of community. Too often, the place of the community is only thought of as a 'presence-to-itself', as an 'object for a subject', as 'what is represented to us': How are *we* to understand processes of globalization? Who are the stakeholders for whom *we* assume responsibility? What do political developments have in store for *us*? What are *our* weak and strong points? With what kind of norms and values do *we* want to engage with the world? What is *our* mission in the world?

According to Nancy, these are exactly not the questions that need to be asked. Again and again, reflection starts with establishing the own identity – in terms of mission, values, nationality, norms, and so on – and then the world and its objects – stakeholders, politics, and so on – are placed within it. The point is that we do not have the freedom to do this. Or rather, doing this is based on a fatally wrong conceptualization, not only of community, but also of freedom. Freedom is not about appropriating the world and then reordering it in ways that we like: this really amounts to subjecting the world to our own immanence. Neither is freedom just a being out of yourself or a kind of self-loss for this wrongly assumes that there was once an immanence that has now finally been transcended. You can only let in the world if you let yourself out in the world. This implies that freedom is neither about autonomy nor about heteronomy As Nancy sees it, freedom is about being present in the world rather than about being opposed to the world. It coincides with what Nancy understands as existence which is always co-existence:

> Understood thus, freedom is not a sense conferred on existence (like the senseless sense of the self-constitution of a subject or freedom as essence). Rather, it is the very *fact* of existence as open to existing itself. This fact *is* sense.
>
> (Nancy 1993: 13)

Freedom is neither a property nor a means to but the 'very being or truth of sense'. In his oftentimes cryptic prose, Nancy (1988: 96) refers to freedom as the 'spacing of space'. Above, we have seen that singular – identity-less – beings open up to space. When Nancy argues that freedom 'spaces' this space, he wants us to understand freedom as what holds space and therefore denies immanence or interiority. Freedom allows for or rather is the division of singular beings understood here as sense-sharing. It can only be maintained if we embrace the indefinite openness and acceptance of intrusion. Freedom, Nancy (2001: 127–38) claims, always comes from the outside. This is what I understand as the gist of his onto-ethics.

What to do with business ethics?

Business ethics asks the wrong kind of questions and therefore lacks substantial moral criticism. It soars between the seductions of communitarians and libertarians alike: the world of business obviously cannot do without libertarian constructs but neither can it do without communitarian ones. Business ethics suffers from the problem of immanentism which becomes manifest in *both* a tendency to organize or plan ideal communities *and* in a willingness to expel all strangeness from the heart of organizations. It therefore merely deploys an enormous list of strategies – ranging from stakeholder analyses to initiatives for the establishment of corporate identities – that help to perpetuate business communities as they are.

How to counteract this? To be frank, I do not know. For me, the ideas put forward by Nancy are suggestive enough, but many scholars in the area of business ethics will no doubt dismiss them as totally unrealistic, if not preposterous. They have good – organizational, financial, academic – reasons for this. *But to understand the ethics of business, we need not be business ethicists.* It is, I propose, very important to keep a discourse going about the ethics of business that comes from the outside. There should be some noise and, indeed, some strangeness in a world that generally does not manifest any doubt whatsoever about the goodness of its own endeavour. Contestation is thus all that matters here. What I hold against the notion of ethical business communities is quite simply the idea that it does not invite us to explore new communal possibilities, that it takes existing communities as a manageable project and that it is therefore profoundly a-political. It is for this reason that business ethics asks the wrong kind of questions. As we have seen, these questions invariably focus on a '*we*' – who are *our* stakeholders? what are *our* norms and values? what is *our* mission in the world? and so on – and therefore preclude a communality with the other, with the stranger, with the non-we. So then, what are the kind of questions that we should ask in our study of the ethicality of business?

Here are some provocative suggestions about a possible ethics of business that I leave you, dear reader, to ponder:

- Is an ethics possible that comes from the outside, that does not play the rule of the games and that is, strictly in this sense, deliberately unrealistic?
- Is an ethics possible that tries to overcome and, indeed, takes issue with the nostalgic craving for communities?
- Is an ethics possible that is both post-communitarian and post-individual?
- Is an ethics possible that is alienating in the sense that it is open to intrusions and visits from elsewhere?
- Is an ethics possible that does not work with a particular kind of community – our community, our company, our department – but from within *the* community? Is there, in other words, an ethics that is truly political or anthropological?
- Is there an ethics possible that does not view the community as a teleological project?
- Is there an ethics possible that is about intra-communal sense-sharing rather than about identity, norm, essence, value, or mission within a particular community?
- Is there, finally, an ethics possible that is present in the world and that, in this sense, embraces freedom?

Notes

1 Thanks are due to Bobby Banerjee, Ignaas Devisch, Campbell Jones and the editors of this volume.
2 As the Dutch prime minister Balkenende put it not long ago: 'The Dutch nation is and will remain a Christian nation'. This political essentialism was a response to president Chirac's declaration that the essence of the French state is neutrality with respect to religion. Mutual differences notwithstanding, in both countries the forced integration of minorities, especially the Islamic one, is a key political issue. Here, one might wonder where secularism and missionary zeal meet. See, for a devastating critique of political essentialism in the institutions of the European Union: Nicole Dewandre (2002) *Critique de la raison administrative. Pour une Europe ironiste*. In this important book, written by a former member of the European Parliament, it is argued that Platonist essentialism haunts the administrative body that should bring Europe together. According to Dewandre, the major problem of this administration is that it is organized as if it has a mission of truth. The alternative she proposes has the following elements: more pragmatics, more irony, less hierarchy, more openness to chance, no language in the name of the collective ('we'), economic use of language, and more countervailing powers at the heart of these administrative bodies.

Chapter 3

The ethics of globalization

Eduardo Ibarra-Colado[1]

Editors' introduction

If in the previous chapter Europeans were imagined as floating somewhere between a nostalgic past and an imagined future, between a dream and a nightmare, one might say, then what of those who can only be envious of the privileges that such floating subjects enjoy here-and-now, irrespective of dreams and nightmares? These are the questions that Eduardo Ibarra-Colado explores in this chapter, writing from the vantage point of an intellectual in the developing world; in his case, Mexico. This is a context for business and management ethics that began its journey into modernity under the harsh tutelage of the Jesuits, and which, for much of its history has been by-passed by the Enlightenment. Now, in the age of globalization, rational calculation operates as the only basis for a progress in which modernity seems to be approaching its own limits, expressed by the exhaustion of its own modes of domination. In this chapter the parameters of this modernity are sketched; the limits of modernity are explored through a series of questions; and the condition of modernity specified in terms of three basic principles that define liberalism: individual freedom, the free market and the limited state. While this project is much vaunted in the metropolitan centres of the world economy it was, in fact, in the Latin American periphery that many of its first applications were made, in Pinochet's Chile.

In contemporary times, Mexico, a country at the margins of modernity, illustrates in a renewed form how the domination that was manifest 500 years ago in the conquest of land is now expressed in the conquest of markets; where previously it was economic, religious and cultural imperialism that subjugated the margins, now it is neo-liberal globalization. As ever, the costs of such a rational project weigh most heavily on those at the margins.

Viewed from the margins, the gap between the liberal project and its realization has widened during recent years, exhibiting an unequal and unjust global world in which a few concentrate wealth and the majority remain in conditions of poverty. In such circumstances, a new ethics, an ethics of the South against the North is required, argues Ibarra-Colado. He proceeds to outline what such an ethics must encompass. As he says, the 'only option is to learn how to live together and to build a real planetary civilization with the basic purpose of preserving life and providing the conditions for a better existence for humankind'. The chapter offers a call for action and reflection.

We live in an uneasy world where discourses imagining a non-existent reality constantly collide with ever greater force against existing realities. Globalization was initially cast as the renewed promise of modernity: progress would finally guarantee the well-being and happiness of society, thus realizing the values of the Enlightenment. However, despite its positive declarations, globalization has led to a resurgence of exclusion; this has largely been caused by inequalities that show the world to be a fragmented space where some people benefit at the expense of others. It is a world that speaks of peace, democracy and development but which in reality operates based on war, totalitarianism, fraud and corruption: as its identity-mark it tolerates a boundless concentration of wealth, forcing many people to live on the *margins* of 'civilization'.

In order to understand this new global configuration it is necessary to recognize that its benefits and promises have been narrated from the Centre, imposing Western truths and projects on the rest of the world, defended through the use of force and the myth of reason. But it is also essential that we recognize that we do not face a new reality but rather the advanced stage of modernity. Five hundred years ago, with the invention of America (O'Gorman 1972) and the beginning of the Conquest of the 'New World', an *ethics of domination* was exercised to integrate the indigenous peoples, imposing the totalitarianism of the 'modern self' (Florescano 1994). The process of conquering the Other, of invalidating the Other's original identity and history, has never been concluded. It remains unfinished, permitting the strengthening and expansion of the empire of Western reason, thereby perpetuating modernity as a process of domination. Thus, globalization represents an exacerbated modernity in which rational calculation operates as the only basis for progress, concealing that which is not European (Dussel 1995).

Today, modernity seems to be approaching its own limits, expressed by the exhaustion of its own modes of domination. Foremost, economic stability is approaching its limits because of vulnerabilities associated with a speculative economy that destroys productive capacities and, in so doing, disrupts employment, consumption and the possibilities of expanding development and well-being. The movement of capital becomes a weapon used to force others to yield to the will of the corporations, which impose their conditions upon governments and entire nations. In the same way, the control of external debt has been used by the creditors as a tool of domination in order to impose economic reforms that are consistent with the global project. *How much longer will this civilization endure that favours the concentration of wealth and pushes ever larger sectors of the population into unemployment, poverty and criminal activity?*

In a similar manner, industrial production is pushed to its limits in the absence of sufficiently dynamic markets because of decreased purchasing power amongst broad sectors of the population, and because of sumptuous, discretionary and extravagant spending by the wealthy minority. The pattern of production and its modes of consumption favour the desires of those who can pay rather than the basic needs of those with limited purchasing power. The predominance of 'throwaway consumption' reaches its limits in the irrational use of energy, provoking a possibly irreversible sickening of the planet that manifests itself through climate change, global warming, the disappearance of an infinite number of species of fauna and flora and the destruction of the ozone layer (Sarukhán and Whyte 2005; Singer 2002; Ziegler 2003). *How much longer will this civilization endure in favouring luxury spending while ignoring the basic needs of the population and the requirements for planetary survival?*

Finally, knowledge is approaching its limits in the standardization of the mentalities of extensive masses of people, dominated by an education based on know-how, information saturation and the frivolity of the mass communications media. It is a force that eats away at culture, producing an 'enlightened ignorance' depriving people of historical memory and cultural roots, increasingly functioning on the basis of emotions and fears, degrading people's reflective capacity and values. *How much longer will this civilization endure in favouring ignorance, conditioned responses, identities made of plastic and McDonald's culture?* (Monsiváis 2002: 19–20; Ritzer 1998).

The modern world promise was to provide development, prevent violence, preserve the planet and promote reason – four goals that have repeatedly remained unfulfilled – such that the project itself is at a crossroads. The contradictions multiply, creating tension between the narratives of progress and the realities of marginalization, failing to resolve problems of development and not silencing the conquered, who maintain a presence based on their historical memory, resisting, acting and demanding justice. *For how much longer will the world be able to tolerate this history of violence, exclusion and domination?*[2]

The current crossroads is a historic moment in which *the world faces the limitations of the use of force to perpetuate domination*, since the capacity to destroy has been superimposed upon the capacity to subjugate.

Reason is used against itself, having produced the knowledge with which the barbarities of modernity are carried out, amongst invasions, despotisms, and resistances. The military might of the great powers is limited by its own growing vulnerability when facing smaller enemies that have found ways to disregard security systems and thus cause great damage.[3] One of the characteristics of terrorism is its capacity to mobilize, appear, act and vanish in order to regroup and attack again, utilizing surprise, taking advantage of the ambivalence of technology, and playing with the defensive resources of its enemies.

The vulnerability of complex systems has been made possible thanks to three products of modernity itself. First, *illegal trade*, dedicated to the trafficking of arms and materials necessary for the creation of attack devices. Second, drug trafficking and money laundering, established in order to finance resistance activities. Finally, the new technologies have allowed for the broad and uncontrolled circulation of knowledge and information, making breeches in security systems possible (Sevares 2003; Ziegler 2003: 91). Due to this growing fragility, modernity has remained trapped in a never-ending vicious circle of *destruction → security-surveillance-control → destruction*, from which there appears to be no escape. Today, this destructive capacity is distributed throughout the entire planet, generating a consciousness that, even though it may not be possible to win, it is possible to prevent the enemy's triumph, leading down the road of no return: *the irrationality of domination is found in its capacity for mutual destruction and, as a consequence, in the annulment, for one side as well as the other, of any possible future.*

Modernity is limited as a project of domination due to the absence of any common rules favouring the discretionary movement of capital, the manipulation of messages and information, and the promotion of irrational consumption, all of which have led to confrontation and violence. Globalization is that historical moment of modernity in which domination ceases to be viable and make sense, opening the doors to the construction of a new ethics, based on principles of respecting differences and negotiating basic agreements of coexistence, as the only alternative. There exists no option other than to *recover reason*, supported by dialogue without exclusions, based on shared responsibility. In order to do so, the vindication of humanity's ethical project proves to be essential. However, the crossroads of modernity does not end here.

The project of modernity confronts its very meaning as Reason and, as a consequence, the shape assumed by economic, social and political institutions that promise progress in order to guarantee the welfare and happiness of society. Modernity, outwardly projected as being universal, is actually peculiar and diverse on the inside (Dussel 1997). What have been debated are the mentality and the principles upon which society is organized, determining in various moments the role occupied by the individual and the reaches of individual liberty, as well as the shape of the State and the limits on its action (Foucault 2003).

The idea of Reason that has been imposed ia an expansion of capitalism on a global level. It has an immanently instrumental connotation based on the domain of things and men through competition and rational calculus (Ibarra-Colado 2006). In the economic realm each individual competes *against* the others. The guarantee of individual liberty, above all other considerations, is the key to this project of domination.[4] Substantive reason as an inter-subjective act from which the ethical orientation of individual comportment is constructed for the benefit of all is lacking: individual action and the economy do not operate as means to achieve progress and the well-being of society. The supremacy of the state as the absolute totality from which individual behaviour is regulated, preserving the rights and well-being of the social whole, has been abandoned.

The pendulum of the history of modernity has oscillated between two extremes, generating tensions between individuals' liberty to pursue personal benefit through domination and force, and the rights of the society that seeks to defend itself through reasoned dialogue and cooperation. Two very different projects of civilization have developed: one based on the utilitarianism of commerce, production, and financial transactions, and the other on justice, solidarity and responsibility to the Other. Undoubtedly, the latter has lost out to the dominance of the first mercantilist project.

The first privatization wave: the corporation as a 'person'

Globalization is the most radical demonstration of disequilibrium between individual interests and the general welfare of society. The domination of politics by the markets is expressed in the relative weight that the state and the corporation have acquired over the last decades, favouring plunder and accumulation as components of the same equation. The corporation has been established as the personification of the individual and individual liberty. Its greatest innovation, as Drucker points out, was that it was the 'first autonomous institution in hundreds of years, the first to create a centre of power that, though within society, is independent of the central government of the national state' (quoted in Sampson 1995: 26).[5]

From this stance, the first task was to defeat the state to allow for the 'natural' development of markets. The key aspect was the privatization of the corporation, an entity that was originally created by the state to carry out public tasks that, because of their great cost or magnitude, the risk implied, or the scant profits represented, could not be realized by individual interests. They were semi-public institutions that often functioned as state concessions, thus it was assumed that they would have a finite life and would exist under strong governmental regulation (Attali 1989; Roy 1997: 71).

Their privatization, promoted throughout the nineteenth century, gave rise to the establishment of a normative framework of the company as a *natural entity*, with rights similar to those of individuals. In the US, for example, the Supreme Court of Justice established in 1886 the fourteenth amendment to the Constitution in order to indicate that a private company is a person and that, as such, it has the right to enjoy the protection that the constitution confers to any person (Bowman 1996: 37).[6] The legal recognition of the corporation as a 'person' established the conditions for the exercise of corporate power, with the goal of being able to always act in its own best interest (Korten 1999: 184).

Law enables corporations to preserve their rights and liberty against other subjects.[7] Their *right to privacy* and *commercial-in-confidence* stipulations strongly impede intervention and favour fraud and illegal business practices protected by bank secrecy and fiscal paradises. The scandals of companies such as Enron demonstrate the limitations of the laws and courts in regulating growing corporate power within globalization (Huffington 2003; Martín 2003: 522; Sevares 2003; Ziegler 2003). Similar cases are to be found globally.

Existing rules and regulations reduce risks for investors, *limiting their liability* (Roy 1997: 158). Socialization of company losses occurs, as corporate assets often are insufficient to cover damages or losses. Managers easily elude responsibility for inefficiency and errors without being obliged to make amends for the damage they cause, since the laws hold the corporation responsible in its condition as a legal individual (Bakan 2004: 79). Externalities are accepted (see Henderson conversation in Capra 1989) and remedies are few and costly. The institutional network of the law affirms corporate power, converting litigation into a new commercial transaction in which it is a commercial decision whether to respect the law or to proceed unscrupulously.

Finally, the laws have also seen to *the protection of the rights of stockholders before the power of the managers*, establishing limits on managers' ability to make decisions. Shareholder interests prevail. Any decision that ties to benefit other individuals constitutes a violation of the law and disloyal behaviour before the corporation (Bakan 2004: 35–6; Micklethwait and Wooldridge 2003: 113, discussing the 1916 legal precedent).

Control of managers is furthered by the design of a corporate governance structure centred on the creation of value for shareholders. Numeric performance, expressed in dividends, is imposed as the basic criterion for determining results. The privatization of the corporation puts private interests before general welfare. The protection of personal liberty, that is to say, the deregulation of economic activity, was achieved paradoxically through the regulation of limits to state and societal intervention, establishing legal regulations that hinder public control over private activities. The dissemination of liberalism as the mentality of an age made these transformations possible.

The liberal project: the invisible hand and its marginal ethical content

Three basic principles defined liberalism: *individual freedom*, the *free market* and the *limited state*. The institutional and regulatory basis established expedited the consolidation of the large private corporation as the basic organizational unit of the economy at the beginning of the twentieth century. Liberalism synthesises the foundations and assumptions that sustain and legitimate a *corporate power of marginal ethical content*. According to the liberal mentality, the natural functioning of the economy needs individual liberty, with people acting rationally in order to try to satisfy their personal interests. The only moral obligation of the individual rests in the maximization of one's own gains and its only limit is the law insofar as it protects others' liberty. Thus, the market provides, through the system of prices, the information that is required by economic agents to maximize their utility by means of voluntary exchange. The will to cooperate is based in the belief of the parties involved in such an exchange that it will be in their interest, with the coordination of such economic activities left to the 'invisible hand' of competition, leading to general equilibrium. Social order occurs spontaneously (Friedman 1962; Hayek 1990a). Liberty of subjects occurs through *homo oeconomicus* acting however it wants to maximize its utility, as long as it complies with the rules and procedures of exchange, stripping the economic act of substantive evaluative content other than winning the competitive struggle.

Every individual is responsible for their own acts and fulfilment. Inequality is naturalized in at least two senses. First, *unequal competition* is made natural because the rules which apply – being previously known and accepted – are the same for everyone. Thus, a principle of formal justice is established, rejecting the real differences between individuals and disregarding the conditions that really bring about competition. Second, *social inequality* is naturalized, as economic success corresponds to the individuals that best adapt to the market in a fortuitous process of selection (Hayek 1990a). Thus, for liberalism inequality is a positive value and unemployment a necessary mechanism for any efficient market economy (Friedman and Friedman 1990; Mises 1979).

The economy is seen to function on the basis of natural relationships of exchange dictated by formal equality. Power disappears and there is no longer any space for consideration of goals other than accumulation. Because of this, 'the common good' or 'social justice' are judged as lacking any basis, alluding to ambiguous goals, the renunciation of the rule of law, and totalitarianism, thus attacking free society itself (Hayek 1990a, 1978).

Interest groups, such as labour unions, are interpreted as a form of mirage, a discrimination that is an affront to liberty (Hayek 1990b: 2). In this way, every individual act, based on intelligence, individual initiative, and liberty, is considered to be an ethical act unlimited by social morality. However, liberalism supposes a very limited concept of ethics – we might even say it has a marginal concept of ethics – that is basically composed of a set of norms that guide humans towards their goal. If that goal is a person's own well-being, then the behaviour of economic agents will essentially be ethical, disregarding the consequences that arise from their acts before others. In a spontaneous order based on natural selection, there is no place for responsibility for 'unforeseen consequences'. These have not been deliberately provoked and no one individual can be held responsible for the fact that such realities 'are produced' (Hayek 1990b). The liberal project is basically concerned with the expansion of individual liberty, specifically defined. Individual liberty and its corollary of freedom of business are the basis of social order: the actions of free individuals create and shape society rather than society socially constructing individuals.[8]

Conservative economic liberalism, based on a *marginal ethics* that defends the operational liberty of the individual in order to guarantee *marginal utility*, contrasts with radical political liberalism based on a reflective ethics seeking to make new modes of existence possible. These two routes show substantial differences. The first route leads to the subjection of the individual by the 'invisible hand' of competition, reducing human existence to the inescapable desire always to obtain the maximum benefit. In this case, a mode of rationality operates that splits the economy from society, facilitating introjections of work routines and rules of conduct based on individual interests. Such ego-ism, projected by liberalism as the new identity of the modern self, disarticulates the social fabric, hindering any alternative mode of existence (Zermeño 2005). The second route leads to the liberation of the individual as a subject, through reflective dialogue with others. Such subjects experience some possibility of transforming the modern type of individuality (Foucault 2000: 336). In this case, subjects are superimposed onto the market, deciding their modes of production and consumption and the terms of their relationships, always accepting responsibility for their acts before others (Ibarra-Colado 2002: 178–80).

Liberty is an unforsakeable freedom for liberalism as there is no acceptable alternative. It is a natural condition so one must always act in one's own benefit, and the natural state of the economy, underpinned by the 'invisible hand' of competition.[9] The state's only obligation is that of preserving liberty, limiting itself to protecting the harmony of the factors of production and to removing obstacles to private property's ability to act in its own favour. It is a limited state, as its functions must be restricted to the protection of the rights of people, those rights that foster the individual's autonomy to decide and act. The state is once again defeated, confronting the society that created it, converting itself through policies that ensure that every participant respects the rules of the game of competition. In its precariousness, the state ends up being at the service of the *individual person* and, above all, the *individual corporation*.

Liberalism, in its most extreme or savage version, would lead to the dissolution of politics and those spaces which are public, the disappearance of society and the general interest, in favour of unlimited individual liberty, ruled by the 'natural' law of survival of the fittest and the related principle that 'the end justifies the means'. Such individualism is the beginning and end of all explanation, leaving no space for collective organization or action, or for the recognition of differences between societies based on different identities, customs, and cultures. A linear evolutionism is adopted that places modern society based on the corporation as its culminating moment; the genealogy of modernity is eliminated, an atemporal stationary totalitarianism is established that negates any possibility for change that might lead to a different future. Market relationships convert all human activity into commercial activity that finds its original meaning supplanted and ends up being reduced to objects of exchange with the only purpose being the pursuit of profit. All human beings who lack work, do not possess buying power, or do not have assets for savings or investment will automatically find themselves invisible in modernity, because they fail to translate their being into meaningful signals.

Nonetheless, this project, in its zeal for the conquest of modernity, ends up betraying itself: even though it reaffirms the rational behaviour of the individual it assumes as an indisputable truth an ideal formulation of human behaviour constantly refuted by reality. Liberalism moves in the sphere of beliefs, defending the existence of that spontaneous social order that depends upon the 'invisible hand' of competition as a revealed truth. The dogma displaces human understanding in favour of the naturalization of markets, under which the *homo oeconomicus* and its freedom are erected as the beginning and ultimate end of its civilizing project.

We have arrived at the moment when the present, dominated by liberalism, meets the past of the conquest of the 'New World'. Five hundred years ago, the mentality of the conqueror deemed the Amerindian peoples to be barbarian societies ruled by the devil, practising human sacrifices in worship of false gods; Christian modernity appeared as its legitimate saviour, through domination it would evangelize the pagans, planting the seeds of civilization that would free them from the power of the devil (Florescano 1994: 65). Today the liberal mentality appears to revive the ghosts of the conquest as it pays homage to the Market God in the temples of banking and commerce, silently and in discreet sacrifice offering up millions of *defective consumers* (Bauman 1998: 96), in exchange for substantial sums of money. Its victims, the poor, unemployed and marginalized, are offered up in order to purify the sinful soul of the individualist, pragmatic and antisocial spirit of accumulation. Faced with this situation, we cannot help but ask ourselves, based upon what modernity, and along with it, based upon what ethical project, will it be possible to restore Reason and return to society the role that the markets have snatched away?

The second privatization wave: the corporatization of the world

While the liberal project has been unable to keep it promises its ideas and arguments increasingly define the reach of politics, not to eliminate the state, whose strengths as a regulatory mechanism were well-known and appreciated by the liberals themselves, but to reinforce the position of the large corporation as the basic space for the structuring of human activity, subordinating state actions and the needs of society to the logic of competition.

After the First World War alternative visions of the functioning of the economy and the role of the state in guaranteeing social progress were created. The crisis of 1929 weakened liberalism, changing the direction of the pendulum of modernity towards a different project. Beginning at that moment and during the following four decades, the state was established as an essential agent in the regulation of economic activity, promoting a set of government actions in favour of development and compensating sectors of the population hurt by the imperfect operation of markets. Growing state interventionism, which translated into a *bureaucratization of the world* (Rizzi 1985; Burnham 1960) led to the establishment of the Welfare State (Jacoby 1997), in which a set of norms and institutions operated in order to protect the general interests of society before individual economic liberty. It seemed clear, as such, that the terms of the liberal scheme had been reversed, restoring the predominance of the state and politics over the power of corporations and the market: in public decisions, society came first, and so one ought always act for its benefit.[10] From this point of view, economic activity was subordinated to the welfare goals of society and the corporation was judged to be one more means, amongst many others, for the realization of society's well-being.

The new government mentality was openly questioned by liberal ideologues, who insisted that it was a historic error that would soon be shown to be less than viable. Beginning with the Second World War, authors such as Mises, Hayek and Friedman argued that Keynesian-inspired interventionist policies were an affront to individual liberties, distorting the natural operation of markets (Gamble 1996: 151–9). They would lead, sooner or later, to profound economic crises which would demonstrate that state welfare aggravates problems instead of solving them.

Despite the momentary successes of a form of government based on increasing public spending to sustain demand, its associated ills would be expressed through low levels of growth with high levels of inflation and, in the long term, through problems of economic stagnation and recession. Beginning in the 1970s, clear symptoms of the failure of state welfarism began to appear, as attention to social necessities translated into growing public indebtedness, provoking a severe fiscal crisis without any sign of possible solution. During this time, the liberal economists redoubled their attacks with the goal of reinstating a regimen of 'good government' based on the free market and free competition in which the large corporations, with help from the state apparatus, would be able to extend their all-encompassing reach.[11] A set of recipes began to be put into place that promised the revival of stable and lasting economic growth, leading to a process of complex and unequal trade being gradually disseminated to all corners of the globe. Thus began the path towards what we can describe as the *corporatization of the world*, produced by a second intensive privatization wave, which will allow nothing to escape from the market and the large corporation's unbridled desires for conquest.

The first neo-liberal experience took place in Latin America. Under the Pinochet dictatorship, Chile established itself as the test laboratory for the neo-liberal prescription, which gave it the 'prestige' of offering itself as an example to be followed all over the region (Foxley 1983; Winn 2004). Towards the end of the 1970s and the beginning of the 1980s, other neo-liberal programs began to operate in England (Thatcher/Major), the US (Reagan/Bush), Australia (Hawke/Keating), Germany (Kohl), and Japan (Nakasone/Miyazawa). The process was reinforced at the end of the 1980s by the fall of communism in Eastern Europe and the Soviet Union and was gradually extended to different regions and countries, until it came to form today's universal neo-liberal globalization (Gray 2000; Amin 2003; Bello 2001; Chossudovsky 2003; Flores-Olea and Mariña 2004).

The neo-liberal formula was conceived via various privatization policies that have allowed just about everything to be given to the corporation. Amongst these privatizations, the sales of public enterprises within diverse areas such as the banking, telecommunications, petrochemical, steel, port, railroad, mining, cane mill, and airport sectors stand out. With these sales, the states lose control over society's energy and natural resources and over strategic sectors, thus weakening national sovereignty.

In a second generation of privatizations we find public services traditionally provided by government agencies – public lighting, water, sewers, cleaning services, security, etc. – and services that safeguard the basic rights of society, such as food, health care, education, housing, recreation, turning all of these into profitable businesses available only to those who can pay. The process is reinforced by the *fiscal discipline and monetary stability* that guarantee the restriction of public spending and, consequently, the strengthening of the markets in which the previously privatized sectors began to operate.[12]

Finally, privatization reaches its most extreme form when the public institutions or organizations still remaining are encouraged to function as if they were businesses. Artificial markets are created to compete for scarce resources, operating through diverse mechanisms of regulation at a distance (Ibarra-Colado 2005). In imposing competition as the logic of their operation, the original goals of public agencies and social organizations are displaced by the inexorable requirement of preserving their ability to survive economically. In this way, nothing escapes the market and everything is found within reach of corporate ambition.

Added to the process of privatizations in their different forms are processes of deregulation that seek to remove legally established limits and restrictions that circumscribe corporations' competitiveness and profit levels. Deregulation involves increasing the degree of freedom that companies have at the time of resource investment, establishing or closing plants, adjusting their personnel force, transferring capital from one country or region to another, or assuming their responsibilities before consumers and the environment. These legal reforms were carried out with new provisions that favoured the reduction of taxes levied on elevated incomes and the elimination of controls over financial movements.

The flexibilization of labour legislation played an especially significant role in that it allowed for the reduction of labour costs and more intense utilization of the labour force. Flexibility translated into the modification of the scope of collective bargaining agreements, or even their elimination and substitution by individual contracts in which the company individually agrees time, mobility, and remuneration. *Salary contention*, repression of unions and the restoration of a 'normal' unemployment level all permit a large excess labour force, guaranteeing discipline, order and profits. Labour flexibility in terms of the systematic push to make work precarious, implies an important reduction in companies' economic costs and the dismantling of the social fabric sustaining worker organization and resistance (Zermeño 2005).

In general the neo-liberal formula, in each of the dimensions that we have discussed, proposes an environment of free conduct providing great advantages for organizations to compete and act in their own benefit, without much consideration of the consequences of this indiscriminate liberty for society.

The other key element of the neo-liberal strategy can now be situated: increasing the *commercial aperture through the establishment of free trade agreements*, an asymmetrical process that results in the promotion of a *protectionist neo-liberalism* in the countries of the Centre, represented in exemplary terms by the US (Amin 2003; Krugman 2003: 385–7), promoting a *self-destructive neo-liberalism* based on an aggressive policy of commercial opening in the countries of the margins, as abundantly demonstrated by the experiences of diverse nations in Latin America

(Demmers *et al.* 2001; Phillips 1998; Zea 1996). The increasing inequality in the region is an unquestionable symptom of the inherent injustice of this model.

In addition to having a greater consolidation of regulatory institutions and the power that is given to them by the great financial capitals that are found in their territories, the countries of the Centre have available to them the wealth generated at the margins, thanks to the export of capital as external debt service payments, the operation of International Financial Institutions (IFIs), and the destruction of the few mechanisms regulating economic activity in its international dimension (Marichal 2003; George and Sabelli 1994; Hawley 2000).[13]

The IFIs are the guardians of neo-liberal globalization, limiting state interventionism in the nations of the margins by means of their adjustment programs. These institutions seek to universalize a mode of rationality based on the market, guaranteeing the accumulation of capital on a global level, in addition to containing local and regional conflicts and attending to the most serious social inequalities that could put the regime of accumulation at risk. One of their basic instruments of control rests in the conditional provision of 'fresh' funds that states require in order to comply punctually with financial obligations and maintain certain priority social programs. In turn, trade agreements have often acquired the character of meta-legislations that are held to above all else, including the constitutional provisions of participating nations, permitting a modulation of the role of the state, thus protecting economic competition and free trade. Such asymmetries explain why the greatest costs of neo-liberal globalization always weigh on those countries at the margins of modernity, illustrating a renewed form of domination that was manifest 500 years ago in the conquest of land, which is now expressed in the conquest of markets.

Self-destructive neo-liberalism in facts: the exemplary case of Mexico

Mexico's experience is exemplary because of its radical nature and its enormous social consequences (Guillén 1997; Otero 1996, 2002). The beginning of the transformation of Mexico's economic model can be traced back to the early 1980s, in the context of a deep crisis that helped to disarticulate some old institutions and weaken certain social forces that were an obstacle to the establishment of a new development model based on a neo-liberal conception (Babb 2004: 171). The 'lost decade' can be characterized as a period of governmental action based on non-action, because government decided not to negotiate or answer the demands of social agents, in a strategy of exhaustion of resistance and the destruction of collective identities. The 1990s was a period of reconstruction based on free market agreements, with the government actively leading the transformation of the country and operating policies and programs already negotiated with some IFIs (Ibarra-Colado 1998).

Within a short period, Mexico transformed itself from a closed economy sustained by an authoritarian government to one of the most open economies in the world, based on the signing of 12 free trade agreements. These agreements, led by NAFTA, involve Mexican commercial relationships with 32 countries across the globe, representing 860 million potential consumers (SEP 2003: 23). The last piece of this puzzle will be the *Free Trade Agreement of the Americas* (ALCA) represented by the 'Plan Puebla-Panama' that was proposed in 2000 by the current Mexican government. In addition, during this period Mexico privatized nearly 1000 public enterprises and dismantled or transformed most of its welfare institutions. The privatization process reported Treasury inflows of US$31.5 billion during the period 1982–2001, an amount that represents only 28.8 per cent of the debt taken by the state to finance the failure and bankruptcy of some of the companies privatized. Some examples are the rescue of banks, highways, sugar cane mills and airlines, calculated at US$109 billion (Ramírez 1995; MacLeod 2004). It has undoubtedly been good business but the question is 'for whom?'. The Mexican government still has 217 public enterprises, most of them in strategic sectors such as oil and electricity, which are now also at risk of being privatized (González 2003). The strategy followed by the state has been the *de facto* abandonment of social institutions, such as the public health sector, or the transformation of other governmental agencies such as social financing of housing or public education, in order to transfer the costs to the final consumer.[14]

Finally, the re-privatization of the banking system was unique in the world because it implied an almost 90 per cent de-nationalization of the industry. The banking system in Mexico was for a long time a national concession placed in the hands of the private sector. Law forbade foreign investment. In 1982, because of the economic crisis, the government nationalized the sector. Its re-privatization began in 1990, resulting now in a system almost completely controlled by nine foreign banks, such as Citigroup, Bilbao Viscaya Argentaria Bank, HSBC, Scotiabank and Santander. These groups control about 90 per cent of the total assets of the commercial banking system of the country (Santillán 2001; Murillo 2002).

All these processes were accompanied by huge scandals of bribery and corruption and have involved incredible social costs. For example, the FOBAPROA-IPAB laws (Bank Savings Protection Fund-Institute for the Protection of Bank Savings), approved in order to carry out the banking rescue after the 1995 crisis, have cost Mexican taxpayers US$42 billion up to 2004, and still represent a debt of US$67 billion (Méndez 2004a). To consider the immensity of these amounts, they are similar to the cost of the Iraq war for the US – estimated at US$120 billion – and less than the cost of the Marshall Plan for the reconstruction of Europe after the Second World

War – estimated at US$90 billion (González 2004a). These data acquire their real dimension when we consider that Mexico's gross domestic product in 2002 was US$637.2 billion.

In summary, Mexico provides a good example of the problems involved with the current globalization process and the ethical implications of the radical application of free market economic principles. It explains why Mexico is a country of deep contrasts, indicating the normality of injustice and exclusion: more than 50 per cent of Mexico's population lives in conditions of moderate poverty and more than 20 per cent lives in extreme poverty (World Bank 2004: 15; Cortés *et al.* 2002), but the country also has a huge concentration of wealth in the hands of few great local millionaires.[15] Let's mention just one example. According to a recent report by Forbes.com, Carlos Slim-Helú, owner of the Carso Group, was in 2005 the fourth richest person on the planet, amassing a fortune calculated at US$23.8 billion (Kroll and Goldman 2005). Such a fortune would be enough to cover the minimum legal salary of 15.5 million Mexicans during one year. As the report establishes, this prominent businessman tripled his fortune in only nine years, amassing on average almost US$2 billion a year between 1996 and 2004.

Mexico also is one of the biggest exporters of labour power in the world: 9 per cent of the total population of the country works in the US. The annual net migratory flux has increased ten-fold in the last 30 years, representing more than 8.9 million Mexicans living in the US in 2001, including 3.5 million illegal workers. Its most important economic impact is related to the remittance of money: in 2003, for example, Mexico received US$13.2 billion, an amount superior to the resources received by direct foreign investment or tourism, and representing 79 per cent of the value of crude oil exports (González 2004b).

Ethics break in markets: towards a new civilizing project

What can the world learn from the Mexican experience? The incorporation of some developing countries into global markets has been a traumatic process, always involving deep tensions between economic imperatives, social demands in emerging democratic systems, and cultural traditions based on a cosmogony very different from those based on Reason in the modern world. The role played by corporations and governments appears central to the process but also there is the role of the IFIs as supposed regulators of the world 'order'. The economy has been placed at the helm of the process, so the old social inequalities, instead of being solved in the short run, have deepened with the argument that wealth must be produced first and then distributed. Can the population wait that long?[16]

The gap between the liberal project and its realization has widened during recent years, exhibiting an unequal and unjust global world in which a few concentrate wealth and the majority remain in conditions of poverty (Chossudovsky 2003; Bauman 1998: 70–1); in which unemployment appears as a problem without evident solution (Forrester 1999); where the constriction of the less developed nations does not have any limit because their external debts suffocate them, placing control of their territory, natural resources, and industry in the hands of transnational corporations. One of the most visible consequences of this new 'order' has been an increasing violence, compelling modern society to become an imprisoned society: wealthy people must live inside their great mansions with very sophisticated systems of surveillance and protection; poor people must be contained by the gaze of police and the army or other special private forces of order, representing more market opportunities, or be contained directly in prison. Thus, instead of progress and social justice there really is recurrent exclusion and endemic violence.

Consequently, the types of problems originally circumscribed in the so-called underdeveloped countries in global times attain a universal dimension: the richest countries of the world are beginning to struggle with similar problems, though to a lesser extent, such as poverty, unemployment, health insecurity and education deficits but also delinquency and corruption. Crisis situations such as Hurricane Katrina in New Orleans expose the miserable underlife for all to see. As a result, increasing opposition from social sectors all over the world is emerging because they no longer believe in the ever postponed and unredeemed promises of globalization. The *citizens of the world* are the only global agents that have not yet arrived at full recognition of their role in the construction of the new global order; the official agents that run the world always consider them to be a problem.[17] Is there any solution?

There is no doubt that modernity is confronting the limits of its historical viability as a civilizing project for humanity. Conquest based on an ethics of domination no longer is feasible or makes sense. Unfortunately, such a project is still represented by the US' vocation of subjugation, which goes to extremes in order to eliminate its adversaries under the old banners of force, occupation and domination, trying to leave no trace of the historical memory or the values of the defeated (Huntington 1997; Amin 2003).[18]

There appears to be no alternative other than an inclusive and just globalization sustained by a new ethics, under principles of respect of differences and the negotiation of basic agreements between communities and nations to guarantee coexistence and collaboration. Instead of an ethics of domination, the world needs a new ethics based on the protection of life. To move in this direction *ethics must break in markets* to restore the essential place of society over economy. It is necessary to move from economic reductionism based only on one's own individual/private best interest to an ethics based in the recognition of 'the Other' that achieves the best interest of communities.

The marginal ethics defended by the liberal economy must be definitively displaced by a new ethics based on the recognition that the world is already saturated and, consequently, that there is no place for conquest and domination (Bauman 2002). The only option is to learn how to live together and to build a real planetary civilization with the basic purpose of preserving life and providing the conditions for a better existence for humankind (Morin and Kern 1998; Singer 2002). Thereby, a successful resolution of the direction to take at the crossroads of modernity depends on the capacity of each culture and community, side by side, one with the Others, to reinvent the ethical commitments of humanity to move towards a new civilizing project.

The complex challenge must be confronted by the inhabitants of the European and North American Centre as well as the communities and nations that are located on the margins. The opening of modernity to a diverse, inclusive and just world demands that the 'modern self' be conscious of the effects of its own actions, which up until now have been hidden by their own narratives (Mignolo 1999; Banerjee and Linstead 2001). It is necessary to understand that the failures of modernity are not simply the price to be paid in order to achieve the universal goal of progress;[19] on the contrary, such failures are the conditions under which the Centre has achieved its own particular progress, demonstrating the historical necessity of conquest and subjugation for the Empire of Reason (Galeano 1998). In order to transcend this ethics of domination that same Centre must accept that modernity, in order really to be considered as such, founds itself on the recognition and acceptance of differences. The modern Centre needs to confront a process of de-modernization, recovering all that the world of the Others offers in fulfilling a better life.

In turn, opening modernity to its own re-creation also demands that the peoples and nations that have been conquered and dominated recognize their own hybrid condition, given that their non-modern origin has been re-created through the avatars of uneven colonization. It is necessary to understand that they are, as Carlos Fuentes points out, 'the *mestizo* sum of contributions, encounters, assimilations, metamorphosis' (Fuentes 1997: 93). Consequently, instead of a clash of civilizations, the world needs a new encounter based on understanding and respect of differences as much as in the recognition of their possible complementary aspects. Thus, if we recognize the world as a mosaic of differences, the modern as well as the non-modern must critically confront each other regarding the history of modernity to facilitate the emergence of a new civilizing project. Each one must review the role that they have played, the responsibilities that they assume and the effects that their presence and their relationships generated, having changed themselves in the presence of the other, but also changed the other with their presence. Only in this way can one respond to the challenges of the present: how to restore the value of the conquered peoples' originating identities, while at the same time preserving the modern ideals of liberty and equality; how to preserve a sense of community side-by-side with the modern principle of individual autonomy, achieving their reconciliation? In synthesis, the challenge consists in substituting the ethics of domination for a new ethics that encourages a plural, inclusive, material coexistence upheld by the indivisible triad of liberty, justice and solidarity.

The *new ethics would be transmodern* because it entails the possibility of creating, from the outside, a multi-polar cultural world that recuperates the best of modern technological revolution, rejecting that which is anti-ecological and exclusively Western, and puts it at the service of differentiated evaluative worlds. It involves a project that goes beyond modernity in its recognition of the multicultural, poly-faceted, hybrid, post-colonial, pluralistic, tolerant, democratic and affirmative condition of the heterogeneous identities that make up the world (Dussel 2002: 236).[20]

The *new ethics is material* because it departs from the recognition of the universal principle that we are all human beings, an obvious and irrefutable material condition in any culture at any time. Therefore, the substantive goal of human existence is the production and reproduction of the material conditions for life, so humans can develop their capacities as members of social communities. According to this basic principle, any organization created by humans must favour protection of life in terms of the attendance of human necessities expressed in food, clothing, health and knowledge for a better existence. Any action, individual or conducted by groups or organizations that attack any kind of life – of a particular person/group or of the planet – must entail an ethical problem. The obvious example is war, but one can also think about an organization that generates problems such as unemployment, malnutrition, ignorance or any social relation that despoils the conditions of life, obstructing its development and, in extreme conditions, producing death.

The *new ethics is inclusive* because it is produced by the symmetric participation of everyone, those in charge of governments and organizations, but also the affected and excluded. In order to decide how society can produce and preserve the conditions of life, it is necessary to guarantee the participation of everyone through dialogue and conversation based on reason instead of force and violence. Debate and judgement about reality – the kind of actions that preserve life versus those that attack it – between different communities, cultures and nations is the only way to arrive to new consensuses to establish the minimum agreements to guarantee equity and justice for everyone. A basic condition to build agreements about what must need to be done is the reflective consideration by communities of their own economic, social, technical, political and organizational feasibility.

Finally, the *new ethics is critical* because it recognizes that any human action always produces some negative effects and then some victims. In its recursivity, social organization never ends and always produces costs for somebody, who then has the right to demand the necessary changes in order to improve their conditions of existence; the recursive reconstruction of the principles and rules of the global community must be founded in the recognition of these negative effects, giving voice to the affected, so society can constantly improve its modes of organization. The reflective condition of society rests in its capacity to recognize critically what is not functioning properly, remembering the fallible condition of human existence. A new ethics entails a 'will of re-organization' as a collective and inclusive process of creative destruction to produce a better planet for life.

The four main characteristics of a new ethics for a better global civilizing project can be summarized in ten main proposals:

1 The basis for ethics is the reflective protection of life.
2 The substantive goal of life is the well-being of humankind.
3 Participative dialogue and conversation based on reason are the foundations to building a new ethics.
4 Human freedom, but not isolation or individualism, is a basic value of society; its un-negotiable limit is the protection of life.
5 The well-being of humankind must be fulfilled by the exercise of free human action via cooperation and agreement.
6 Wealth is only a means for preserving life and providing the conditions for a better existence for humankind, so the economy must be at the service of society.
7 If corporations are a means to fulfil the well-being of humankind, then they are essentially social/public entities.
8 Therefore, managers are at the service of the people under the principle of 'the best interests of society'.
9 Society must regulate the economy and corporations, protecting life to build a free and diverse global society, trying to minimize the production of victims by its recursive re-organization.
10 In a transmodern ethical world there is space for everyone.

Although these ethics are not yet apparent, there is room for optimism. Recovering the spirit of Victor Hugo (Zea 1996: 56), modernity must transcend its own history in order to create the opportunity for the conformation of a new extraordinary nation in the twenty-first century, woven of different experiences, that we may call *Humanity*. In it rest the possibilities for constructing a different sort of globalization, a *civilized globalization* which does away with its vocation for domination in order to begin a new phase that reshapes relations between society and economy and, in the everyday spaces of human existence, between organizations and their members. The possibilities for constructing a transmodern globalization that can, upon assuming responsibility for the past acts of savagery colonization, build a more just and inclusive planetary civilization depend on this reshaping of relationships.

Notes

1 I would like to acknowledge and thank the members of the Research Project on *corporate ethics, corruption and governance* at UAM-Iztapalapa for helping me discussing earlier drafts. I also express my appreciation for the revision that Stewart Clegg did on the translation from Spanish to English done by Ian MacDonald. The responsibility for the outcome is entirely my own.

2 It suffices to remember the conflicts of the last decade in Zaire, Rwanda, Liberia, Bosnia, Chechnya, the Middle East, Algeria, Sudan, Cashmere, Sri Lanka and Chiapas, the Palestinian-Israeli problem, the US' confrontation with the Islamic world and the serious problem of hunger in Ethiopia, Rwanda, Somalia, Sudan, Liberia, Mozambique and Angola. Or the economic crises in Mexico, Brazil, Peru, Bolivia and Argentina, to mention just a few in Latin America, and in the countries of East and Southeast Asia. For a summarized account, see Bello (2001) and Chossudovsky (2003).

3 The latter is confirmed by the attacks on the World Trade Centre (11 September 2001), the Bali bombing (11 October 2002), the Atocha train station bombing in Spain (11 April 2004), the Chechen attack on a primary school in North Osetia (1 September 2004), and the London Underground and London Transport bombing (7 July 2005).

4 The ethics of domination associated with competition is clearly appreciated by Humberto Maturana when he writes: 'Healthy competition does not exist. Competition is a cultural and human phenomenon and not essential to biology. As a human phenomenon, competition is based on the negation of the other. Look at the emotions involved in sporting competitions. In them there is no healthy competition because one's victory arises from the defeat of the other and, most critically, under the discourse that values competition as a social good, one does not see the emotion that constitutes the praxis of competing, which is what gives rise to the actions that negate the other' (Maturana 1990: 13).

5 Corporate power has expanded in a permanent way since the beginning of the twentieth century (Berle and Means 1968). The incomes of the 200 mega-corporations that dominate world markets have achieved sales for a combined total greater than the total incomes of the planet's countries with the exception of the nine largest economies, employing less than one-third of one per cent of the population in doing so. Of these corporations, 98 per cent have their headquarters in eight countries of the Centre, within which the US and Japan predominate (Bergesen and Fernández 1999).

6 Therefore, the reader must consider that when the constitutional order mentions 'the individual' or 'the person', it refers indistinctly to the human person and to corporations.

7 The role of normativeness as a mechanism that protects and regulates the power of corporations before the state and society can be appreciated by reviewing the laws and judicial decisions adopted over the course of the past century (Bowman 1996: 42). In a general appraisal, everything indicates that the balance up until now has tended to favour the corporation. However, it is not a linear process nor is it free of contradictions, and variations according to periods and countries are quite large (Levy 1998). In any case, what we wish to highlight is that the pronouncement of laws and judicial resolutions, which in certain moments expands the power of corporations and in other moments restricts them, shows the oscillations of the pendulum of modernity, clearly indicating the relative force of social agents in their disputes for the imposition of their projects.

8 Not even Adam Smith would agree with this statement. A close reading of his work allows us to understand that he always placed the national economy within

the wider framework of a moral philosophy based on prudence, justice and goodwill (Smith 2000). According to Küng, 'The motivations (economic, above all) that are based on self-interest have to be led by prudence, and economic interaction has to be balanced out by justice. But the basis of all moral justice and all ethical self-criticism also has to be made of human kindness (*benevolence*)' (Küng 1998: 195). In this sense, Smith would be closer to *ordoliberalism* or that which has been called an *economy of social markets* than to classical liberalism or neo-liberalism (Küng 1998: 196; Foucault 2003). For a discussion of the propagandistic and interested use of Smith's work, we recommend Méndez's excellent study (2004b).

9   The 'invisible hand' of the market, before being a natural self-regulated mechanism, is constituted as the pretext for the power of the large corporations and their managers, which currently manage the economy by regulating the terms of exchange and the appropriation of its benefits. Because of this, market and bureaucracy have been the basic ingredients of the ideal formula for doing business in modernity. Administrative and organizational theory have taken advantage of the neo-liberal boom in order to position themselves amongst the most relevant disciplines since the second half of the twentieth century (Clegg 2003), as they provide the wisdoms and techniques from which the visible hand of administration pulls the puppet strings of the invisible hand of the market (Ibarra-Colado 2006).

10 This is only partly true, as the government in turn acted to take advantage of society with the primordial goal of obtaining the support of the electorate that would guarantee its permanence in power. The liberals have deemed this political regimen to be populist, criticizing the economic dis-equilibriums provoked by excessive spending and the social costs of promoting a handout economy that inhibits the human spirit and the care that every individual should take of his or herself. For a discussion of this point, see Demmers *et al.* (2001).

11 When economic power was extended to the logic of the operation of governmental power, the *political market* was incorporated in order to finance the media campaigns of candidates and parties that guarantee unrestricted protection of their freedom to act in their own benefit. Moreover, apart from electoral situations, legislative lobbying was established as a fundamental means for corporations to intervene in the political decisions that could affect their interests.

12 The restriction of social spending on health care and education, for example, implied an accelerated deterioration of their quality and drastic reductions in access. This translated into the *de facto* encouragement of private consumption markets for such services, as there is no other option for families than to turn to pay schools or private hospitals. The circle of government action is then closed with the promotion of financing and credit programs that mortgage people's futures.

13 Latin America is a good example of this subjugation: '... poor countries produce wealth and rich countries produce Financial Institutions to collect that wealth. Mexico, a poor country, has paid in the last ten years almost US$350 billion for the so called "service of the external debt". ... Just during the "government of change" [the Vicente Fox Administration] Mexico annually spends in the payment of "debt service" about six times the amount applied in the battle against poverty. From the total paid by Mexico, a poor country, in the last ten years, a quarter has been for the World Bank, the International Monetary Fund and the Inter-American Development Bank (who are not poor or they dissimulate it very well), and about two thirds have been for the banks of the rich countries (mostly those of the US, but also the European, Japanese, Canadian and Asian

banks). Latin America, a region of poor countries, pays eight dollars for each one received as a loan and still owes four. The creditors? North American and European banks (essentially British, French and Spanish)' (Marcos 2004; see also Galeano 1998).

14 At the time of writing Congress is debating legal amendments to the Public Health Security Laws so that the government can reduce the costs of pensions negotiated in past collective bargaining agreements. The opposition from workers has been enormous from now on, so if there is not a negotiated solution, a deep social confrontation could result.

15 The World Wealth Report 2004 establishes: 'Compared to 2002, when Latin America experienced a decline in the number of HNWIs (high net worth individuals), the region fared much better in 2003. However, it had relatively slow growth in both HNWI numbers and wealth, despite impressive equity market gains across the continent. *Latin America continues to epitomize the polarization of economic fortunes between rich and poor: Latin American HNWIs have the highest average wealth per HNWI of any major region*' (Capgemini/ Merrill Lynch 2004: 7).

16 The Zapatista Revolt represents the social resistance of the excluded in Mexico in global times – especially the indigenous. The Zapatista Army of National Liberation declared the war to the Mexican government on 1 January 1994, precisely the day NAFTA began its operation (Vodovnik 2004; Volpi 2004). A decade after the problem is still there and the low intensity war could transform in any moment in a new confrontation between the Mexican government and the excluded, the people without voice, the invisible. The conditions are given, so Mexico could experience a new wave of conflict and revolt in the scenario of the Presidential succession of 2006, writing another chapter of the resistance of society against the savage globalization commanded by the huge transnational corporations. The excluded nature of globalization under the neo-liberal recipes is also in the centre of the dispute in Latin America, a coveted region because of its oil and potable water reserves, and the advantages of its geographical position and biodiversity. Latin American recent movement to the left, clearly represented by the political profile recently adopted by governments in countries like Venezuela, Brazil, Uruguay, Peru, Bolivia, Argentina and Chile (Paramio 2003; Lozano 2005), is a clear message for the rest of the world about the limits of the neo-liberal project of domination.

17 Any conference called by the IFIs gives voice to society, perhaps because the economic and political powers still think that society must simply obey. Nevertheless, social agents all around the world have been organizing themselves and being increasingly visible, confronting the current model of organization of the world with socially oriented alternative options (Cavanagh and Mander 2004; ATTAC 2002). This scenario places ethics as one of the main issues facing humanity for the future.

18 A less radical variation of this project has begun to be timidly insinuated in Europe: through the creation of a common space constructed through the negotiation of common rules there is an attempt to combine strengths while preserving identities and cultures in order to try to re-establish their hegemony as the centre of the world (ATTAC 2002; Mignolo 2001: 44). Of course, it is an inclusive project for Europe, but it is also an excluding project for the 'no-Europeans' of the world.

19 Hegel clearly assumed this posture when he stated: '*But a great figure must trample some innocent flowers and destroy something on its way*' (quoted in De la Garza 2002: 111). In turn, according to the first chronicler of the Indies, the discovered natives '... were cannibals and addicts to sodomy, had a cranium four

times larger than that of Europeans and an inferior rational capacity' (Florescano 2000: 299–300). As such, the conqueror established himself as their saviour, even though this implied mass killings, the rape of women, the murder of Indian chiefs, captivity and slavery (Florescano 2000: 307). Such was the cost, it was assumed, to be paid for civilization and progress. Euro-centrism that assumes the Other to be simply defective natural material, usable but finally expendable, gave rise to this linear history inevitably built upon the sacrifice of its victims. The future, if we wish to improve, requires us to recognize these acts in order to promote a different way of thinking that restores justice and eliminates the usually unrecognized barbarism of the modern conqueror.

20 The following ideas benefited from arguments developed by Enrique Dussel in a public dissertation entitled 'Globalization, organization, ethics', that took place at UAM-Iztapalapa on 12 September 2004.

Chapter 4

The ethics of corporate social responsibility

Subhabrata Bobby Banerjee

Editors' introduction

While in Chapter 3, Ibarra-Colado writes from the margins of modernity as he defines them – in fact, given the overarching presence to the north, it is perhaps better to say he writes in the shadow of modernity – in this chapter Banerjee reflects on the form that most exemplifies that modernity, the modern corporation. This is an invention that is, as he outlines, rather recent in the historical scheme of things. Furthermore, while it may have begun life as a legal fiction, the corporation seems recently to have acquired a moral status with significant and real effects and implications. In exploring this, Banerjee provides a critical perspective on the ethics of corporate social responsibility (CSR).

The academic literature and business press generally talk about CSR in positive, if not glowing, terms because it provides an ethical framework for corporate decision making that appears both rational and calculable. CSR is often viewed as a 'practical' way for corporations to discharge their ethical obligations to society. Despite its emancipatory rhetoric, discourses of CSR are defined by narrow business interests and serve to curtail interests of external stakeholders, he argues. Here the ethical becomes subsumed within the managerial and, as a result, its practical potential becomes severely bracketed.

To counterbalance the CSR position Banerjee uses this chapter to develop an alternate perspective. Incisively critical, this perspective considers CSR as an ideological movement intended to legitimize the power of large corporations. And there is a great deal of perfidy to whitewash, as he argues. Despite the warm and inclusive rhetoric about the 'stakeholder corporation', stakeholders who do not toe the corporate line are either co-opted or marginalized in a form of stakeholder colonialism that serves to regulate the behaviour of those stakeholders. Banerjee's conclusions are compelling, but not optimistic: CSR cannot provide an adequate ethical basis for business and seems to be unreformable.

Did you ever expect a corporation to have a conscience, when it has no soul to be damned and no body to be kicked? (And by God, it ought to have both!).

First Baron Thurlow (1731–1806)
Lord Chancellor of England

In the corporate economies of the contemporary West, the market is a passive institution. The active institution is the corporation ... an inherently narrow and shortsighted organization ... The corporation has evolved to serve the interests of whoever controls it, at the expense of whomever does not.

(Duggar 1989)

These two quotes, made 150 years apart, reflect a particular perspective of corporate social responsibility that is rarely found in the management literature. The first quote attributed to First Baron Thurlow was made in the glory days of what was probably the world's first multinational corporation – I refer of course to the infamous East India Company. In an era of British colonial expansion, this company was engaged in conquering markets, eliminating competition, securing cheap sources of raw material supply, building strategic alliances: in short, the empire did everything our current strategy textbooks now teach us. Colonial expansionist practices of the British empire in the 1800s involved both capital appropriation and permanent destruction of manufacturing capacities in the colonies – the 'technological superiority' of the British textile industry for example, was established as much by invention as by a systematic destruction of India's indigenous industry involving innovative competitive strategies such as the severing of the thumbs of master weavers in Bengal, forced cultivation of indigo by Bihar's peasants and the slave trade from Africa that supplied cotton plantations in the US with free labour (Dutt 1970; Shiva 2001: 34).

The second and more recent quote seems to be more relevant today in light of the recent corporate scandals that have rocked the US, Europe and Australia. For instance, from an ethical perspective what are the outcomes for society that result from 'an inherently narrow and shortsighted organization'? What is interesting in Duggar's quote is the reference to serving the interests of the people who control corporations 'at the expense of whomever does not'. This seems to imply that corporate strategies of wealth creation – including corporate social responsibility – are zero sum games, which is a debatable point. If this is true then we as a society have to decide how much minimum negative externalities we are prepared to accept for wealth creation. The current debate about CEO compensation is a case in point. Two recent studies have shown that the relationship between CEO pay to stock performance are negative: the CEOs of 10 large US corporations that posted negative returns in terms of their 2003 stock performance received significant pay increases in terms of salaries, bonuses and stock options (Strauss 2003). Another study found that the biggest CEO raises were linked to the largest layoffs. While the median pay increase for CEOs was 6 per cent in 2002, the figure for CEOs of 50 companies that announced the biggest layoffs in 2001 jumped to 44 per cent (Kristof 2003). Of course all of these 50 companies produce slick, glossy corporate social responsibility reports annually. The argument that this is somehow good for the global economy begs the question: whose globe and whose economy?

In this chapter I provide a critical perspective on the ethics of corporate social responsibility (CSR). The academic literature and business press generally talk about CSR in positive, if not glowing terms because it provides an ethical framework for corporate decision making. CSR is often viewed as a 'practical' way for corporations to discharge their ethical obligations to society. However, I argue that despite its emancipatory rhetoric, discourses of corporate social responsibility are defined by narrow business interests and serve to curtail interests of external stakeholders. I provide an alternate perspective, one that views corporate social responsibility as an ideological movement intended to legitimize the power of large corporations (Mitchell 1989).

Social responsibility and the modern corporation

A brief historical tour of the emergence of the modern corporation will help contextualize my analysis of current discourses on corporate social responsibility. An understanding of the historical role that the 'social' played in the development of the corporation in its modern form will allow us to see how shifting power structures in the economy, society and polity construct the terrain of corporate social responsibility. In his excellent book *Organizing America*, Charles Perrow (2002: 31) described the economic, political, and social forces that combined to create the 'legal revolution that launched organizations' in the US. Initially state legislatures in nineteenth century America were the only bodies that had the power to grant special charters of incorporation, charters that specified what a corporation could or could not do, how long it could exist and how it was obliged to serve the public interest.

In the legal environment of the 1800s, the state in the initial formulation of corporate law could revoke the charter of a corporation if it failed to act in the public good and routinely did so. For instance, banks lost their charters in Mississippi, Ohio, and Pennsylvania for 'committing serious violations that were likely to leave them in an insolvent or financially unsound condition'. In Massachusetts and New York, charters of turnpike corporations were revoked for 'not keeping their roads in repair' (Derber 1998: 124). However, by the end of the nineteenth century, restrictions around incorporation had all but disappeared. As Perrow (2002: 41) argues, this was not 'a mistake, an inadvertence, a happenstance in history, but a well-designed plan devised by particular interests who needed a ruling that would allow for a particular form of organization'. This then begs the questions: What are the discursive and material effects of these new forms of organization? How have the power dynamics been shifted in this new regime? What are the possible conflicts that could arise from unrestricted corporate activity? If the corporation is no longer legally required to serve the public interest what is the role of non-governmental organizations in this regime? While the wealth creating ability of modern corporations is unquestionable, some of their social and environmental effects – and indeed some economic effects – are unquestionably damaging as well. It is interesting that 170 years after corporations freed themselves from state charters, consumer and environmental activists of the 1960s and 1970s were campaigning for a system of federal charters to 'reign in the power of large corporations'. In a call for a congressional hearing on the issue, Ralph Nader declared, 'The corporation is, and must be, the creature of the State. Into its nostrils the State must breathe the breath of a fictitious life' (Nader *et al.* 1976: 15).

This legal revolution that gave birth to the modern corporation essentially removed all major restrictions around corporate activity and rules of incorporation. Since the legislative authority of states for regulating corporate behaviour was removed there was now no 'official' requirement to serve the public interest except in the economic realm. As the legal personality of the modern corporation evolved in the 1800s, contestations in the public, political and legal spheres revolved around the conflict between public and private interests. Now that the corporation was defined as an entity that could enjoy property rights the focus shifted to developing systems of enforcement and mechanisms that protected these rights. While this system of property rights gave more power to corporations in a post-charter era, it also served as the primary incentive to maximize economic return for shareholders. Any reference to 'social good' was at best symbolic and derivative in that the economic function provided the social good. The separation of the economic from the social in defining corporate identity is, in itself, a political process, also mirrored in the tenets of economic theories of the time – the notion of 'externalities' for instance, where governments and other agencies, not economic actors were responsible in managing the negative social and environmental effects of economic growth.

The landmark decision of the US Supreme Court that bestowed property rights on private corporations was *Dartmouth College v. Woodward* in 1819. The case typified the inherent ambiguities that arise in defining the role of a corporation – ambiguities between the economic and social – that are yet to be resolved today. Lawyers for Dartmouth Corporation in its move to free itself from state control argued that the rights of private corporations and private rights in general must be 'protected from the rise and fall of popular parties and the fluctuations of political opinions' (Perrow 2002: 41). Chief Justice John Marshall concurred, declaring that '… a corporation is an artificial being, invisible, intangible. And existing only in contemplation of law' (Chief Justice John Marshall, *Dartmouth College v. Woodward*, 1819). Establishing the legitimacy of a 'fictitious legal person' or an 'artificial legal entity' distinct from its owners and officers (Hessen 1979: xiv) had two effects: first, it effectively put an end to the argument that the corporation was a creature of the state thus limiting public representation and, second, by conferring private rights on corporations, rights normally held by individuals the court automatically guaranteed a system that would protect those rights. Thus, an artificial legal entity like a corporation is entitled to protection under the Fourteenth Amendment of the US Constitution. As we shall see these legislative requirements were designed to protect private interests, often at the expense of the public. The legal personality of the modern corporation was created by certain interests to deliver specific outcomes that needed a particular form of organization and a strong state presence was inimical to these interests. In fact, over time the state view also mirrored the corporate view as new laws were created in the US that allowed states to allocate property to private corporations. Perrow (2002) describes how powerful private interests in the railroad industry, the 'big business' of the 1800s, with a combination of creative legal interpretations of property rights along with more than a few illegal activities were able to obtain rights of way on public land at virtually no cost. Public legal actions in most cases were decided in favour of corporations in a socio-economic climate where public purpose was defined so broadly that eminent domain and corporate privileges could always be justified in the name of 'prosperity and growth; and in general for the freedom to externalize costs' (Perrow 2002: 45). For instance, a court decision on a petition by Louisville residents protesting the company's decision to lay rail lines across their neighbourhood declared:

> A railroad will be allowed to run its locomotives into the heart of Louisville despite the noise and pollution from its smokestacks (the externality), because so necessary are the agents of transportation in a populous and prospering country that private injury and personal damage must be expected.
>
> (1839 Kentucky court decision, cited in Perrow 2002).

If a corporation had the legal right to externalize the social and environmental costs of its business activity with impunity, its responsibility to the larger community was less clear and definitely not one mandated by law in the new regime of incorporation. While the property rights of the private 'agents of transportation' had to be respected, the 'necessary externalities' should be dealt with not by the corporation but by someone else. Contemporary notions of corporate social responsibility and corporate citizenship that deploy the 'legal fiction' argument of the corporation in order to create a legal soul for the artificial corporate person run the danger of conflating citizenship with personhood. A corporation cannot be a citizen in the same way a person can. A corporation can, however, be considered a person as far as its legal status is concerned. Current notions of corporate citizenship conflate citizen – which as Windsor (2001) argues a business corporation cannot be – and person – which a corporation can be but only as a 'legal fiction'. Thus, as Windsor (2001: 4) points out 'fictional personhood is not a sound basis for artificial citizenship' and theories of corporate social responsibility that take the citizenship approach will tend to be limited in defining the scope of responsibility. The problem is compounded in the case of multinational firms (MNCs) where there is no constitutional or legal basis for MNCs to becoming 'world citizens'. We do not have a system whereby international bodies like the United Nations can charter a particular business.

While the law recognizes a corporation's metaphorical personhood allowing it to enter into contracts and promote private property rights, the metaphorical soul of the corporation and its corresponding responsibilities cannot be legally prescribed. Thus, social responsibility, an integral part of a corporation's identity and existence in the 1800s now becomes an activity devolved to the corporation, a strategic choice influenced by market and competitive factors. This process of redefinition was an exercise of political and economic power by a minority interest group promoting a particular ideology that 'redefined the character of the Republic in order to justify the new opportunities that the corporation offered for the accumulation of private wealth' (Harvard Law Review: 1886–7). Changes in the legal environment also shifted the onus of addressing the 'social' from corporations to governments. However, while new organizational forms were proving to create wealth for the few people that owned them, social and environmental costs continued to be passed off as externalities. There was little recognition, at least in legislative circles, that the kind of organization profit-seeking corporations build 'determine social costs that the society will bear, and the powers and freedoms that the organizations will have' (Perrow 2002: 143). However, these anxieties were voiced in several sections of the business press of the time by intellectuals, workers, union officials, artisans and entrepreneurs.

It would be naïve of us to assume that the 'legal revolution' was launched uniformly and spontaneously with the public interest in mind. Large corporations in the 1800s wielded considerable economic and political power and some nineteenth century underhand skullduggery strategies would bring a blush even to the crooks that ran Enron. In his historical analysis of the railroad industry in nineteenth century America, Perrow (2002) describes an impressive list of activities that could hardly be considered 'social'. Judges and legislators were routinely bought. Shady financial dealings like watering stock, misuse of stock in paying dividends, obtaining public funds through deception, misuse of public funds, and violation of legal statutes were common. In fact, the level of corruption was such that Perrow (2002: 143) argues ease of corruption should be added to the usual factors of production such as land, labour, capital, technology and organizational form. He rightly points out that corruption involved considerable social costs in terms of wasting a society's resources, risking the lives and health of communities and workers due to evasion of environmental health and safety laws, and increasing negative externalities. Corrupting the legislature and judiciary meant that corporations could shape their own powers and freedoms. As he argues:

> Corruption meant that the profits were not returned to either the government that subsidized so much of the railroads, or even to many of the private investors, but to a small group of executives and financiers. This concentrated wealth and the power that comes with it. Corruption counts, but few historians and social scientists have done any counting. Instead, they tend to blame the victims, not the perpetrators – the large organizations. There are no accounts of railroads as corporations engaged in lobbying, joining with merchants and shippers in getting public funds, fighting regulation and accountability, and generally using the organizational tool to shape the commercial world to their liking.
> (Perrow, 2002: 144)

It is important to realize that the legal developments that created the modern corporation did not go uncontested. Anti-corporate protests were strong in the mid-1850s as they were on the streets of Seattle 150 years later. But, as Perrow (2002) points out, these protests were more a reflection of the anxiety about the growing powers of corporate capitalism as opposed to any resistance to capitalist ideals per se. Individual entrepreneurs, workers and artisans with restricted access to capital supported private property rights for individuals because it could provide freedom from wage dependence. However, they opposed easy incorporation of corporations without a state charter because opportunities for self-employment would be limited. A community of self-employed artisans and traders with shared interests was seen as a public good which was threatened by permanent wage dependence (Perrow 2002). In fact, a union publication declared in 1835:

> We entirely disapprove of the incorporation of Companies, for carrying on manual mechanical business, inasmuch as we believe their tendency is to eventuate in and produce monopolies, thereby crippling the energies of individual enterprise, and invading the rights of smaller capitalists.
> (cited in Harvard Law Review 1989: 1989)

Concerns about the effect of 'commerce' on society and 'political virtue' were the source of early public hostility towards corporations. Easy incorporation laws that would dramatically expand the power of corporations were seen as creating new forms of dependency that 'threatened the capacity of citizenship' (Harvard Law Review 1989: 1891). There was a fear that in the Republic a new form of aristocracy would be created, 'depending for its wealth on government privileges and therefore with an interest in corrupting government by diverting it from the public good' (Harvard Law Review 1989: 1891). Small entrepreneurs, artisans and farmers were also concerned their livelihoods would be destroyed because of the new privileges granted to corporations.

Debates about the role of corporations in their new entity centred around two assumptions: that the corporation was inherently guided by self-interest or that a corporation has an 'enduring capacity to operate on the basis of civic virtue' (Regan 1998: 305). The first notion is also reflected in economic theories of the firm where the focus is on efficiencies required to maximize rent-seeking opportunities. The second notion refers to the legitimacy of a corporation and its role in society. Thus, to quote Dahl (1973):

> Business corporations are created and survive only as a special privilege of the state. It is absurd to regard the corporation simply as an enterprise established for the sole purpose of allowing profit-making. One has simply to ask: Why should citizens, through *their* government, grant special rights, powers, privileges, and protections to any firm except on the understanding that its activities are to fulfill *their* purposes? Corporations exist because we allow them to do so.
>
> (Dahl 1973: 11)

The problem with the efficiency-legitimacy dichotomy is that in public policy it is often the case that legitimacy becomes subordinate to efficiency because notions and terms of legitimacy are discursively produced and defined by economic efficiency criteria. As Regan (1998) has argued both assumptions are problematic for society. Assuming that the corporation is solely guided by narrow economic self-interest tends to reinforce structures that will lead to this outcome. According to Regan (1998: 305) it also denies agency to the multitude of people who work in corporations and are 'denied the exercise of full moral autonomy'. Here, Regan seems to refer to the received view of corporate social responsibility that recognized institutional, organizational and individual levels of responsibility where the 'principle of managerial discretion' meant that managers could exercise their own autonomous moral judgement on business decisions (Carrol 1979). According to Wood (1991: 698), 'managers are moral actors. Within every domain of corporate social responsibility, they are obliged to exercise such discretion as is available to them, toward socially responsible outcomes'. The fallacy of managers as 'moral actors' is easily revealed by the Foucauldian notion of subjectification, a mode that reveals how managers become constituted as subjects who secure their meaning and reality through identifying with a particular sense of their relationship with the firm (Knights 1992). Individual managers' role in accommodating stakeholder interests is predefined at higher levels and practices at this level are governed and organized by organizational and institutional discourses. Do managers really have genuine freedom to make socially responsible decisions?

A second outcome of the self-interest assumption is that it leads to a free rider scenario where corporations will not usually take the socially responsible course of action unless it meets their profitability criteria (Regan 1998). This view is reflected in the 'corporate social responsibility is good for business' refrain heard from many CEOs, government officials, academics, NGOs and the like. If the sole obsession is with profits then governments and other agencies need to regulate business to produce socially beneficial outcomes, which is another shortcoming with this approach. Laws are usually created after the fact and cannot anticipate every instance of social evil. Monitoring compliance in a command and control system can be an expensive process involving high transaction costs. Moreover, it is naïve to think that laws governing the behaviour of corporations are made in isolation and not without active involvement from industry. Political lobbying as a corporate strategy has more than a 200-year history.

Disputes between 'social' and corporate interests that entered the legal arena tended to muddy social responsibilities of the modern corporation and narrow the focus of the board of directors to generating shareholder wealth. In one celebrated case, the Ford Motor Company was taken to court by its shareholders who contested the company's plan to forego the payment of special dividends. Henry Ford, in the middle of implementing one of his social engineering plans declared to the court that he chose to forego the dividend payment because the company wanted '... to employ still more men; to spread the benefits of this individual system to the greatest possible number; to help them build up their lives and their homes' (Henry Ford, 1919, cited in Regan 1998). The court disagreed, ruling that:

> A business organization is organized and carried on primarily for the profit of the stockholders. Directors cannot shape and conduct the affairs of a corporation for the mere incidental benefit of shareholders and for the primary purpose of benefiting others.
> (*Dodge v. Ford Motor Company 1919*, cited in Regan 1998)

Now a vulgar interpretation of this ruling could mean that it is illegal to be socially responsible. However, managers do have some discretion in determining the best way to enhance shareholder value. Had Henry Ford chosen to be a little less modest about his plans for society and restated his argument concentrating on the long-term financial benefits of his 'social investment', the court may well have accepted his argument. Hertz (2001) mentions a similar case where the court ruled that a donation to a civil rights group by Kodak was not a 'financially responsible' investment and ordered the company to accede to shareholders' demand to pay the amount as dividends instead. However, some recent rulings have attempted to include some level of stakeholder recognition by emphasizing that directors do not 'have a duty to the shareholders but instead have a duty to the corporation' (Cunningham 1999: 1294). Another ruling stated that directors in considering the best interests of the corporation consider 'the effects of any action upon any or all groups affected by such action, including shareholders, employees, suppliers ...' (Cunningham 1999: 1294). However, this simply allows company directors to consider public interests; it is not legally binding in any way, thus limiting whatever attention corporate elites will pay social concerns. As Regan (1998: 305) puts it, 'the operation of both law and the market therefore systematically tend to deprive corporations of the capacity to cultivate civic virtue'.

If the legal revolution that launched the modern corporation was one that served particular interests, the same can be said of the current rhetoric in corporate boardrooms about 'corporate social responsibility' and 'corporate citizenship'. The power of this rhetoric lies in its ability to validate a particular form of ideology along with its accompanying epistemological and ontological assumptions. Thus, from a critical perspective corporate social responsibility becomes an ideological movement designed to consolidate the power of large corporations. In the next section I will discuss how 'progressive' discourses of corporate social responsibility, corporate citizenship, and sustainability create a particular form of corporate rationality that despite its emancipatory intent serves to marginalize large groups of people.

Corporate social responsibility, stakeholders and sustainability: holy trinity or praxis of evil?

Research on CSR is not new and dates back at least 50 years. The two major camps hold divergent views – from the almost tiresome Friedman cliché of 'the business of business is business' to a vastly more accommodating – although ultimately meaningless if taken to the extreme – stakeholder framework. While the Friedman camp is dismissive, in fact downright suspicious about corporate social responsibility outside the shareholder value framework, the fact remains that corporate social responsibility is publicly espoused by almost all the major corporations of the world. Margolis and Walsh (2003) in a study of 127 empirical studies conducted during 1972– 2002 measuring the relationship between corporate social performance and corporate financial performance found that about half the studies found a positive relationship. The research findings are not convincing however, and recent reviews have pointed out serious shortcomings ranging from sampling problems, measurement issues, omission of controls, and more significantly lack of explanatory theory linking CSR with financial performance (Margolis and Walsh 2003). However, the authors found little evidence of a *negative* relationship, which would certainly weaken the Friedman case of CSR having negative financial effects. In other words there is no evidence to state that CSR can harm the wealth-generating ability of business firms which should lead to alleviating concerns about shareholder value. In any case corporate rationality dictates the nature and scope of acceptable CSR practices engineering the inevitable compromise of making a business case for corporate social responsibility. Corporate social responsibility in this framework is limited to win-win situations starting with the assumption that it makes good business sense and enhances shareholder value.

I will not review the vast literature on corporate citizenship and social responsibility here. More than 50 years of research in the field has produced a variety of theoretical concepts along with some limited – and somewhat dubious – empirical evidence on the relationship between corporate social responsibility and firm performance. An examination of the literature indicates that the rationale and assumptions behind the corporate social responsibility discourse are: (1) corporations *should* think beyond making money and pay attention to social and environmental issues; (2) corporations *should* behave in an ethical manner and demonstrate the highest level of integrity and transparency in all their operations; and (3) corporations *should* be involved with the community in which they operate in terms of enhancing their social welfare and providing community support through philanthropy or other means. These notions of corporate citizenship should be operationalized through engagement and dialogue with *stakeholders* – another term that seems to be unproblematically and uncritically accepted in the literature – and corporations should always engage their stakeholders and build relationships with them (Waddock 2001). The normative core of this discourse is not hard to ascertain: the assumption is that corporations should do all these things because: (1) good corporate citizenship is related to good financial performance – despite the dubious nature of empirical evidence of this relationship; and (2) if a corporation is a bad citizen then its licence to operate will be revoked by 'society'. Both of these are simplistic assumptions with little theoretical or empirical support. Large transnational corporations responsible for major environmental disasters and negative social impacts in the Third World – Union Carbide, Nike, Exxon, Shell to name a few – rather than lose their licence to operate have actually become stronger and more powerful whether through mergers, restructures or relentless public relations campaigns.

There is a remarkable lack of critical examination in the literature of these concepts of corporate citizenship. The literature on corporate social responsibility easily identifies 'bad' corporate citizens: tobacco companies, weapons manufacturers, environmental polluters. However, the fact that these companies regularly publish corporate citizenship and social performance reports tends to muddy the waters more than a little. Thus, a recent report released by the Vice President, Corporate Affairs and Social Responsibility of Phillip Morris, outlines their 'values-based culture' that demonstrates 'integrity, honesty, respect and tolerance' while promising 'transparency' and 'stakeholder engagement' (Phillip Morris 2002). How tobacco firms can use these concepts to produce 'socially responsible' cigarettes is of course another matter. These concepts are echoed by academics as well: for instance, Birch (2001: 59–60) in developing a conceptual framework of corporate citizenship outlines '12 generic principles of corporate citizenship' including 'making a difference, employee and stakeholder empowerment, transparency, accountability, sharing responsibility, inclusivity, sustainable capitalism, a triple bottom line, long-termism, communication, engagement and dialogue'. It is interesting to see how these theoretical principles are seamlessly integrated into corporate policies. Consider, for example, the following excerpt from the corporate responsibility annual report of a large multinational corporation:

> The principles that guide our behaviour are based on our vision and values and include the following:
>
> - Respect: We will work to foster mutual respect with communities and stakeholders who are affected by our operations.
> - Integrity: We will examine the impacts, positive and negative, of our business on the environment, and on society, and will integrate human, health, social and environmental considerations into our internal management and value system.
> - Communication: We will strive to foster understanding and support our stakeholders and communities, as well as measure and communicate our performance.
> - Excellence: We will continue to improve our performance and will encourage our business partners and suppliers to adhere to the same standards.

This corporation, voted by *Fortune Magazine* for six consecutive years as the most 'innovative company in North America'; for three consecutive years as one of the '100 best companies to work for in America' and on *Fortune Magazine*'s 'All star list of global most admired companies' is of course none other than Enron (Enron 2002). Glossy corporate social responsibility reports are a form of 'greenwashing'[1] that often do not reveal the grim realities that lie behind them. To quote the words of a famous philosopher, Marx – Groucho, not Karl – 'The secrets of success in business are honesty and transparency. If you can fake that, you've got it made'.

While stakeholder empowerment is indeed a noble goal, one wonders how this would affect the economic performance of a firm when the stakeholders it is supposed to 'empower' have opposing agendas to industry, for example in the current conflicts between mining and resource companies and indigenous communities (Banerjee 2000, 2001a). In my work with two indigenous communities in Australia I sought 'stakeholder input' about the presence of a mine on indigenous land. The response was unanimous: both communities wanted the mining company – a very, very, very large multinational company – to 'clean up, pack up, leave and never come back', to quote the words of one traditional owner. The company's response was to hire an anthropologist to 'consult' with communities on how best to expand its operations. The fact that these 'consultations' take place under drastically unequal power relations remains unaddressed. As Tatz (1982) points out, Aboriginal communities are the *receivers of consultation*, that is, that Aboriginal people are from time to time *talked to* about the decisions *arrived* at' (Tatz 1982: 176, original emphasis). In every case involving 'consultation' with traditional owners in Australia, the focus was not whether or not mining should proceed but under what conditions should it be carried out. Royalties, promises of jobs, pitting one community against another are some strategies that have proved useful for mining companies.

Any analysis of the history of corporate citizenship must also reflect the history of corporate power. North American corporations for example, originally conceived in the eighteenth century as entities serving the public interest, have over the past 200 years systematically diminished the power of state and federal governments in regulating or governing their activity. There are no legislative requirements that corporations serve the public interest, thus opening up what Alan Greenspan calls more 'pathways to greed'. This is quite apparent in the emergent discourse on 'sustainability', which originally promoted sustainable development as an alternate paradigm to the growth model but like the modern Western environmental movement, has been hijacked by corporate interests.

The World Commission for Economic Development provides the most commonly used definition of sustainable development, describing it as 'a process of change in which the exploitation of resources, direction of investments, orientation of technological development, and institutional change are made consistent with future as well as present needs' (WCED 1987: 9). Discourses of sustainable development are becoming increasingly corporatized. For instance, the Dow Jones recently launched a 'Sustainability Group Index' after a survey of Fortune 500 companies. A sustainable corporation was defined as one 'that aims at increasing long-term shareholder value by integrating economic, environmental and social growth opportunities into its corporate and business strategies' (Dow Jones Sustainability Group Index 2000). It is interesting to observe how notions of sustainability are constructed, manipulated and represented in both the popular business press and academic literature. As evidence of the deleterious effects of development mounted, the discourse shifted from sustainable development to the more positive sounding sustainability and then shifted the focus to corporate sustainability. Corporate discourses on sustainability produce an elision that displaces the focus from global planetary sustainability to sustaining the corporation through 'growth opportunities' (Banerjee 2003). What happens if environmental and social issues do not result in growth opportunities remains unclear, the assumption being that global sustainability can be achieved only through market exchanges. Even national governments and international organizations like the United Nations promote sustainability as a business case a consequence of which is that business, not societal or ecological, interests define the parameters of sustainability.

Business, government and international institutions

If one role of governments is to promote democracy while looking after the welfare of the poor and needy, a richer but needier client seems to be getting most of their attention. Corporations are one of the largest receivers of welfare in the US in the form of direct subsidies that run over $75 billion (Hertz 2001). The poorer states in the US having the greatest income inequality not surprisingly offer the largest tax concessions and other subsidies, not to mention the non-financial benefits of lax environmental regulation and a 'flexible' labour force – meaning no unions. Caring for the corporation has become a bigger business than the caring corporation. The impact of multinationals in the Third World is even more powerful. As 'carriers of democratic values' multinational companies often take on the role of governments in these regions, as in the case of Shell. Here we have one company that generates 75 per cent of the Nigerian government's revenues and nearly 35 per cent of the country's GNP. As a Shell manager put it: 'Things are back to front here. The government's in the oil business and we are in local government' (Brian Anderson, Shell senior manager, cited in Hertz 2001: 173). The distribution of this wealth is, of course, another matter.

The rhetoric of corporate social responsibility also seems to confuse democracy with capitalism. While the rhetoric behind American foreign policy over the last 70 years is to 'spread democratic values', the reality is that foreign policy decisions promote a brand of American liberal democracy that seeks to create a global system 'based on the needs of private capital including the protection of private property and open access to markets' (Hertz 2001 p. 78). There is also more than an element of hypocrisy as far as 'open access' is concerned in dozens of cases where the US government has restricted foreign access to their markets to protect national economic interest in several industrial sectors. Iran, Guatemala,

Brazil, Chile, Philippines, South America are just a handful of countries where democracy took a back seat to American corporate interests. Jean Kirkpatrick, former US ambassador to the UN in an admirable act of political doublespeak was able to reconcile these opposing positions. Kirkpatrick distinguished between authoritarian regimes – Philippines, apartheid South Africa and Chile – and totalitarian regimes – Cuba, the former Soviet Union. Although authoritarian regimes were not democratic and often used violence to suppress dissent they 'shared' American beliefs about open markets and free trade and hence it was acceptable for American corporations to do business in these regions. Free markets first and democracy would follow was the motto. Totalitarian regimes on the other hand were evil for Kirkpatrick because 'they controlled every part of society especially the economy which was closed to private enterprise and foreign access' (Hertz 2001: 79).

Thus, Woodrow Wilson's declaration that the world must be made safe for democracy must therefore be seen in light of the kind of market fundamentalism that defines the parameters of democracy. American style liberal democracy where multinational corporations become the carriers of democratic values to Third World regions is perfectly capable of functioning in authoritarian regimes, in fact these regimes are preferred, as long as a market economy is allowed. Property rights and the rule of law are a must, other aspects of democracy such as 'mass participation, an active civil society, regular free and fair elections' are optional and in fact expendable (Hertz 2001: 80). Democracy also seems to be conveniently forgotten in many of the decisions taken at international trade or environmental summits. For instance, at the 1992 Rio Summit there were open conflicts between corporations, their trade associations, NGOs, and indigenous community leaders over environmental regulations. The demands of NGOs were shelved and a voluntary code of conduct developed by the Business Council for Sustainable Development – consisting mainly of multinational corporations – approved instead in what was supposed to be a democratic process of developing an action plan for sustainable development (Hawken 1995). While the policies from the Rio Earth Summit and the more recent Johannesburg Earth Summit – an even bigger failure according to many NGOs and environmentalists – stressed the role of multinational corporations in promoting sustainable development, they are silent about corporate responsibility and accountability for environmental destruction. Development, sustainable or otherwise, in a globalizing world is inherently anti-democratic as several indigenous groups have found. As Subcomandante Marcos, a spokesperson of the Zapatista movement in Chiapas, Mexico stated:

> When we rose up against a national government, we found that it did not exist. In reality we were up against financial capital, against speculation,

which is what makes decisions in Mexico as well as in Europe, Asia, Africa, Oceania, North America, South America – everywhere.

(Zapatista 1998)

The story is depressingly familiar to indigenous communities all over the world. In this case, officials of the World Bank met in Geneva and decided to give a loan to Mexico on condition they export meat under the agreements laid down by the World Trade Organization. Land used by indigenous communities in Chiapas to grow food is now used to raise cattle for fast food markets in the US to feed American consumers while locking out local communities from participating in the benefits – there is no McDonald's in Chiapas. This is an inherently undemocratic process where peasant populations do not have the right to decide how they want to live. This is another example of how imperialism operates in the Third World: where one 'state' – in this case representing the interests of the rich countries, the international institutions they support and their transnational corporations – controls the effective political sovereignty of another political society, by force, by political collaboration, by economic, social or cultural dependence. The following was a response to the Zapatista uprising by a multinational bank, a major financer in the restructuring of Mexico's economy:

The government will need to eliminate the Zapatistas to demonstrate their effective control of the national territory and security policy.

Mexico, Political Update, Chase Manhattan Bank

(Zapatista 1998)

If this is an example of a corporate 'triple bottom line' strategy to integrate social and environmental issues, the future for resistance movements is very bleak indeed.

The recent North–South conflict over the World Trade Organization's controversial Trade Related Aspects of Intellectual Property Agreement (TRIPS) is another case in point. The TRIPS agreement legitimizes private property rights through intellectual property even over life forms. These rights are for individuals, states and corporations, not for indigenous peoples and local communities. In effect, governments are asked to change their national intellectual property rights laws to allow patenting of 'micro-organisms, non-biological and micro-biological processes'. There are two related problems that arise from imposing a regime of intellectual property rights on indigenous knowledge. First, 'traditional' knowledge belongs to the indigenous community rather than to specific individuals. Second, as indigenous communities all over the world have discovered, national governments are increasingly employing neoliberal agendas – some willingly, a majority through coercion – that have adverse impacts on their livelihoods by restricting community access to natural resources. 'Equitable' sharing of commercial benefits through mutually beneficial contracts between indigenous groups and multinational corporations are unlikely to occur given the disparities in resources and capacities to monitor or enforce the terms of any contract.

The TRIPS agreement at the Uruguay Round of the GATT was developed 'in large part' by a committee called the Intellectual Property Committee (IPC) consisting of many transnational firms including Bristol Myers, Merck, Monsanto, Du Pont and Pfizer. Monsanto's representative described the TRIPS strategy as follows:

> ... [We were able to] distil from the laws of the more advanced countries the fundamental principles for protecting all forms of intellectual property ... Besides selling our concept at home, we went to Geneva where we presented our document to the staff of the GATT Secretariat ...What I have described to you is absolutely unprecedented in GATT. Industry identified a major problem for international trade. It crafted a solution, reduced it to a concrete proposal, and sold it to our own and other governments ... the industries and traders of the world have played simultaneously the role of patients, the diagnosticians and the prescribing physicians.
>
> (cited in Rifkin 1999: 52)

This is another example of how corporate power is wielded in the area of international trade and why any analysis of corporate social responsibility at the level of an individual organization cannot address broader social concerns. If the 'industries and traders of the world' dictate global trade and environmental policies that serve certain interests then the question to ask is who gets excluded from these policies? WTO policies such as TRIPS are developed to ensure protection of corporate rights, not community rights. The TRIPS agreement resulted in mass protests by indigenous and peasant communities along with NGOs in Asia, Africa and South America that continue to this day (Dawkins 1997).

The distinction between national and corporate interests becomes particularly important in the way these disputes are resolved in the WTO. National environmental legislation, safety regulations, social welfare nets, ethical buying policies are all examples of 'unfair trade practices' as far as recent WTO rulings are concerned. In 1996, the state of Massachusetts ruled that it would stop awarding government contracts to companies operating in Burma because of the country's brutal human rights record. A number of European companies – Unilever, Siemens, ING, ABN-Amro among them – lobbied their governments and as a result the EU threatened to take the case to the WTO, arguing that the ban was an unfair trade practice. The courts ruled in favour of the corporations. Lawyers representing Massachusetts argued that Nelson Mandela 'would still be in prison had current trade rules been in force in the 1980s' (Hertz 2001). In every environmental case considered by the WTO, national laws of democratically elected governments have been overridden by an organization that is accountable to no one. And exactly who are the institutions and people that play a highly influential role in global trade negotiations? Trade advisory bodies representing business interests of member countries are key players. However, the problem is about whose interests the trade advisory bodies represent. For example, in three of the main trade advisory committees of the US trade representative's office, representing a total of 111 members, only two represented labour unions (Korten 1995). Ninety-two represented individual companies and 16 were trade industry associations – ten from the chemical industry. More than a third of the member companies represented at these meetings – referred to in WTO parlance as 'the green room meetings' which are essentially closed door meetings with no access to the public – had been fined by the Environmental Protection Agency for failure to comply with environmental regulations (Korten 1995). A third of the member companies had actively lobbied state and federal governments opposing higher environmental standards. It is quite clear not only whose interests are being promoted in these world bodies but also who is being excluded from this process.

Thus, despite all the strident rhetoric about the 'stakeholder corporation' the reality is that stakeholders who do not toe the corporate line are either coopted or marginalized. The stakeholder theory of the firm represents a form of stakeholder colonialism that serves to regulate the behaviour of stakeholders. That – perceived – integration of stakeholder needs might be an effective tool for a firm to enhance its image is probably true. However, for a critical understanding of stakeholder theory, this approach is unsatisfactory. Effective practices of 'managing' stakeholders and research aimed at generating 'knowledge' about stakeholders are less systems of truth than products of power applied by corporations, governments and business schools (Knights 1992). As Willmott (1995) points out the establishment of new organization theories are very much the outcome of the historical development of capitalism and create value only for particular people and institutions. A view of the full picture of the consequences of stakeholder theory and practice requires a stepping out of the frame. A more critical examination of stakeholder theory, for instance understanding that stakeholder relations are systematized and controlled by the imperatives of capital accumulation, may produce a very different picture. Notions of power, legitimacy and urgency and the resultant practice of identifying stakeholder salience are contingent on the interests of nation states, industries, organizations or other institutions (Wilmott 1995) and in the process of stakeholder integration, either negate alternative practices or assimilate them.

Conclusion and implications for management ethics

As Clegg and Rhodes state in the introduction, the core questions of this book are: 'What are the ethics of organizing in today's institutional environment and what does this mean for the practice of management and the organization of work and business?'. In the context of corporate social responsibility we might ask what are the ethics of CSR? How can we make corporate social responsibility work for society and not just for corporations? What are the outcomes of CSR activities for the broader society? While much of the research focuses on the financial consequences of corporate social initiatives, we know little about the social consequences of these strategies. To what extent do current corporate initiatives actually achieve their intended outcomes? Instead of focusing on win-win situations, perhaps identifying and describing the conditions, challenges, and consequences of lose-lose or win-lose situations might reveal more interesting theoretical and practical challenges. Much of the strident voices against corporate power draw attention to issues such as exploitation of labour in developing countries, abusive practices and environmental destruction. These are practices that are easy targets. We need more research on the social consequences of apparently beneficial economic development policies at the level of people, for example detailed ethnographic accounts of the social transformations and dislocations created by foreign direct investment, industrial development, industrial agriculture, privatization, offshore production and export processing zones (Harvey 2003; Ong 1987).

It is unlikely that any radical revision of corporate social responsibility will emerge from organizations, given how this discourse is constructed at higher levels of the political economy. Focusing on the individual corporation as the unit of analysis can only produce limited results and serves to create an organizational enclosure around corporate social responsibility. For any radical revisioning to occur, a more critical approach to organization theory is required and new questions need to be raised not only about the ecological and social sustainability of business corporations but of the political economy itself. Radical revisions at this level can only occur if there is a shift in thinking at a macro level. We need to open up new spaces and provide new frameworks for organization-stakeholder dialogues as well as critically examine the dynamics of the relationships between corporations, NGOs, governments, community groups and funding agencies. Contemporary discourses of organizations and their stakeholders are inevitably constrained by 'practical' reasons such as the profit-seeking behaviour of corporations (Treviño and Weaver 1999). While the vast literature on corporate social responsibility, stakeholder integration and business ethics is based on the assumption that business is influenced by societal concerns, the dominance of societal interests in radically reshaping business practices is in some question

(Mueller 1994). The domain of corporate social responsibility cannot be assessed by primarily economic criteria and neither can an environmental ethic be developed through an 'ethically pragmatic managerial' morality that primarily serves organizational interests (Fineman 1998; Snell 2000). The limitations of a market-based model of corporate social responsibility mirror the shortcomings of economic rationalism. The term economic rationalism itself is problematic and needs to be unpacked. It assumes first that there is something inherently 'rational' about economics, which needs to be debated. Second, it disallows alternate imaginaries from emerging because of its discursive power automatically to label them as 'irrational'. Perhaps market fundamentalism is a more appropriate term where fundamentalism is less about the content of any belief system and more about the strength with which it is defended.

Corporations cannot replace governments and contribute to social welfare simply because their basic function – the rhetoric of triple bottom line aside – is inherently driven by economic needs. What will happen to a local community that is completely dependent for its economic, social and environmental welfare on a multinational company once the latter decides to move its location? On economic grounds of course, not social or environmental reasons. Markets, however efficient they may be in setting prices, cannot be counted upon to ensure that corporations will always act in the interests of society. Social investment and social justice can never become a corporation's core activity – the few companies that have tried to do this, Body Shop and Ben & Jerry's come to mind, have failed and even worse been accused of fraudulent behaviour (Entine 1995). In the political economy we live in today, corporate strategies will always be made in the interests of enhancing shareholder value and return on capital, not social justice or morality. And emerging attempts to conceptualize social responsibility as 'social capital' will still fall short unless there is a radical restructuring of the political economy and fundamental rethinking about the role of a corporation in society. Social capital is not a universal good, often times it is generated for one group of people at the expense of some other segment of society. The Mafia has considerable amounts of social capital. So has Al Qaeda.

A radical ethics of corporate social responsibility will go beyond a managerial position and whose purpose will be 'not performativity but emancipation' (Grice and Humphries 1997: 422). Much of current critical work in management focuses on the same questions and tries to provide better answers. As we have seen, even theories of social responsibility despite their emancipatory intent, are avowedly managerialist and do not contribute to a critical understanding of the consequences of managerial decision-making. Changing organizational theorizing needs a different way of thinking that asks new questions rather than obtaining more answers to the same questions. It needs to ask questions from different, often oppositional perspectives, while being constantly suspicious of all answers. It asks why certain questions are asked, why others are not asked, 'why some approaches are chosen over others and what interests are included or excluded in this process' (Grice and Humphries 1997: 423). An overwhelming proportion of research in management focuses on traditional profit-oriented corporations. The bulk of research on not-for-profit organizations is also framed by similar corporate goals: how can we raise more money for charity, how can we get more people into museums or libraries or zoos? There is very little research on strategies for activist groups and organizations, and the theories and practices required to oppose corporate actions (Frooman 1999). Contemporary discourses of stakeholder theory often distort its 'normative core' for 'practical' reasons such as profit seeking (Treviño and Weaver 1999).

A critical-ethical perspective on stakeholder theory would not just focus on documenting 'best practices' in stakeholder management. It would involve examining how knowledge and theory development in the field constitutes social relations between different stakeholders and perhaps even set the ground for a different set of conditions, which in turn needs to be critiqued. It would also question the autonomy of corporate law and focus attention on the power dynamics between different groups in society. Let us not forget laws also represent the interests of a specific class despite its self-representation as an expression of 'universal will'. Questions that need to be addressed include: What are the power dynamics underlying the political process of stakeholder partnerships? What are the material and discursive effects? How do institutions reinforce hegemonic structures? What institutional structures can overcome the narrow self-interest of the financial elite? How can we create alternate structures of decision-making, conflict resolution and accountability?

Mahatma Gandhi was once asked by a newspaper reporter in London about what he thought of Western civilization. Gandhi replied that it might be a good idea. Perhaps the same thing applies to CSR – it may be a good idea provided it creates genuine change rather than reacting to changes in the political economy. As Frank (2001: 143) states, management theory teaches us that the corporation is capable of resolving all social conflict 'fairly and justly within its walls'. It is this theory that an ethical-critical perspective seeks to subvert. Restoring a sense of social justice and equity cannot be achieved through 'some final triumph of the corporation over the body and soul of humanity, but some sort of power that confronts business' (Frank 2001: 143). As we debate issues of CSR, corporate citizenship, sustainability and stakeholders let us never lose sight of the fact that companies are not the only inhabitants of this planet. Perhaps the words of Subcomandante Marcos can serve as a guide:

> En suma no estamos proponiendo una revolución ortodoxa, sino algo mucho más difícil: una revolución que haga posible la revolución. (To sum

up, we are not proposing an orthodox revolution, but something much more difficult: a revolution that will make the revolution possible.)

Note

1   The Oxford English Dictionary defines greenwash as 'disinformation disseminated by an organization so as to present an environmentally responsible public image'. The non-governmental organization CorpWatch has a less charitable definition of greenwash: 'the phenomenon of socially and environmentally destructive corporations attempting to preserve and expand their markets by posing as friends of the environment and leaders in the struggle to eradicate poverty'.

Chapter 5

The ethics of corporate legal personality

Robert van Krieken

Editors' introduction

Robert van Krieken begins this chapter by quoting some of the more realist contributors to ethical debate, notably Thomas Hobbes and Max Weber. What characterized both of these thinkers was a keen concern with the application of ethics to practice in troubled times. Indeed, from a business ethics point of view almost all times appear troubled because a concern with ethics is rarely characterized by an absence of trouble. It is often when situations are constituted as 'problems' that managers reach for ethical accounts. As van Krieken puts it, it is when 'we become concerned with contradictions or conflicts between managerial conduct and widely-shared ethical principles, [that] it is important to see that there are two ways of approaching such conflicts'. These two ways are described as 'thick' and 'thin' respectively; the former is something not too dissimilar to the framework that Ibarra-Colado prepared, which looks at ethics against the backdrop of a whole civilization. By contrast, thin accounts focus on matters of organizational design, abstracted from the thick context and from the motives of the managers who run them; they stress the normative character of the organization as a whole, rather than those of managers as individuals.

But there is an internal contradiction which cuts across both the 'thin' and the 'thick' dimensions of managerial ethics, which is seen in the tensions between explicit normative standards and implicitly constituted practical forms of behaviour. This is the problem of 'hypocrisy' that is manifest in the ways in which otherwise 'good' men and women can still end up doing 'bad' things, and the ways in which good things can be done for bad reasons. In this chapter van Krieken seeks to reconcile institutional design and socially constituted individual habitus not simply as alternatives between which one can choose, but as linked and interacting with each other within a broader overall process of the 'civilization of management'. Thus, van Krieken is involved in an ambitious project to further develop the application of the ideas of the great German social theorist, Norbert Elias, to theorizing contemporary organization and management practice.

Van Krieken finds the 'ethical form' of management conduct somewhat inaccessible. In part this is because of the role that idealized standards play in fixing ethical responsibility. In practice, the ethical dimensions of management occur within a complex field of differing ethical interests and orientations. These provide for relatively autonomous, self-referential ethical sub-systems with no necessary consistency between them. The relation between them thus becomes a central problematic. Indeed, somewhat pessimistically, in the context of the recent cases of corporate corruption, such as Enron, van Krieken concludes that contemporary management ethics may well be a testing ground for the character of contemporary civil society itself. If that is the case, then the prognosis is not apparently good.

> In the design of human institutions Hobbes must be taken seriously. He showed what in human nature we must guard against; and he found in rational self-preservation a reliable, if limited, source of moral ordering. For the most part, it is self-interest, not virtue, that underpins reciprocity, compromise, and fidelity to obligation. (Selznick 1992: 208)

- **ethics:** code of morality, a system of moral principles governing the appropriate conduct for an individual or group [15th century. Via Old French *ethiques* from, ultimately, Greek *ethika*, from *ethikos* 'ethical', from *ethos* 'character, nature']
- **ethos:** shared fundamental traits: the fundamental and distinctive character of a group, social context, or period of time, typically expressed in attitudes, habits, and beliefs

It is difficult to overemphasize the centrality of management ethics to the constitution of modern social life. Like politicians, managers and administrators exercise enormous control and influence over the distribution of resources, power and, indeed, of the means of violence. The question of the lines of responsibility and accountability surrounding the actions of managers is, therefore, just as significant as it is for the actions of politicians and any powerful social actor.

The complexity of the issue was outlined by Max Weber (1948) in 'Politics as a Vocation', where he pointed to the paradox of the poor fit between good intentions and good outcomes. As he put it:

> No ethics in the world can dodge the fact that in numerous instances the attainment of 'good' ends is bound to the fact that one must be willing to

pay the price of using morally dubious means or at least dangerous ones
– and facing the possibility or even the probability of evil ramifications.
From no ethics in the world can it be concluded when and to what
extent the ethically good purpose 'justifies' the ethically dangerous
means and ramifications.

(1948: 121)

For Weber, then, the more important 'test' for ethical conduct was not
whether it corresponded to abstract principles, but its final outcome. He
took it for granted that there was no such thing as 'purely ethical' action, the
forces governing the exercise of power and the actual relationships between
intentions and outcomes were so 'diabolical' that one would inevitably have
to risk the salvation of one's soul to a greater or lesser extent, forced to end
up saying 'Here I stand; I can do no other'.

Weber's perspective may have been coloured by the particular historical
events taking place around him, but this does not dispose of the saliency
of his observations, which still highlight how problematic it is to work
with a simple distinction between 'ethical' and 'unethical' behaviour, and
suggest that just as there may be no purely ethical conduct, there may also
be no purely unethical action. It is just as likely that all human action is
guided by some set of moral principles, so that the question becomes one of
disagreements about what those principles are. Obedience to orders remains
itself an ethical position, despite its consequences for other ethical concerns.
Behaviour described as corruption and nepotism can also be understood
and experienced as loyalty to family and friends. Peter Drucker (1981)
highlighted this point pointing out the alternative ethical explanations of
some key business scandals, such as the General Electric cartel case in the
later 1950s and the Lockheed bribery case in the 1970s. He did so in order to
discredit the casuist approach to ethics in business, but the piece is probably
more usefully read as identifying a real problem, namely the range of often
competing and cross-cutting ethical concerns that run through any business
and any organization.[1]

This leads us to question, then, whether it is correct to describe events
like the Holocaust simply as the product of normatively empty instrumental
rationality (Bauman 1991), rather than regarding them as, say, the outcome
of the alliance of such instrumental rationality with particular normative
orientations. Is it really a case of 'ethics v. instrumental reason', or should
we also see things in terms of competing ethical orientations? It may be
important to develop a more differentiated understanding of ethically driven
action, with the jury being out on whether such action necessarily produces
outcomes which we regard as positive, or as consistent with *all* our ethical
principles. Certainly a very large proportion of the violence and abuse
human beings have inflicted on each other throughout history has been the
product precisely of normative concerns, and many of the arguments for

the development of capitalism were based on the idea that 'interests' were ultimately a more civilized basis for human action than 'passions' (Hirschman 1977; Holmes 1995).

When we become concerned with contradictions or conflicts between managerial conduct and widely shared ethical principles, it is important to see that there are two ways of approaching such conflicts. One is based on 'thin' conception of human conduct, presuming that what people do is largely situationally defined (Bendix 1952), focusing on questions of institutional design, so that one engages primarily with the framework of organizational action, addressing issues like the concept of the corporate legal personality and everyday organizational practices. Among the more important examples here are the arguments of Dennis Thompson (2005) and John Braithwaite (1998) concerning the combination of maximising interpersonal trust, but also institutional *distrust*, which means 'deploying sound principles of institutional design so that institutions check the power of other institutions' (Braithwaite 1998: 343). As Thompson puts it, 'If we recognize the importance of distrust, we will make sure that the institutions on which we depend are designed in such a way to encourage good behaviour in the absence of good character, and in the absence of trusting personal relations' (2005: 249). Such an orientation focuses more on the normative character of the organization as a whole, rather than those of managers as individuals.

The other derives from a 'thick' conception of human psychology, in which human beings are understood as having a relatively stable set of habits and dispositions – what Norbert Elias (2000) and Pierre Bourdieu (1984) refer to as *habitus* – which has emerged in the course of their biography and which drives the individual's conduct as much, if not more so, than the demands and requirements of their immediate organizational context. This is the realm of culture, norms, values in the social world beyond the organization itself, which individual members bring with them and which constitute their normative orientation towards the kinds of indeterminate choices they are daily confronted with. In this approach, ethical questions are treated primarily as questions concerning the character of key individuals, and the emphasis is on increasing the trustworthiness. Such an understanding of human psychology, I will argue, requires a discussion of the emergence of particular psychic structures which have changed over time, and which can only be understood in connection with changes in the forms taken by broader social relationships, and the sociological theorizations of processes of civilization and decivilization originally inspired by Elias have been the most useful here (van Krieken 1998, 1999).

The particular problem I will use to draw these points together is that of the *internal* contradictions which cut across both the 'thin' and the 'thick' psychological dimensions of managerial ethics, the tensions between explicit normative standards and implicitly constituted practical forms of behaviour – the problem of 'hypocrisy' – the ways in which otherwise 'good' men and women can still end up doing 'bad' things, and good things can be done for bad reasons. The chapter will work towards a sketch of the ways in which this problem might be better understood through seeing these two concerns – institutional design and socially constituted individual *habitus* – not simply as alternatives, between which we need to choose, but as linked and interacting with each other within a broader overall process of the 'civilization of management'.

The corporation's legal personality

One of the most important features of the institutional design of managerial action is the way in which 'the organization' is constructed in law as a distinct legal entity or actor separate from the real human beings that make it up. The example which generally receives most attention is that of the private corporation as an entity possessing 'legal personhood' apart from its members or shareholders, but it is also more broadly true that legal responsibility is often attributed to collective entities. To understand management ethics across the spectrum of organizational forms, a useful place to begin is to attend to the effect of this separate entity doctrine in the corporate world of increasingly complex networks of multi-layered, multi-national corporations sub-divided into a number of subsidiaries, with share-holding being as much a characteristic of relations between corporations among themselves as between corporations and their members, as well as to the ethical problems concerning accountability thrown up by the particular approaches dominating Anglo–Australian corporation law.

Many of the central features of the concept of corporate legal personhood are often traced, in English and Australian legal thinking, back to the nineteenth century dispute between Aron Salomon the bootmaker and his creditors. In 1892, Salomon ran a successful boot-making business in High Street, Whitechapel. His five sons had expressed an interest in acquiring an interest in the business, and Salomon wanted to provide for his family, so he formed his business into a limited company, fulfilling all the requirements of Companies Act 1862. The only shareholders were Salomon himself, his five sons, and his wife. However, the business fell prey to a downturn in the boot and shoe trade, and in an attempt to save it, Salomon borrowed £5,000 from a Mr Broderip at 10 per cent interest, transferring £10,000 of debentures to Broderip as security. The decline continued, and it became impossible to pay the interest on the loan. Liquidation came shortly after, and in the process of meeting Broderip's claim, the liquidator turned on Salomon, holding him accountable for losses incurred by the company, constructing it as a fraud to shield Salomon from creditors. Both the Court of Chancery and the Court of Appeal upheld the liquidator's claim, arguing that the company was merely an agent of Salomon's, creating a crisis in the legal position of the ever-increasing number of one-man companies. However, the House of Lords came to their rescue in 1896, arguing that the principle of limited liability, well-established in relation to joint-stock companies, also applied to individual companies. The point of the House of Lords' judgment was that limited liability holds even when a company is under control of a single individual, so that the corporate form can be used to limit even an individual owner's liability.[2] This is often referred to as the 'veil' of incorporation, in the sense that the courts generally do not look behind that veil to identify who 'really' controls the corporation.

The case established the unwillingness of the legislature and the courts to supervise the 'real' relations between shareholders, or the 'authenticity' of their association, in contrast to the view of 'corporations as partnerships' which had held sway up to and including the Court of Appeal's judgment in the *Salomon* case (Grantham and Rickett 1998: 8). What Salomon and all individual proprietors *gained* in terms of limiting their liability has to be seen also, however, as part and parcel of an overall *reduction* of shareholders' power in relation to corporate management and the *abolition* of their interest in the corporation's assets. The decision pushed corporation law much further towards the more autonomous operation of corporations from shareholder influence (Pickering 1968: 502; Ireland 1999: 41, 48).

The decision was also part of the process of the separation of *shares* from *company assets:* shares as autonomous forms of property, and company assets as independent from shareholders – who only had rights to dividends and to assign shares (Ireland 1999: 41). The *Salomon* case is thus a watershed in addressing the problem of defending the distinction between two distinct forms of capital: company assets and shares, a distinction embodied in the distinct legal entity that is the corporation. In addition to extending the principles of limited liability to the one-person company, by establishing that full control did not prevent the operation of those principles, Grantham and Rickett have pointed out that the judgment also laid the foundations for the subsequent twentieth century development of corporate groups (Grantham and Rickett 1998: 5), allowing for the fragmentation of a single corporate entity into a multiplicity of corporations, each with their assets partitioned off from each other and from the parent company. One of the more significant effects of the concept of corporate legal personality, then, has been to distinguish, not just real human beings from the organizations they make up, but different parts of networks of corporations from each other, essentially creating ever more complex firewalls or bulkheads within lines of corporate accountability. In Anglo–Australian law there have basically been two types of response to this evolving complexity in the structure of corporations.

The first has been to work within a tension between, on the one hand, continuing to apply the same principles to the relationship between holding companies and their wholly owned subsidiaries as were applied to the relationship between Aron Salomon the boot-maker and *Salomon & Co* the boot-making company and, on the other hand, looking for *exceptions* to those principles, especially any contrary intention on the part of Parliament. The doctrine of the corporation as a separate legal entity is held generally to apply, but with some exceptions under certain circumstances, when the courts choose to 'lift the corporate veil', where it can be shown that there is sufficient evidence of fraud, unlawful purpose, or a relationship of agency. The second approach has been to sidestep the question of the corporation's legal identity altogether and look beyond the entity doctrine to, say, a nexus of contracts approach, or agency law, or equitable principles. Christos Mantziaris (1999) describes the two approaches as an 'inner' and 'outer' view of the corporation, the former focusing on a formalist account of the corporation as a construction of law itself, and the latter approaching it in terms of its instrumental and pragmatic effects in the world of economic action.

However, neither approach really provides the conceptual tools required to deal with contemporary corporations; the continuing reliance on *Salomon* reveals a fundamental conceptual problem in corporation law, a failure to adapt to the very distinct reality of corporate groups (Ireland 1999: 44), but the turn to a nexus of contracts approach also fails to grasp the essentially de-personified nature of corporation. Both are inadequate for dealing with the reality of corporate groups, producing a core problem of legal uncertainty as well as an inability to deal effectively with the problems of accountability they throw up, and it remains unclear how the entity and contractual approaches might be articulated with each other, or how they might evolve into a completely different approach.

What is apparent is that corporation law's construction of limited liability writes a particular ethical script for organizational action, and once one begins to pay attention to this aspect of the legal construction of the organization, it becomes clear that it has to be seen as having a *dual*, in many senses *contradictory*, ethical effect. On the one hand, it is obviously true that legal mechanisms are central to the regulation of organizations and the establishment of consequential lines of accountability and responsibility; it is through the law that individuals and groups are able to hold corporations, government and non-government agencies to account and to enforce some consistency with broadly accepted ethical principles, to the extent that they have found their way into the legal system. The criminal prosecution of the wide variety of corporate fraud is the most obvious example.

However, at the same time, writers such as Harry Glasbeek (2002) and Joel Bakan (2004) point out that there are a number of elements of the basic legal design of corporations which themselves *underpin* a weak relationship between socially accepted ethics and managerial conduct. Their work draws out the ways in which corporation law, and especially the concept of limited liability, actively encourages particular forms of organizational conduct breaching a wide range of generally accepted ethical norms, and positively obstructs a variety of mechanisms of accountability and responsibility. The economic firewall protecting shareholders from financial liability for corporate action also generally rules them out of consideration for ethical responsibility. There have been some attempts to encourage a greater sense of moral accountability among investors, with a little effect at the margins, but on the whole the moral sensibility which reigns among shareholders is 'just show me the money'. As Joel Bakan (2004) emphasizes, the corporation's legal 'personality' has a lot in common with that of a psychopath, and the concept of legal personality stands in the way of attributing genuine responsibility to real human beings capable of modifying their thoughts and actions in response to ethical concerns. This was why the English Lord Chancellor Edward Thurlow once complained 'Did you ever expect a corporation to have a conscience, when it has no body to be kicked and no soul to be damned?' – a point also drawn on by Banerjee in Chapter 4.

Managerial accountability

If shareholders are shielded from both financial and ethical liability, and the corporation as a fictional legal 'person' does not have a psychology amenable to moral regulation, that leaves only the real human beings within organizations. As we all know, the formal structure of an organization only tells you a part of the story, it is equally if not more important to examine its informal structures and dynamics, the character of the live human beings that make it up, what Philip Selznick calls 'thick' institutionalization (1992: 235). Against the background of the legal construction of the corporation, the fabric of the structuring of responsibility and accountability within organizational life also establishes a very particular kind of ethical 'space' which generates its own patterns of conduct and organizational action. One of the most useful insights into the ethical space of business organizations – although it is probably not that different for other kinds of organizational settings – remains Robert Jackall's 1988 study of three US business corporations in the early 1980s, *Moral Mazes*. The specific concern of Jackall's research was 'the moral rules-in-use that managers construct to guide their behaviour at work, whether these are shaped directly by authority relationships or by other kinds of experiences typical in big organizations' (1988: 4). The importance of the book lies in its uncompromising empiricism: it goes beyond measuring management action against an ideal normative standard, to identify the actual distinct ethical form of managerial conduct, and the ways in which organizational life 'makes its own internal rules and social context the principal moral gauges for action' (1988: 192). This ethical form has a number of key elements, all of which contribute to the *differentiation* of management ethics from that of the social life outside the organization, a historical shift from an ethical subjection to a Protestant ethic or its equivalent, to a different and equally powerful set of gods. For the purposes of this chapter I will highlight two of them.

First, Jackall observes the ongoing *combination* of what Weber identified as the ideal-typical form of bureaucracy and its patrimonial predecessor – what Elias (1983) called 'court society'. Weber's well-known outline of the 'pure' form of bureaucracy emphasizes ways in which modern social life is increasingly characterized by an emphasis on instrumentally rational action, in preference to affective, traditional or value-rational action, and the dominance of rational-legal forms of power instead of the charismatic and traditional forms characteristic of patrimonial bureaucracies, both of which have the effect of minimising the significance of particular human beings and their particular personalities and biographies in the service of the organization's overall goals and functions. Organizational rules, policies and procedures impose strict discipline and control, leaving little room for personal initiative or discretion. The 'ideal official' performs his or her duties in 'a spirit of formalistic impersonality ... without hatred or passion, and hence without affection or enthusiasm' (Weber 1978: 225). The activities of bureaucrats are governed by the rules and the impersonal purposes of the organization, not by personal considerations such as feelings towards colleagues or clients, or their personal relationship of loyalty or obligation to their 'rulers' (Weber 1978: 1028–31). Business is conducted 'without regard for persons' (Weber 1978: 975). It is this aspect of modern organizational life that is being highlighted when a critique of the ethical dimensions of modern organizational society is pursued. Bauman (1989, 1991), for example, argues that adherence to impersonal rules on its own does not do sufficient justice to the human moral impulse, indeed that reducing ethics to rules reduces rather than increases our moral capacity, with the Holocaust as a key example. Weber himself articulated a similar viewpoint in his ambivalence about bureaucracy: he recognizing the superior efficiency and effectiveness of the rational-legal approach, but he was also critical of its broader impact, and seeking to articulate bureaucracy with the realm of politics, where value-rationality and charisma would play a much stronger role.

If we return briefly to Weber's account of the difference between patrimonial and bureaucratic officialdom, a central issue is the extent of the significance of personal relationships, ties, commitments, obligations and loyalties in determining the form and content of the work done in the organization. Weber suggests that patrimonialism is characterized by a demand for 'unconditional administrative compliance', because:

> ... the patrimonial official's loyalty to his office (*Amtstreue*) is not an impersonal commitment (*Diensttreue*) to impersonal tasks which define its extent and its content, it is rather a servant's loyalty based on a strictly personal relationship to the rules and on an obligation of fealty which in principle permits no limitation ... the official partakes in the ruler's

dignity because and insofar as he is personally subject to the ruler's authority (*Herrengewalt*).

(Weber 1978: 1030–1)

The selection of personnel is based on 'personal trust, not technical qualifications', and their position derives from their 'purely personal submission to the ruler' (Weber 1978: 1030). However, Jackall observes that in reality contemporary organizational life actually displays many of these features of patrimonial forms of organization; it is by no means true that impersonal, objectives considerations have displaced questions of personal loyalty and obligation. It appears that the Weberian ideal-typical bureaucracy did not *replace* patrimonial forms of organization, but *combined* with it to produce a multi-layered hybrid (Jackall 1988: 11–12).

Jackall himself explains this in terms of American particularism: a number of factors, including the frontier experience and the poor education of many American immigrants together constituted a setting for organizational evolution in which American corporations 'instituted as a matter of course many of the features of personal loyalty, favouritism, informality and nonlegality that marked crucial aspects of the American historical experience' (Jackall 1988: 11). But it is more likely that this persistence of a patrimonial model of bureaucracy is more broadly characteristic; human history is generally marked by a combination of continuity with change, rather than abrupt transitions from one type of society or social form to another (Ginzburg 1981).

This combination of patrimonial with rational-legal organizational form has a number of consequences: it generates an authoritarian mode of governance, in which the wishes and will of those further up the hierarchy play a strong role in determining individual action, not least because every individual's survival can depend on it. Jackall suggests that it 'ties' management ethics to a particular set of concerns more closely related to the nature of a particular network of personal bonds than to a stable set of moral principles, anchored either in the individual themselves or in the surrounding society and culture. Managers' work is framed by 'structures of personalized authority in formally impersonal contexts, fealty with bosses and patrons, and alliances shaped through networks, coteries, cliques, and work groups that struggle through hard times together' (Jackall 1988: 192). It generates a structuring of responsibility that makes it difficult, if not impossible, ever to pin down the lines of accountability of any given set of organizational actions. A hierarchical division emerges between knowledge and responsibility, so that those higher up the hierarchy are in principle more responsible, but also less knowledgeable about detail, which means they can choose to dodge responsibility for any given action or outcome. Those further down the hierarchy in principle are more knowledgeable about the causes of particular outcomes, but are also able dodge responsibility by virtue of their hierarchical position.

Jackall also observed a general tendency towards the use of language to obscure rather than pin down lines of causality and accountability, again in the service of personal ties and obligations. He quotes one senior manager pointing out the poor relationship between the explanatory narratives circulating in an organization and anything that might be identified as an objective account:

> What's interesting and confusing at the same time is the way guys around here will switch explanations of things from day to day and not even notice. It is astonishing to hear the things people say. Like they explain the current stagnation of our stock one day by referring to the Falkland Island war; the next day, it's the bearish stock market; the next, it's the Fed's interest policy; the next, it's unsettled political conditions. And so on and on. And they don't remember the explanations they gave a month ago. They end up going around believing in fairy tales that might have no relationship to reality at all.
>
> (Jackall 1988: 146–7)

An Alice-in-Wonderland kind of linguistic world is thus more the rule than the exception, putting up still another obstacle to identifying, let alone realizing moral accountability.

Second, paralleling this persistence of patrimonialism in modern organizations, Jackall notes the profoundly *symbolic* nature of organizational life, in the sense that any individual's worth, position and status is heavily dependent on how one is perceived, how adroitly one manages one's image in the organization, and this may have almost no relationship to one's actual skills, capacities, actions and performance. In this respect the dynamics of modern organizational life correspond closely to Elias's (1983) account of seventeenth century court society, in which the representation and display of position and status was of enormous consequence, and the primary skill was the 'public relations' one of *representing* and securing *recognition* of one's position, rather than necessarily building an objective foundation for it. Vitally important here was the management of emotions, for 'the competition of court life enforces a curbing of the affects in favour of calculating and finely shaded behaviour in dealing with people' (Elias 1983: 111). Jackall gives the following description of managers' emotional stance:

> Managers also stress the need to exercise iron self-control and to have the ability to mask all emotion and intention behind bland, smiling, and agreeable public faces. One must avoid both excessive gravity and unwarranted levity. One must blunt one's aggressiveness with blandness ... One must be able to listen to others' grievances and even attacks

upon oneself while maintaining an appropriately concerned, but simultaneously dispassionate countenance. In such situations, some managers don masks of Easter-Island-statuelike immobility; others a deadpan fisheye; and the most adroit, a disarming ingenuousness.

(Jackall 1988: 47)

This corresponds almost word-for-word with Elias's account of the constant self-observation required in the symbolic world of court society. He quotes a contemporary observer, Jean de La Bruyère : 'A man who know the court is master of his gestures, of his eyes and of his face; he is profound, impenetrable; he dissimulates bad offices, smiles at his enemies, controls his irritation, disguises his passions, belies his heart, speaks and acts against his feelings' (Elias 1983: 105).

This in turn contributes to the uncoupling of extra-organizational ethical concerns from the internal dynamics of organizational life. Both individual and socially-sanctioned ethical orientations fall into the same category as emotions: they are not infinitely flexible, they resist being bent to particular strategic aims, they reveal an attachment to concerns other than those characterizing the ebb and flow of power relations within the organization. As Jackall put it, 'moral viewpoints threaten others within an organization by making claims on them that might impede their ability to read the drift of social situations. As a result, independent morally evaluative judgments get subordinated to the social intricacies of the bureaucratic workplace' (Jackall 1988: 105).

Both these long-term historical continuities in organizational dynamics contribute to what Jackall calls the 'bracketing' of management ethics from extra-organizational normative concerns, the creation of a distinct ethical framework within the organization, and the generation of a profound ethical 'splitting' of all members of modern organizations. He quotes the former vice-president of a large firm as follows: 'What is right in the corporation is not what is right in man's home or in his church. *What is right in the corporation is what the guy above you wants from you.* That's what morality is in the corporation' (Jackall 1988: 6; respondent's own emphasis). An important feature of this ethical 'bracketing' is that it can never be admitted publicly, so that it also involves a constant process of 'massaging' the tension between the private and the public, back-stage and front-stage (Goffman 1959), what is understood, admitted and lived with within the organization and the public face of the organization.

Against this background, there are many other accounts of the various mechanisms apparently built into the structure of modern organizations which persistently undermine lines of accountability and responsibility, and thus effectively create ethical 'no man's lands'. Dennis Thompson, for example, speaks of the 'problem of many hands' characterizing all human action arising from the complex and differentiation interaction of any number of individuals, that is, all organized action. He defines the problem as follows: 'Because many different officials contribute in many ways to decisions and policies of government, it is difficult even in principle to identify who is morally responsible for political outcomes' (Thompson 2005: 11). This is in turn connected with the question of the unintended consequences of human action, the ways in which the outcomes of collective action generally have a weak relationship to the intentions and goals of the individuals participating in it. Mark Bovens (1998) has also complemented Jackall's study with an analysis of how responsibility and accountability work in complex organizations, and in particular all the mechanisms which undermine their effective operation. His account includes an examination of Thompson's 'problem of many hands', or the paradox of collective responsibility, the difference between passive and active responsibility, the limited rationality of complex organizations, the lack of external insight, the ways in which the ethical orientations of individuals operating within organizational settings tend to get undermined and weakened by the combination of instrumental rationality and the 'collectivization' of action in organizational life. He identifies the ten most frequently used explanations people give for their participation in organizational action which they agree breaches their ethical principles:

(1) I was just a small cog in a big machine; (2) Other people did much more than I did; (3) If I had not done it, someone else would; (4) Even without my contribution it would have happened; (5) Without my contribution, it would have been even worse; (6) I had nothing to do with it; (7) I wash my hands of the whole business; (8) I knew nothing of it; (9) I only did what I was told to do; (10) I had no choice.

(Bovens 1998: 113–24)

These kinds of analyses converge on a concern to address management ethics at a structural level, at the level of the design of the frameworks of action within organizations. As Thompson puts it, 'we should stop thinking about ethics so much in terms of individual vices (bribery, extortion, greed, personal gain, sexual misconduct) and start thinking about it more in terms of institutional vices (abuse of power, improper disclosure, excessive secrecy, lack of accountability)' (Thompson 2005: 4). Bovens then goes on to identify a number of ways in which the issue can be dealt with in terms of institutional design, such as pursuing greater clarity in the lines of responsibility, the notion of 'sluices' in the chain of responsibility and accountability rather than chains – 'the buck stops here' – attaching individual names to actions, the extension of personal accountability within organizations – for example, requiring individuals to accept full legal liability for their actions – and the creation of more space for active individual responsibility. However, they all work within a 'thin' conception of human psychology and moral formation, and there are also other observations to be made from the standpoint of a 'thick' conception which pays more attention to the formation of psychological dispositions outside organizational life itself.

Processes of civilization and managerial habitus

Questions of institutional design, significant as they are, do not entirely exhaust the effective understanding of the moral dimensions of organizational and managerial action. It may be true that instrumental legal rationality on its own *can* generate action that will later or from other quarters be morally condemned, but much of it does not, and we need to look further afield to explain the difference. Networks of social relations and their accompanying 'deep structures' of organizational action also have histories extending beyond organizational life itself which require examination and understanding. Both the current operation and the historical development of organizational forms can only be properly understood alongside the operation and historical development of more general social modes of constituting human subjectivity, their embeddedness in social relations in the sphere of society and culture. Subjectivity is a crucial medium for the establishment of 'institutional isomorphism' across organizations and for the 'deep structure' of the tacit rules governing organizational action. This is particularly significant in a world 'characterized by increasingly dense, extended, and rapidly changing patterns of reciprocal interdependence, and by increasingly frequent, but ephemeral, interactions across all types of pre-established boundaries, intra- and interorganizational, intra- and intersectoral, intra- and international' (Scharpf 1993: 141).

Weber's analysis of bureaucracy, in other words, needs to be read alongside his account of the Protestant ethic (Weber 1930), in which it becomes clear that the production of a disciplined psychological disposition suited to the routines and procedures of organizational life was both *preceded* and *accompanied* by the more general ideological development of Christian asceticism's methodical, calculative organization of conduct. Capitalist work organizations found at least some workers already possessed of an 'adequate lifestyle' through which it 'gained massive control over life in the manner that it has' (Weber 1978: 1119), so that Protestant asceticism unintentionally prepared the foundations for the development of organizational discipline (van Krieken 1989). The psychological dispositions on which organizational life depends, including its ethical orientations, thus has been and continues to be formed as much outside organizations as within them (van Krieken 1996).

One particularly useful account of the construction of human identity and subjective experience beyond the organization, particularly the changing standards to which it is subjected, has been Norbert Elias's analysis of what he called 'processes of civilization'. Although the concept of civilization is often used to capture the self-understanding of the West as superior to the rest of the world, for Elias it meant something much more specific connected with the particular form taken by social relations at certain times and in certain contexts. Elias argued that as an increasingly complex web of social interdependencies and networks of competition develops, and increasing numbers of people have to coordinate their actions with others:

> ... the web of actions must be organized more and more strictly and accurately, if each individual action is to fulfill its social function. Individuals are compelled to regulate their conduct in an increasingly differentiated, more even and more stable manner ... the more complex and stable control of conduct is increasingly instilled in the individual from his or her earliest years as an automatism, a self-compulsion that he or she cannot resist even if he or she consciously wishes to.
>
> (Elias 2000: 367)

It is the foresight required by this increasing interdependency which in turn makes it necessary for every individual to develop increasing constraint of their drives, impulses and affect, and constituted much of the foundation of behavioural adherence to norms of civility, what would be referred to in psychoanalytic terms as the superego. Increasing social interdependence thus produces a development from external to internal constraint, or a 'social constraint towards self-restraint' which becomes part of human personality structure: 'The web of actions grows so complex and extensive, the effort required to behave "correctly" within it becomes so great, that beside the individual's conscious self-control, an automatic, blindly functioning apparatus of self-control is firmly established' (Elias 2000: 367–8). For Elias the question of why people's behaviour, ethical norms and emotional dispositions change 'is really the same as the question of why their forms of living change' (Elias 2000: 172).

Elias's emphasis was thus on the broadest possible range of networks of interdependent, interweaving plans and actions, the notion of a patterned 'fabric' of social relationships from which arises 'an order *sui generis*, an order more compelling and stronger than the will and reason of the individual people composing it' (Elias 2000: 366). The civilizing process is not simply a process of rationalization; its production of a disciplined personality structure cannot be linked with the impact of a particular structuring of organizations. Civilization, said Elias, 'is not "reasonable"; not "rational", any more than it is "irrational"'. It is set in motion blindly, and kept in motion by the autonomous dynamics of a web of relationships, by specific changes in the way people are bound to live together' (Elias 2000: 367). One of the earliest commentators on the ways in which Elias's work can be applied in organizational analysis, Jacques van Doorn (1956), argued that Elias's conception of the civilizing process 'laid the foundation for our concept of social controllability, also the organizability, of the modern person' (Jacques van Doorn 1956: 200). He suggested that there was a dialectical relationship between the psychological and ethical worlds inside and outside the organization, so that the production of self-disciplined subjectivity both within and outside organizations enabled new, more flexible forms of organizational discipline. The modern organization thus constituted a formalization of existing relationships, a process which seemed less enforced than before, because the enforcement, intended and unintended, had already succeeded in the previous generations and in the early life-phases of the individual (van Doorn 1956: 202; for more recent applications of Elias to organizational studies, see van Iterson *et al.* 2002 and van Vree 1999).

However, there is not a bright line between processes of civilization and conformity to particular ethical principles. First of all, self-constraint and a disciplined personality is not the same thing as conformity to any particular set of ethical principles. Indeed, the organizational life described by Jackall constitutes exactly the same kind of evolving framework for what Elias called the civilizing process in his analysis of court society. The crucial determinant of the civilizing process is the increasing coordination of human action within an ever-widening network of interaction, and the 'compulsion' driving people to regulate their conduct is a *strategic* one related to the potential advantages of doing, not a *normative* one. Elias emphasized that the changing patterns of requirements imposed on individuals did not act directly on them, but indirectly, mediated by their own reflection on the consequences of differing patterns of behaviour. 'The actual compulsion', suggested Elias, 'is one that the individual exerts on himself or herself either as a result of his knowledge of the possible consequences of his or her moves in the game in intertwining activities, or as a result of corresponding gestures of adults which have helped to pattern his or her own behaviour as a child' (Elias 2000: 372–3). The important question then becomes the *relationship* between such attunement of individual conduct to a wider network within particular individuals' settings on the one hand, and in relation to broader social contexts on the other, the 'bracketing' phenomenon that Jackall spoke of.

Second, Elias in his later work (1996) paid more attention to the question of contradictions within processes of civilization as well as what he called processes of 'decivilization' which may develop simultaneously. He proposed that the example of the Nazi regime showed 'not only that processes of growth and decay can go hand in hand but that the latter can also predominate relative to the former' (Elias 1996: 308), and also suggested that the monopolization of physical force by the state, through the military and the police should be seen as having a Janus-faced character (Elias 1996: 175), because such monopolies of force can then be all the more effectively wielded by powerful groups within any given nation-state. Elias also argued at another point for the *reversibility* of social processes, and suggested that 'shifts in one direction can make room for shifts in the opposite direction', so that 'a dominant process directed at greater integration could go hand in hand with a partial disintegration' (Elias 1986: 235). In a discussion of the idea of social norms itself, he argued that the integrative effect of norms is often emphasized at the expense of their 'dividing and excluding character'. Elias argued instead that social norms should be seen as having an 'inherently double-edged character', since in the very process of binding some people together, they turn those people against others.

Third, the workings of the civilization of conduct are complex, and can produce outcomes which will seem counter-intuitive if we see 'civilization' as homogenous and unitary. As social restraint becomes increasingly 'second nature' to individuals, overt social rules and sanctions become less significant and we can observe a more relaxed and informal attitude to manners and etiquette. Elias referred to a general relaxation of social norms in the period after the First World War, and argued that this should be seen as 'a relaxation which remains within the framework of a particular "civilized" standard of behaviour involving a very high degree of automatic constraint and affect-transformation, conditioned to become a habit' (Elias 2000: 157). Elias saw this as a process of 'informalization' which was part of the civilizing processes. Using the example of sexual behaviour, Elias argued that a less authoritarian system of sexual norms actually increases the demands made on each individual to regulate their own behaviour, or suffer the consequences. In relation to intimate relationships, he said that:

> ... the main burden of shaping life together ... now lies on the shoulders of the individuals concerned. Thus informalization brings with it stronger demands on apparatuses of self-constraint, and, at the same time, frequent experimentation and structural insecurity; one cannot really follow existing models, one has to work out for oneself a dating strategy as well as a strategy for living together through a variety of ongoing experiments.
>
> (Elias 1996: 37)

Elias said the same of the more informal relations between superiors and subordinates in organizational life, which also requires a greater degree of self-restraint in the absence of formal, explicit rules and formulae governing everyday conduct.

As power relations change and the rules of human interaction become less formalized and routinized, and more flexible, we are all compelled to develop a more self-reflexive and sophisticated apparatus of self-regulation to be able to negotiate such an ever-changing and contingent network of social relationships. Cas Wouters sums the overall line of development up as follows:

People have increasingly pressured each other into more reflexive and flexible relationships, and at the same time towards a more reflexive and flexible self-regulation. The status, respect and self-respect of all citizens became *less directly* dependent upon internalized social controls of a fixed kind – on an authoritative conscience and *more directly* dependent upon their reflexive and calculating abilities, and therefore upon a particular pattern of self-control in which the more or less automatic and unthinking acceptance of the dictates of psychic authority or conscience has also decreased.

(Wouters 1999: 423)

What might be seen as an increase in individual 'freedom' is part and parcel of an increased demand for self-compulsion and self-management, but then also a changed structuring of ethical disposition as well. Elias had used the concept of a 'second nature' to capture the ways in which adherence to behavioural standards become an automatic part of one's personality or *habitus*, and Wouters suggests the notion of a 'third nature' to capture the reflexive moral self, in which self-regulation is much less automatic, and more accessible to reflexive, flexible strategic management to suit ever-changing fields of social possibilities and expectations. In a sense this analysis parallels those of Ulrich Beck, Anthony Giddens and Scott Lash (1994) concerning 'reflexive' or 'second' modernity, in which adherence to established norms or ethical principles gives way increasingly to a 'reflexive project of the self' which 'has no morality other than authenticity' (Giddens 1992: 198). The process that Wouters refers to as the emergence of a 'third nature', Ulrich Beck and Elisabeth Beck-Gernsheim frame as a process of individualization, a core aspect of which is that 'more people than ever before are being forced to piece together their own biographies and fit in the components as best they can ... the normal life history is giving way to the do-it-yourself life history' (Beck and Beck-Gernsheim 2002: 88).

Lifting the corporate veil: towards the civilization of management

What this chapter has been working towards is an avoidance of seeing whatever is regarded as problematic about managerial conduct in terms of normative 'failure' or the failure of 'virtue', in favour of an ability to locate the bases of that conduct in contradictions between explicit ethical and implicit structural and cultural expectations, between the normative and the structural, between organizational and extra-organizational subjectivity, and to at least reflect on the changing dynamics of those contradictions in terms of the overall long-term trends in the 'civilization of management'. The aim has been to emphasize the importance of attending *both* to legal and institutional design *and* socially constituted *habitus*, *as well as* to the complex ways they interweave to generate the managerial conduct in evidence today, and a number of conclusions can then be drawn from this account about the future analysis of contemporary management ethics.

First, part of the difficulty in grasping hold, both conceptually and practically, of the conflict between broader ethical principles and actual managerial behaviour is the very inaccessibility of the 'ethical form' of management conduct. The fact that its normative dimensions are assessed primarily with reference to ideal standards of behaviour, rather than in its own terms, makes it a 'dirty secret' which is then even less accessible to coordination with the ethical standards which other parts of society may want to at least argue should play a more prominent role in organizational life. Concepts like 'corruption' thus have a number of drawbacks, constituting the action in question simply as 'immoral', at the expense of grasping the particular ethical dimensions of that action.

Second, related to this, rather than presuming a single, relatively homogeneous set of norms and values, from which the instrumental rationality of organizational, especially corporate, life diverges, it is important to see the ethical dimensions of management behaviour as placed within a complex *field* of differing ethical orientations: management, shareholders/market, employees, civil society, public administration, the state. In addition, in many ways these differing ethical orientations are radically distinct from each other, constituting relatively autonomous, self-referential ethical sub-systems with no necessary consistency between them. This is especially true of the distinction between *the ethics of pragmatism, outcomes and obedience to authority* and the *ethics of values*, in which the latter are 'bracketed' off from the former, and it is this distinction that much of the discussion of management ethics is essentially about.

Third, this in turn has two analytic consequences: it makes it necessary both to grasp how distinct the different ethical orientations in organizations and society can be, but also how they interrelate. When Jackall's former Vice-President says 'What is right in the corporation is not what is right in man's home or in his church' (Jackall 1988: 6), this raises two problems: how to recognize the various ways in which this ethical distinction works, and how to grasp the relation between the two sorts of 'what is right', how the tension between the two plays itself out, how it has changed over time, and what its constituent foundations are.

Finally, however, the 'what is right in the corporation' comment does not in fact capture all we need to know about the relationship between what is right in the home and what is right in the corporation. One of the important implications of accounts of the production of a 'third nature' and the changing dynamics of processes of individualization, is that the strategic, instrumental orientation which appears to characterize much of organizational life may not in fact be that distant from everyday ethical dispositions in social life beyond the organization. It may be that it is the very calculative and flexible self-controls demanded by contemporary social relations which generate a similarly calculative and flexible normative orientation within organizational settings. In other words, it is important to attend to the extent to which managerial behaviour which we might suppose contradicts more general ethical principles – say, 'greed is good', or an explicitly instrumental orientation to the world – is actually *consistent* with the normative *habitus* being generated by contemporary social relations. The question of the management ethics, as well as being one of the civilization of management, is also a testing ground for the character of contemporary civil society itself.

Notes

1 Drucker himself framed the debate in terms of a choice between a casuist (or consequentialist) approach, an 'ethics of prudence' and an 'ethics of interdependence', but of course in reality all three ethical orientations run through all organizational action, depending on the issue, the nature and position of the organization actor in question, and the particular social, economic, political and legal context.
2 For another example of the legal distinction between an individual as such and as 'the corporation', even if they are the same, *see Lee v Lee's Air Farming Ltd* [1961] AC 12, [1960] 3 All ER 420, Privy Council.

Part II

Management ethics in organizations

Chapter 6

Management ethics and public management

Michael Muetzelfeldt

Editors' introduction

In this chapter Michael Muetzelfeldt considers ethics in relation to public management – an area often sidestepped in the private sector focus that dominates much of business ethics. Muetzelfeldt starts from the sociology of organisations and power, and moves from there towards considerations of ethics in discourse and practice. In his view ethics, when considered as a practice, are shaped by and respond to organisational and professional power in contemporary public management and administration. His focus is on the 'new professions' and current understandings of ethics as a knowledge practice.

The newness of the new professions alerts us to the fact that the notion of the professions is not static; the scene is characterized by changes in professionalism, knowledge and corporate ethics accompanying the emergence of post bureaucratic public sector organisational forms. This leads Muetzelfeldt to an elucidation of how, in everyday knowledge, ethics-in-practice relate to organizationally defined ethics. Rather than being monologically authoritative, in this practice, dialogue is not only the aim of ethics but also its source. Such an ethics is not something just read off from codes of practice and applied to decision making scenarios; instead it is a processual aspect of the distinct practices through which decisions are reached. A critical point here is the unlikeliness that ethics documented in codes of practice and ethics-in-practice will normally align. It is also unlikely that they will become more closely aligned in future. The difference between the two spheres of ethics-as-code and ethics-as-practice is the world of everyday work. The possibility of ethics for professionals in public sector management rests in their ability to become skilled practitioners in negotiating these differences.

In this discussion of ethics in public management, I start from the sociology of organizations and power, and move towards considerations of ethics in discourse and practice. I focus on ethics as shaping and responding to organizational and professional power in contemporary public management and administration, and how this works itself out in the everyday practice of people as they interpret and implement public policy through delivering government funded services. The chapter has three sections. It starts from the conventional sociology of ethics and the professions, developing this in the context of the 'new professions' and current understandings of knowledge. This suggests ways in which ethics can be understood as a knowledge practice. The second section considers changes in professionalism, knowledge and corporate ethics that have accompanied the emergence of post bureaucratic public sector organizational forms. The final section explores on-the-ground ethics as everyday knowledge practice, and relates this to corporate ethics.

Ethics and the changing sociology of professions

According to the post-functionalist 1960s sociology of the professions, ethics is a response to the interests of clients, individual professionals, and the profession as a whole, with clients' interests being least salient and the profession's interests being most salient (Johnson 1972; Carlin 1966; Elliott 1972). Professions were characterized by their legitimate monopoly over the use of a body of knowledge, and their ethics supported that legitimacy and their associated market power. Academic inquiry was concerned with the content of professional knowledge – e.g. scientific medicine and clinical medical practice; the institutions through which it was generated and transmitted – e.g. large teaching hospitals, university medical schools, and professional associations; and the sources of the power through which those institutions were developed and supported – primarily the state in its relationship to dominant classes or groups, together with the profession's use of ethics to protect and regulate its members and manage their relationships with clients. This was a realist socio-political account of ethics, standing in contrast to more idealist value based accounts.

Today, several things have changed in this conventional picture. In this chapter I aim to apply to contemporary professions, especially those involved in interpreting and implementing public policy, the socio-political perspective of the conventional realist account. I start by detailing changes to professions, professionalism and knowledge that have occurred over the last 20 or 30 years.

The first change is that there has been a double shift concerning the professional-client relationship and the way knowledge is understood. In some areas – particularly in general health care and in human services, to some extent in finance and accounting, but less so in law and specialist medicine – clients have become more important. They are now more often seen as active partners in the professional-client relationship, rather than as passive recipients of the professional's expert practice. In health and human services, this partly reflects a change in the profession's self-perception, and its increasing prevalent views that, for a combination of social and economic reasons, clients and professionals co-produce health and well being outcomes (e.g. Brechin and Swain 1988; Gallant et al. 2002; Swain and Walker 2003). In financial services, this arguably has to do with constructing as clients people who previously were not engaged with finance advisors (Aldridge 1998).

The emergence of clients as partners also partly reflects their increased access to more or less accurate and useful information through the internet. For example, Ziebland et al. (2004) found that there was widespread use of the internet by British cancer patients in 2001–2 to gain information about their illness, and Brotherton (2004) reports that in 2001, 46 per cent of cancer patients at two Sydney hospitals got information about their illness from the internet. The use of the internet by patients is likely to have increased since then. The president of the Australian Medical Association is recently reported as saying that '[g]one are the days when patients dutifully accepted their doctor's advice without so much as contemplating questioning it. ... today's patients have become more inquisitive, discerning and informed about their health problems, thanks in no small part to the internet' (Kerbaj 2005). This may have its downside through patients bringing misinformation or inappropriately applied information to the doctor–patient engagement, as Kerbaj reports. However, the internet also has the potential for patients to find out about effective new treatments that are less radical or more efficacious than conventional treatments, and seek out practitioners who use them. So patient use of the internet is likely to promote the uptake of effective new treatments by otherwise conservative practitioners.

In parallel to the – perhaps overstated – rise of the client, and closely connected to it, there has been a change in the way knowledge is understood. Both academics and practitioners now recognize that professional knowledge is no longer the exclusive property of the professional, who in their practice applies it to the passive client. Instead, at least part of professional knowledge is co-produced in the relationship between professional and client, and effective knowledge practice draws on the client's as well as the professional's knowledge. This co-produced knowledge has been referred to as 'mode 2' knowledge (Gibbons et al. 1994). Compared to the earlier view of conventional sociology, there are now somewhat changed answers to the questions: What is professional knowledge? How is it generated? Who has it? How do they get it? and How do they use it?

Institutions are still crucially important in providing access to and legitimating professional knowledge, although as well as the institutions of state and class that were central to the analysis of the 1960s and 1970s, we would now recognize the increasing importance of cultural institutions including the media. There are two reasons for this. Most immediately, the media provides current information on health and illness, finance and taxation, legal interpretations, and other areas of what had previously been more or less exclusive professional knowledge. More generally and possibly as importantly, cultural institutions including the media also give attention to stories and ethical interpretations concerning professional action in areas as diverse as: continuing or withdrawing life support, providing financial advice without disclosing commissions, and engaging in 'creative' corporate accounting practices. This media coverage has become an important part of the continuing dialogue that may shape the ethical understandings not only of clients and potential clients, but also of professionals. As professional ethics face major challenges because of changes in prevailing attitudes and values, and because of changing technology, both professionals and their clients watch or engage in these debates as they are conducted through cultural institutions.

The second change to the conventional socio-political view is a result of two new analytical perspectives that let us see things that were not highlighted previously. First, risk management that was latent in knowledge and its practices is now apparent, and is increasingly more or less consciously used in professional decision making. So now ethics can be understood as a way of distributing risk between players, clients and stakeholders so as to minimize risk to the profession and to professionals. However, any use of ethics to re-distribute risk may be contested, given that consumers now have a heightened awareness of risk and its allocation (Flynn 2002: 155). As such, risk management is a resource – although a potentially problematic one – that can be used by professions and professionals in their knowledge practices.

As well, and importantly, we can now not only distinguish between explicit and tacit knowledge, but also distinguish between monological and dialogical knowledge. Dialogical knowledge is emergent through interactive practices. It constitutes identities, categories and values – it embodies the discursive foundations of practice, and so is central to sustaining and reproducing practices and the organizational forms in which they occur (Mezirow 1985, 1991, 2000). It differs from monological knowledge – variously named as technical, instrumental or empiric-analytic knowledge – which is produced through analytical, technical or empirical practices (e.g. Wilber 1997; Gurevitch 2000; Meyer 2003). Instrumental knowledge, which organizes recognized practices within organizations, derives from and is dependent on dialogical knowledge (Mezirow 1985, 1991, 2000; Smart 1999: 252). Instrumental knowledge is located within a more basic but less apparent dialogical knowledge system that substantially frames, contains and organizes it, and gives it sense and substance. For example, historically, nursing followed an understanding of professional knowledge being monological, as being owned and applied by the professional. This was expressed discursively in language such as 'care of' patients. However, contemporary nursing tends to apply a mode 2 understanding of dialogical knowledge. This is expressed discursively in language such as 'care for' or 'care towards' patients, which recognizes the patient as a co-producing participant in developing and carrying out the program of care. Dialogical knowledge is an analytical category that shares ground with its substantive counterpart tacit knowledge, which 'entails information that is difficult to express, formalize, or share' (Lubit 2001: 165). However, tacit knowledge does not necessarily have the constitutive potential of dialogical knowledge.

The third and final change to the conventional socio-political picture has to do with the rise of the so-called new professions. The conventional analysis was based on the established old professions, such as medicine, law and accountancy. These were characterized by self-employed individual professionals who practiced within state sponsored institutions such as hospitals, courts and legislated domains of autonomy, protection and legitimacy. Members of the new professions, such as social workers, teachers and engineers, typically work as employees within large organizations. Indeed, increasingly, members of the old professions now also do so. Nearly all the staff of large organizations now work within an organizationally given overlay of values, ethics or codes of conduct, and are to a greater or lesser extent knowledge workers using knowledge that substantially comes from outside the organization. This brings them within the ambit of being members of the new professions.

The focus of this chapter is on professionals working in public sector or publicly funded organizations. In studying these professionals, the realist socio-political approach to the sociology of the professions leads to questions such as: What interests are furthered and legitimated through the ethics of organizationally based professions, and what power structures are they based on? To address these questions, I discuss the changed organizational paradigm of the public and publicly funded sector, which is generally called new public management or managerialism.

New public management and the ethics of monological knowledge

The new public management paradigm has been conceptualized, developed and implemented through post-bureaucratic organizational forms, reflected in managerialism, internal service agency agreements within government departments, and outsourcing. The contractual model of the 1990s was built on the foundations of the managerialist style of the 1980s. It had as a key feature the reduction of the public sector by privatizing or contracting out its functions (Alford and O'Neill 1994), and more recently by negotiated partnership arrangements with service providers (Linossier 2000). The state has reduced its direct service delivery in many sectors and devolved many functions to private corporations or to non-government, third sector community service organizations. This has had some rather perverse effects. Rather than loosening government control, it has tightened management and accountability arrangements between government and service provider organizations, with a strong emphasis on business principles of quantitative measurement and output-based funding. Rather than facilitating coordination at the local geographical level, it has fragmented the organization of service delivery and inhibited knowledge sharing and organizational learning. And in narrowing the links between service delivery and government policy development, it has exposed government to the risks of losing contact with its electoral constituency's political mood and perceived needs.

This has had complex effects on professionals in the government funded sector. On one hand, it has reduced the skill and discretion of these professionals (Grugulis *et al.* 2002). On the other hand, government has become increasingly dependent on the formal and informal inter-organizational links, communication and learning that can be provided by networks of professionals that include and cross between government departments and contracted service providers in the private sector and NGO sector (Muetzelfeldt 2003).

Corporate ethics as an organizational resource became an important issue in the public and publicly funded sectors during the rise of new public management and post-bureaucratic organizational forms. This is no accident. Ideal type bureaucracy was rule governed and process driven. Staff were assessed on their competencies, were career motivated, and gained knowledge, competencies and appropriate values more through on-the-job training and experience rather than through professional academic education. They worked within and expressed a culture based on: organizational commitment, appropriate values and behaviours, rule governed rationality applied to well structured explicit instrumental knowledge, relatively secure expectations about careers, etc. This culture appeared to be well internalized – or at least was carried as substantially tacit or latent knowledge. Before the rise of new public management, there was little or no talk of ethics, although much of the organizational culture could in contemporary terms be described as expressing an ethical system.

Under new public management, organizational forms typically are cus-tomer service and performance based, and output driven. Staff are assessed on their results, and are expected to be risk managing and entrepreneurial in achieving them. To do this, they mobilize and deploy a range of knowledge and skills that in substantial part they bring to the organization rather than acquire from it. Careers are more fluid and problematic, and less secured by and within the organization. There is reduced organizational loyalty, but there is increased connection to, interest in, and perhaps loyalty towards, networks of like-minded and knowledge sharing colleagues within and beyond the organization, who are potentially important career resources.

This outward-looking orientation of staff, who increasingly associate with interests, knowledge resources and networks beyond their employing organization, means that they too can be considered to be members of the new professions.

In government and the public sector, management interest in formal codes of corporate ethics and codes of conduct strengthened during the 1990s. Some Australian examples are given in Table 1, which also shows the OECD's relatively late contribution to this literature. The Royal Institute of Public Administration Australia, which is a professional association of public sector managers, showed an early concern for ethics and in their *Ethics Education and Training Guide* recognized the complexity of making appropriate ethical decisions. However, governments quickly shifted the focus from ethics to codes of conduct – even when, as in Western Australia, it was called a 'code of ethics' even though it formed the basis for disciplining staff. This rise in codes of conduct paralleled the rise of a strong managerial discourse, and the associated weaker but still significant practice of reducing bureaucratic rule-governed behaviour and encouraging risk managing entrepreneurialism.

I consider that the rise of corporate ethics was a way of re-implementing rules and controls over staff within a discursive context that overtly devalued rule based control. As Mulgan observes in his discussion of corporate ethics in The Australian Commonwealth Public Service Act of 1999:

> The broad thrust of the Values [in the Act] builds on a consensus about public sector ethics that evolved within the senior public service over the previous decade … The articulation of values was seen as a substitute for cumbersome rule-bound employment procedures and part of a strategy to reduce the level of controls and regulations generally.
>
> (Mulgan 2005:3)

Table I Examples of documented public sector codes of ethics, conduct and values

1994	Royal Institute of Public Administration Australia – *Ethics Education and Training Guide*
1995	Commonwealth of Australia Public Service Commission – *Guidelines on Official Conduct*
1996	Commonwealth of Australia Management Advisory Board/Management Improvement Advisory Committee – *Ethical Standards and Values in APS*
1996	Western Australian Public Sector Management Act, Commissioner for Public Standards, included Code of Ethics as grounds for discipline
1998	OECD – *Recommendations on Improving Ethical Conduct in the Public Sector*
1998	New South Wales *Code of Conduct and Ethics for PS Executives*
1999	Australian Public Sector Values and Code of Conduct included in *Public Sector Act*
2000	Commonwealth of Australia Public Service and Merit Protection Commission – *Values in the Australian Public Service*

Staff in government departments and in contracted service agencies were told to find new ways of doing things, to show initiative, manage risks, and work smarter not harder. But this could lead them to doing things that might cause political embarrassment to the government or their organization. For example, some departments that deliver social services have devolved responsibility for managing limited resources to their regional offices, and told those offices to establish service priorities based on their local prioritization of needs within their region. This means that services may be denied to one family, yet provided to another family in apparently identical circumstances, because the two families are in different regions that have established different priorities. From the viewpoint of organizational administration, this may be good risk management and resource prioritization. However, it is hazardous politics, because it may lead to media reports and anecdotal stories about the denial of service to some families who are as apparently deserving as others who received it, leading to electoral judgements of inconsistent, arbitrary and uncaring government. Here there are multiple risks, reflecting diverse stakeholders and interests, and articulated through various administrative and political discourses. In such situations, risk management is inherently problematic, and corporate values may become retrospective criteria for judgements as much as pro-active guides to action.

Government departments, and the agencies through which they deliverer services, face very high public exceptions and political vulnerabilities. The same does not apply to private sector organizations to nearly the same extent, yet during the years of aggressive public sector reform the public sector was being urged to adopt private sector practices. The response was to introduce corporate ethics and codes of conduct as ways of containing, constraining and channelling the innovative entrepreneurialism within public sector organizations that was being encouraged by the reforms.

Before new public management, government bureaucracies had an organizational culture that arose through and was in many ways resonant with the bureaucratic organizational form. So staff tended to carry this culture as internalized knowledge, including knowledge of the ethical and value framework that was expected and that was rewarded through the career and status structure. They were likely to enact it in their everyday interactive organizational practices, and so transmit and reproduce it through those practices.

By contrast, under new public management most organizations have an explicit corporate ethics expressed as corporate values and codes of conduct. These corporate ethics are produced and imposed, or at least strongly led, by senior management. They may not resonate with the lived work experience of staff, which comes from as organizational form that conveys expectations of individualized career risk and a focus on results, and that involves personal professional engagements and career building networks that extend beyond the organization. These corporate ethics are communicated through explicit rhetoric that is not consistently sustained by everyday organizational practices. This invites the questions: How well are these management based ethics internalized? and Are they understood by staff to be sham or genuine? A recent Australian case suggests that many see them as fraudulent. Don Watson, historian and speechwriter to former Prime Minister Keating, recently published two scathing rhetorical critiques of managerial corporate discourse (Watson 2003, 2004). These books were warmly welcomed and widely acclaimed, notably by participants in radio talkback programs on the government owned Australian Broadcasting Corporation (ABC) networks – a demographic that includes many educated and professional people with public sector experience or contacts. Regardless of how sound Watson's critiques are, their public success is evidence that he has touched an exposed nerve of resentment and scepticism. This suggests that the prevailing political and corporate rhetorics of ethics and values have certainly failed to convince, and probably are seen as inauthentic cant that invites widespread scorn.

In short, knowledge of and about corporate ethics as promulgated in public sector and related organizations is strongly led or imposed by organizational leaders to serve organizational purposes. For many staff, it is not well integrated into their lived organizational practices, and they have had little contribution to producing and reproducing it. That is, it is monological knowledge: it is not embedded in dialogues and practices between leaders and staff, or among staff, or between staff and their clients. And it does not cultivate or enhance the synergies between knowledge and practice that is characteristic of professionalism.

The ethics of dialogical knowledge

Despite this, within managerial public sector organizations there is extensive dialogical knowledge that informs everyday organizational practice. So, within these organizations there may be veins of ethical values and practice that stand apart from the corporate ethics, and that are produced and reproduced through dialogical knowledge and associated practices. In this final section, I explore this possibility, focusing on human service agencies within or funded by the government sector.

Contemporary professionals are involved in ethical work as an integral aspect of their knowledgeable professional practice, that is, as an integral aspect of their knowledge practice. Knowledge practice is more than knowledge in use, which is how McElroy uses it, although without definition. (McElroy 2002a, 2002b). I follow a constructivist use of the term, which invokes an appreciation that:

subjectivity and objectivity are interlocked in a reciprocal social relationship (Schultze, 2000). Social reality in which knowledgeable practices are sought and found is understood in terms of an ongoing dialectical process with individuals simultaneously externalising their being into the social world, and internalising the social world as objective reality (Berger and Luckman, 1966). In Weick's (1995) terms, individuals make sense of their world by interacting within it.

(Cushman et al. 2002: 2)

This understanding of knowledge practices fits well with a recognition of the importance of dialogical professional knowledge, because from this perspective dialogical knowledge and knowledge practices are mutually constitutive of one another. Närhi (2004: 12) has noted this for social work professionalism.

Social workers and related professionals are engaged in multiple dialogical knowledge practices. As well as structured meetings and everyday interaction with colleagues, and scheduled and ad hoc contact with clients, they have regular personal supervision sessions with their supervisors. For these professionals, supervision generally goes well beyond task oriented consultation, advice and decision making. It is likely to include important inter-personal engagement and dialogical knowledge production through learning that is based on discussing specific cases and general ethical and professional principles, and that is closely linked to emotional de-briefing and support (Jones 2003). Not only supervision, but all these knowledge practices include engagements that lie beyond the instrumental accountability of managerialism. These engagements occur across a range of levels of formality/informality, of impersonal and personal interaction, and of practical and emotional focus.

These knowledge practices generally involve several discursive frames. I illustrate this with an example of one type of knowledge practice – fortnightly allocation meetings where social workers and allied professionals make decisions about which services are most appropriate and available for specific client families. In these meetings, managers or senior workers from several branches or agencies discuss new cases that have been documented and provisionally assessed through the intake process, and make decisions about the services to be offered to each client family. I have observed four discursive frames providing reference points for the dialogue in such meetings. Generally, three of these frames are consensually shared, and one is contested or negotiated. The consensual frames referred to shared human service values, legal constraints, and organizational/resource constraints. The problematic frame concerned divergent values or priorities.

Values that are widely shared in the human service professions, and in their wider knowledge context including the mass media, are embedded in and carried through the everyday discourse of practitioners as they engage in their knowledge practices. For example, the notion of clients' 'challenging behaviour' has replaced previous notions of disruptive, disabled or bad behaviour. The notion of challenging behaviour invokes and calls for staff responses that are self aware, and that are respectful of the person showing the behaviour and of others who may be involved. And it sets the context within which staff will be held accountable for their decisions and conduct. This accountability is not only to their supervisors and to their employing organization, but also to the client and their immediate family and carers, and to the wider society. In the meetings I have observed, the language expressing these values is consistently and effortlessly used, and within formal meetings the values themselves and their accompanying implied accountabilities are unquestioned, and frame the way discussion and decision making proceeds.

These meetings also operate with group understanding of legal constraints or ramifications, and of organizational or resource constraints. The legal issues particularly relate to two matters: how much information can be shared with others at the meeting while respecting the level of informed consent that the client has given; and whether or not providing detailed information might legally oblige others at the meeting to give formal notification to the relevant government department of a child being at risk. These legal issues are consciously dealt with by withholding the client's name, and by detailing the nature of the client's informed consent as part of the case description. Practical resource and organizational constraints typically involve whether the most appropriate service is available quickly, what suitable substitute service could be provided, and which budget or organizational unit will resource the service.

Workers who have direct experience of the client may or may not be present at such meetings, and this can affect the level of detail that is provided and the emotional tenor of the discussion. In my observation, such meetings are conducted quite formally, with scrupulous attention to shared values and the language that signifies them, to legal constraints, and to organizational and inter-organizational practicalities.

However, there are some areas where there is not necessarily a consensus about the priorities of competing values. For example, one case involved discussion of a family with an emotionally disturbed and angry father, a distressed mother, and young children. The family worker had provisionally assessed the children and mother as being at moderate risk of angry abuse from the father. The meeting reviewed the case and quickly confirmed this assessment. There was then discussion of the legal options available to the mother to protect herself and the children from the father, including excluding him from the family home. This line of discussion was developed with some detail and enthusiasm by some of those at the meeting, with others mostly silent. Finally, there was some discussion, only tentatively initiated and not fully developed, of the father's possibly high risk of self-harm, particularly if he was excluded from the family home. During this, it was noted that the mother was strongly attached to the father, and continued to try to help him deal with his problems. Discussion ensued about what advice and assistance the family worker should give the mother, and which specialist services – social work, legal, financial, psychiatric, etc. – should be offered.

The formal function of this meeting was to deal with risks to children, and risks to families' capacities as the primary structure for supporting and nurturing children. The dialogue over this case maintained that general purpose, but within this dialogue there was a contested view of the family – Did it include the father, or not? Were risks to the father and his capacity to contribute to the family part of the risks facing the children, or was the father to be seen primarily as a source of risk to the children, effectively external to the family unit? This contested view of the family reflected contested values around issues of potential domestic violence and men as its perpetrators, the role of fathers in family life, and the meeting's possible responsibility or ability to propose actions that would assist the father even though that was outside its formal function.

Through this dialogue the meeting did make consensual decisions about what to do in this particular case. However, only time and subsequent cases will tell whether the underlying contested issues were in part resolved through this discussion. The meeting engaged in a knowledge practice in which dialogical knowledge was mobilized, and possibly developed. But, as is its way, the dialogical knowledge remained provisional and contextual, and was emergent through the dialogical practice rather than being able to be 'read off' from some monological reference point.

Using dialogical knowledge, risk assessment and risk management are embedded in knowledge practices that call for difficult judgements that are negotiated through dialogue. They depend on narratives of accountability that acknowledge that decisions will be problematic and will depend on adjudicating between competing values all of which have contested relevance, validity and weight in the specific circumstances. At this level, risk assessment and risk management are deeply ethical practices that are based in the use of dialogical knowledge.

Ethics as a dialogical knowledge practice cannot be reduced to instrumental procedures and formalized codes of conduct, which are based on monological knowledge. In social work's contemporary context of managerialism and contractualism, Jones (2003) advocates a reflexive professionalism that incorporates ethics based in knowledge that is produced through critical reflection in professionals' dialogues with clients as well as with colleagues. The dialogical risk assessment described above is a partial example of such reflexive professionalism. It stands in contrast to the monological risk assessment of, for example, the advice to professionals that 'Patient suicide is the most frequently identifiable cause of loss in claims and lawsuits against behavioural healthcare providers. ... Proper documentation helps to avoid costly litigation' (Cash 2005: 21).

Concluding observations

In his consideration of the monologic and dialogic, Gurevitch (2000) uses Bakhtin's discussion of dialogical plurality to caution against an overstated dialogic ethics, based on views that dialogic engagements lead to unity through Habermasian rational communicative action, or through the Schutzian construction of intersubjectivity. He draws attention to the tacit agreements that maintain the social action that participants call dialogue, despite the tensions, breaks, silences and 'the struggle for a voice' (Gurevitch 2000: 249) that are part of the dark side of the dialogic. And he advises against exaggerating the split between the monologic and the dialogic.

In the knowledge practice described above in the example of the allocation meeting, contests over some values were hesitantly aired and never explicitly resolved, yet the meeting did make decisions about how to proceed with the case it was discussing. That knowledge practice drew on monological knowledge and corporate ethics – for example, concerning legal constraints – as well as dialogical knowledge and associated ethicality. Some of this dialogical knowledge was shared – for example, concerning shared commitments towards child centred outcomes, and towards maintaining partnership between the individuals and organizational units represented at the meeting; and some was contested – for example, concerning men as fathers as potential perpetrators of domestic violence. All of this provided the basis for the ethicality of the meeting's decisions about this case. In this knowledge practice, we can see 'dialogue as the source and aim of ethics – the way we speak, the way we listen, our experience of conversation' (Gurevitch 2000: 245). Such ethics is not just read off from decisions, but is a processual aspect of the practice through which decisions are reached.

In this instance, as in many others, both monological and dialogical knowledge, and their associated ethics, are together involved in knowledge practices. The distinction between them remains, despite them being intertwined in practices. This distinction comes from the different institutional loci through which they are produced and reproduced. A map of the institutions relevant to corporate ethics may look similar to the maps relevant to the knowledge and meaning systems of the traditional professions and of the corporation. However, the map relating to the dialogical knowledge that supports everyday ethical practice will be more extensive, and give much importance to cultural institutions including the media, and to the penetration of popular dialogical knowledge into the institutions of professional education.

Because of these different circuits of re/production, it is unlikely that corporate ethics and practice ethics will normally be aligned, or will become more closely aligned in future. The different expectations coming from corporate ethics and practice ethics, which staff may experience as conflicts in their everyday work, is more than just an inconsistency based on unresolved issues. These differences are sustained through differences between the institutional processes of re/production. They remain an ongoing feature of dialogical knowledge practices, and in many ways are central aspects of these practices.

In this situation, staff may be more than passive recipients of these contradictory pressures. Staff are – or at least have the potential to be – mediators that enable corporate public sector organizations to manage risk and contradictory expectations, and to carry on. As such, staff have the possibility of taking a professionally advantageous position, and enhancing the standing of the various professions within the organization and of their shared general professionalism, through the ethicality of their knowledge practices.

Chapter 7

Management ethics, accountability and responsibility

Stephen Cohen

Editors' introduction

Central to any discussion of the practice of ethics in management is a consideration of the individual in the moment of choice. Nevertheless, few solitary individuals are able to choose what they will do in the modern world in a way that is institutionally unencumbered. Instead, we are far more likely to find actors making choices in the context of complex organizations: ethics thus exists simultaneously at the organizational and structural level and at the level of individuals within an organization. Yet, within such a context, it is still the case that at the heart of any ethical choice are the matters of judgement and responsibility. While in recent times management scholars have been concerned to focus on high performance organizations, or excellent organizations, usually defined in terms of economic benefits, in this chapter Cohen focuses on ethical excellence in terms of the question: What are the characteristics of good judgement, responsibility, and high performance in an ethical choice context in organizations?

Cohen is quite clear in asserting that these characteristics cannot be achieved simply by a substitution of organizational action for individual action, as for instance where organizations seek to make the exercise of individual choice impossible – the project of a great deal of management theory ever since its inception in scientific management. What organizations can attempt to achieve, however, is avoidance of incompetence in dealing with ethical issues in the first place, through avoidance of 'moral negligence', 'moral recklessness', 'moral blindness', and, more positively, the cultivation and exhibition of 'moral competence', terms that Cohen defines and develops in the chapter.

The contribution of much of the chapter, however, is on what constitutes 'accountability' and 'responsibility' as they relate to ethics and managerial practice. The terms are explored from several directions, including notions that have become institutionalized within the higher education system of

Australia. As Cohen demonstrates, in what reads as a heartfelt plea, the degree of sophistication around much of this discussion is quite low compared to some of the well-honed tools that are available. In creating and limiting systems of ethical responsibility, the central point, Cohen argues, is to distinguish accountability systems from responsibility systems, and to call research attention to some of the serious limitations and misconceptions of the former and the necessity of attending to the latter. All of this is empirically illustrated with the failures of university systems to get hardly any of these matters right.

In this chapter, I will be directing some comments in relation to ethics at the organizational and structural level and some at the level of individuals within an organization. The centerpiece in all aspects of the discussion is the importance of judgement: cultivating good judgement, encouraging and authorizing the exercise of judgement, and calling attention to dangers associated with failure to do this. The focus is not on minimum ethical requirements, considering concerns such as corruption, fraud, developing appropriate constraints, and, importantly, developing accountability systems. Rather, the focus is on ethical excellence: thinking about the exercise of good judgement, responsibility, and high performance. The concern is with the 'high-end' of ethics rather than with the establishment of minimum ethical requirements.

Regulating for ethics

A first reaction to an ethical failure or breach or shortcoming is often, 'we need more regulations'. It need not be literally with trains running off the rails, as it was for State Rail – the government run train service in the Australian state of New South Wales – where the causes of whatever ill effects had been occurring were seen as largely ethics. The case I am referring to occurred when train drivers' lack of judgement and attempts to shortcut some procedures resulted in more than one terrible accident. The response from the organization was to try to install new mechanical devices and tougher rules and regulations on drivers' behaviour. In short, the organization's approach was to try to make the 'dead man brake' foolproof. Its approach was to do that, rather than to institute whatever training and selection processes might be desirable to ensure that fools do not drive the trains in the first place. This, of course, is an overstatement; and perhaps it is a glib characterization of a very serious and dangerous situation, with its attendant history. The point is that rules and regulations cannot do the job of replacing judgement – they cannot remedy all behavioural difficulties. Focusing on such things fits with a view that if we can just get the procedures, the rules, the equipment, and the hardwiring right, and then get people complying with these requirements, then we will not have these difficulties any longer.

The attraction of such a view is clear. It implies that a reasonably quick and certain remedy can be produced to handle a recognisable difficulty. It also fits nicely into any accountability or compliance regime. Later I will talk more about this particular problem. First, however, I am concerned with the issue of how, in many types of situations which are ripe for ethical failure or shortcomings, such mechanical fixes simply do not work. And, more problematically than that, they sometimes make matters worse. I am certainly not the first to point out that general rules cannot handle all cases. This is what Aristotle had in mind with the notion of 'equity' (see Aristotle, *Nicomachean Ethics*, Book V, Chapter 10). It amounts to the necessity of judgement making a correction to a rule – not because there must be something wrong with the rule, but because of the generality of a rule, which will necessarily make it inappropriate to some cases which it would seem to govern. Trying to accommodate, or replace, equitable judgement with additional rules simply will not work. Rules and regulations are certainly important, but they are not everything; and sometimes they are not the correct remedy for an ethical difficulty.

Consider this brief, somewhat potted, story concerning the role of auditors in the catastrophic corporate collapses of Enron in the US and HIH in Australia. The auditors in these failures were either complicit or unbelievably negligent or inexcusably morally blind in their behaviour. One result of the collapses was a spotlight being shone on auditors. Regulatory bodies and lawmakers basically told the auditing profession, 'clean up your act, or else'. That is, do something so that the types of ethical breaches which occurred here do not happen again. So, 'either you people do something to up your game ethically, so that shareholders and the public are not misinformed like this in the future, or else outside regulators are going to come in and take this self-regulation, with its attendant responsibility, away from you'. In response to the situation, accounting bodies – e.g. the Institute of Chartered Accountants in Australia, and also CPA Australia (Certified Practising Accountants), as well as their counterparts in the US and in the UK – addressed the specific questions of how to improve auditor independence, accuracy, and transparent and understandable information to shareholders and the public at large. There were important suggestions about things like peer review, improvement of judgement, and clear purpose of auditing. In short, the professional bodies began seriously to consider this ethical dimension and ramifications of the problem. They understood that the problem was, at root, an ethical one, and that it had to do with appropriate judgement on the part of the auditors.[1]

Before the dust had settled new regulations were introduced through the Financial Services Reform Act in Australia and the Sarbanes-Oxley Act in the

US. In the climate in which these new pieces of legislation were introduced, the auditing profession knew basically what the problem was and what they were supposed to be looking at to improve the situation. That is, they were to be focusing on rectifying ethical breaches, ethical shortcomings, and bad ethical judgement, which had contributed – and could contribute in the future – to seriously misleading the public. This was the requirement of the threat: 'clean up your act, or else'. However, with the introduction of the new legislation, the focus was removed from matters of judgement and making things better, and placed squarely on the prescriptive requirement of the legislation itself. So, the question for accountants, 'How can we remedy the ethical problems?', was replaced by the question 'What does it take to satisfy the specific prescriptions of the new legislation?', or worse, 'How can we get around the new requirements?'. In this respect, the initial concern has, to a great degree, become lost in the legislation.[2] The legislation is, of course, trying to remedy the problem. However, given that the problem has much to do with the exercise of good judgement, by not focusing on that important aspect of the difficulty, the solution, at best, works on only part of the problem, neglecting the rest, but represents that it is a solution to the entire difficulty. It inhibits further development toward remedying what was accurately perceived to be the serious difficulty in the first place: ethical breaches, and the bad exercise of ethical judgement. It has replaced this with putting the focus squarely on satisfying specific prescriptions. In this respect, more regulation can simply function as a distractor, rather than calling attention to the appropriate places to focus attention. It is, of course, easier to create specific prescriptions than it is to work on improvement of judgement.

Four areas of moral judgement

Systematic, organizational attention can, in fact, be directed at improving moral judgement. It can be focused on each of, roughly, four requisite areas involved in reaching justifiable ethical decisions, each of which is discussed below.

1 *Avoidance of 'moral negligence'*. Moral negligence amounts to a failure to consider something that one should consider. Maybe this is because of lack of awareness.
2 *Avoidance of 'moral recklessness'*. This amounts to a failure to give adequate consideration to something; dealing with it in too hasty a fashion, not paying enough attention, or not particularly caring to get it right.

   As a step toward addressing these dangers, a number of organizations have used or developed their own 'ethical decision-making models' (see Cohen 2004).[3] An ethical decision-making model is a set of systematically organized trigger questions, 'Have you thought about this …? Have you thought about that …? Have you considered these values …?'. These instruments are for the purpose of assisting the reasoner in navigating through something that the reasoner has perceived to be an ethical issue.

Most ethical decision-making models take account of the different perspectives that anyone in an organization must be aware of in dealing with ethical issues. In particular, they typically recognize that the ethical requirements of the particular organization – and the ethical requirements of being in an organization *per se* – might not be identical with people's own individual ethical outlooks. There are, in fact, nearly certain to be conflicts in this realm. In any such case, the reasoner should certainly be aware of the conflicts that are present; and the reasoner must make up their mind accordingly. Sometimes it will be appreciated that the requirements from within the organization should take precedence over one's own individual view; and sometimes it will be the other way around. In any case, among the points to which attention should be called by an ethical decision-making model will be the possibility of this tension. And, the ethical decision-making model should make it clear that whatever decision the reasoner ultimately reaches, it will be the reasoner as an individual who reaches that decision. Perhaps the decision will be to defer to the ethical perspective of the organization; perhaps it will be to buck the organization's perspective in favour of the perspective of the individual. Whatever ethical conclusion is reached, it is important to appreciate that it is the reasoner as an individual who must make it, and that it is the reasoner as an individual who must bear the responsibility for it.

3 *Avoidance of 'moral blindness'.* This amounts to a failure to see that there is an issue at all. As a remedy for this failure, ethical decision-making models do not go very far – for two reasons: (a) A person will only ever think of using an ethical decision-making model if they perceive there to be an ethical issue to reason about. If one is blind to the possibility of an ethical dimension to a problem, then one would not consult an ethical decision-making model at all, and so would get no benefit from it. (b) A person might stare at an ethical consideration all day long, and simply not get it. They are not negligent or reckless, in that they did, in fact, focus on the relevant consideration – it did not escape their attention – but when they did think about it, they were absolutely blind in their comprehension.

Here is an example of something quite like moral blindness. In the Clemenger BBDO television advertisement for Hahn Premium Light beer aired in 2005, titled 'Sex Bomb', a woman sets the relaxed, romantic mood, and begins to luxuriate in a serene bubble bath. A short while after she has begun, her male partner enters and does a 'bomb' into the bath, thus destroying the mood. She is clearly annoyed by what has happened. As he then pops the top on his Hahn Premium Light, he notices her expression, and, with a bewildered look on his face, says, 'Whaaaat?'. He simply has no idea as to how what he has just done could have been other than enjoyed. He just did not see it. We could even imagine that he considered the mood, his partner's enjoyment, and 'decided' that this would be a good thing to do. He was simply blind to the situation. It is not difficult to imagine someone who behaves this way in the face of – and with some sort of recognition of – might acknowledge a serious moral dimension to a situation. So, 'Did you think about this?, ... this?, ...this? ...'. The answer is 'yes', 'yes', and 'yes'; but they did not really see those things in any serious way.

4 *Cultivation and exhibition of moral competence.* This is difficult. Partly, this is the cure for moral blindness. Partly, it is not a cure for anything. It is the requirement for engaging in moral recognition, reasoning, and decision-making well. It involves developing adequate preparation, sensitivity, awareness, knowledge and conceptual apparatus to deal with ethical issues. It is precisely in this area where exercise of judgement is concerned. This is dealing in areas where situations are not black and white, and where judgements are better or worse not because they are correct or incorrect, but because their justifications paint more attractive pictures or tell more attractive stories. They are better or worse because they are more convincing, and reveal a more understanding and sympathetic appreciation for the situations that they are judging; not because they are truer or more correct. These are the characteristics that are integral to moral competence. Encouraging, cultivating, and maintaining them throughout an organization are at the core of the creation and maintenance of an organizational culture that promotes and supports ethical excellence.

Accountability and its limits

I want to spend some time examining the separate notions of accountability and responsibility, particularly with respect to their roles in an environment which nurtures ethical judgement, promotion of ethical culture, and development and maintenance of ethical excellence. I will try to indicate that focusing on creation and maintenance of accountability systems can be like focusing on rules and procedures, rather than on judgement. And in this respect, accountability systems might, in fact, be counterproductive if the goal is ethical excellence. But this is getting to the conclusion. Let me explain.

Accountability is a very important notion these days. Serious concerns about accountability have developed in areas where, not all that long ago, 'accountability' did not receive even a mention. People in various roles –

employees, employers, directors, managers, CEOs, professionals, academics etc. – are held accountable. It used to be that, for better or worse, we simply trusted people – particularly in directorial or managerial positions – to get the job done. This was managerialism at its height. There were serious problems. Accountability systems – and, in general, a focus on accountability – signal a diminution of an environment of trust. Again, this is for better or worse. Accountability systems are important. Accountability systems focus on various elements of job requirements. They identify these and keep track of performance in the various areas. Partly, such systems are historical, in that they keep track of who did what when. People have to sign off. This can make for clearer lines about where the buck stops, and who will be liable for what.

Accountability requirements not only keep account of who does what. They also define what activities, decisions, etc. are to be kept track of. They have to do this. We are not accountable for *everything*. Accountability systems not only keep account; they also declare what is to be accounted for, and what counts. They define those activities, decisions, and so forth, for which people are to be held accountable, and they themselves set standards: 'You are expected to do this, this, this, and this; and you are to sign off after having done them'. In this respect, accountability systems declare baselines such as:

> In the name of X (say, 'satisfaction of your job requirements', or 'excellence in performing your function in the organization'), it is these things which count. We are going to count them, and hold you accountable accordingly.

Later, I will have more to say about declared baselines, and the need for a scepticism about the status of what they actually declare.

To hold people – or institutions – accountable for particular things, those things must be declared, the methods of counting must be specified, and a timetable must be introduced. 'Inputs', 'outcomes', 'milestones', 'key performance indicators', 'productivity', 'quality check', 'schedule', 'timetable': these are some of the notions that apply. Timeframes become important. For example, the people in the materials procurement section are accountable for ordering in, paying, and sending out to the appropriate departments the materials that those departments need. These people can keep records, and can show the incomings and outgoings over a specified period. We can see not merely that there was no fraud, but also that there is efficiency in the operation, in terms of what and how much they are ordering and what and how much is being distributed to the organization's departments. We might also have in place an accounting requirement for how the people are spending their time. The idea is the same: we need to see evidence of inputs and outcomes, and perhaps procedures followed, over a specified period of time. Accountability systems go a fair way toward discovering and helping to weed out freeloaders, or free riders. If someone is not doing the job or is doing it inefficiently, accountability requirements can help to discover this. The periods of time involved are usually relatively short term. Sometimes, they *have* to be short term, because our interest is in the short term. Other times, they are short term, because we need to have some evidence in the short term, even if our interest is in the longer term.

An argument has been mooted to extend somewhat further than this. As mentioned, accountability systems can function well to weed out freeloaders. Under a strong accountability regime within an organization, there will undoubtedly be many fewer freeloaders than where there is no such regime. Accountability regimes make it difficult, if not impossible, to hide; they also make it more difficult to pass the buck. The accountability system will discover that the particular individuals are not doing their share. This itself can be an important consideration for any practice (see for example Condren 1998). What accountability systems do not do very well, however, is to encourage and promote excellence. Accountability systems do not sit very well with the creation and nurturing of good judgement. They keep track of and report what people are doing – those declared items which have been specified and are now countable, the identified items which are produced, or the identified procedures which are followed. They establish and keep track of the norm. They fail to look at, let alone pay recognition to, anything else. And it is precisely in the 'anything else' basket that 'excellence' will belong. If we have become so preoccupied with prescribing, recording, and counting the ordinary, then there becomes little opportunity for even tolerating, let alone promoting, the extraordinary. By its nature, an accountability system defines and then records the ordinary. Now – and here is where the argument extends – in defining the norm, defining what is to be regarded and what is not, the declaration, in specifying some activities as accountable, actually *prescribes* those activities and, in effect, *proscribes* others – or, at the least, offers no encouragement or incentive to engage in those others:

> Your brief is to make widgets. You are to produce however many of them you can; and this will be recognised. This recognition will play a part in whatever promotions, benefits, and remuneration you are to receive in the organization.

Under this regime, when you are giving an account of your achievements, as well as your job description, within the organization, this must all be referable to your widget-production. The prescription to make widgets offers incentive to make them. It also offers disincentive to make anything else. If the business is simply the manufacture of widgets, and the accountability regime is aimed only at those whose jobs are hands-on on the assembly line, then this is probably not a bad effect. However, let us suppose that the business is not so clearly defined, or that you are focusing on those whose job descriptions are not as easily specifiable, or have a more obviously qualitative aspect to them. Let's say, for instance, your business is a university.[4] There are a number of activities that employees of this institution engage in; and there are, of course, a number of activities for which they are accountable. Let's focus on only one, the research activity of academic staff as it is governed in Australian universities.

Accountability in higher education: an example

In Australia, universities receive part of their funding based on the research that they do: simply, the more research, the more money. Research is defined in terms of guidelines set down by the Department of Education, Science and Training (DEST) – a federal government department.[5] A significant portion of funding to universities is now based on research, as defined by DEST. Of this portion, 80 per cent is based on 'research income' – i.e. grants received – 10 per cent on 'publications' – as defined in various categories by DEST – and 10 per cent on 'research completion' – research students completing their degrees. Further, it has recently been suggested that not only will DEST nominate the accepted publishers – i.e. the ones which can figure in the counting for published research – but also that DEST will nominate the accepted periodicals, i.e. which professional journals count – and so, which do not count – for the purpose of ascertaining the amount of published research. DEST also defines quite specifically what 'kind' of books count as research publications at all. The stimulus for this is clear – and it is laudable. Academics should not be immune from a requirement for being accountable for what they do. And, if they – universities, faculties, schools, departments, and individuals – are engaged in research, then they should be able to demonstrate that they are, in fact, participating in this area. If this can be quantified, so much the easier.

Consider this, however: recently it has been pointed out by some people in the scientific community that the focus on accountability is a serious obstacle to 'curiosity research', or 'blue sky research'. This type of research might or might not produce results, and it might take a very long time. 'Schedule', 'milestones', 'timetable' can have little applicability. Wonderful breakthroughs, elements of genius, and much pure research does not seem to fit into the mould of accountability in these respects. Some such work goes on for years and years before producing anything; and some of it gets nowhere at all – ever. If we believe that any such research should be promoted – or even tolerated – then we have to admit that accountability systems as we have designed them to date should not be applied to it.

Further, consider this: with DEST guidelines and categories of research, we have a situation like this:

Is the book used as a text? If 'yes', then it isn't research; it doesn't count.

Is the book a new edition? If 'yes', then it isn't research; it doesn't count.

Is the book published by a publisher not on the DEST list? If 'yes', then it isn't research; it doesn't count.

Does the periodical in which the essay appears have an ISSN? If 'no', then the essay is not research; it doesn't count.

These and other similar questions are, of course, important, inasmuch as recognition, reward, encouragement, and funding at all levels depend on quantity of research. Further, definitions of 'research' which easily produce these answers are being employed to determine what is research, how much research is being done, and who are 'active researchers'. By employing such criteria, it becomes a relatively easy matter to determine what is and what is not research for the purpose of DEST recognition. Arguments, explanations, justifications, and descriptions become largely unnecessary – and even inappropriate – and the system can function smoothly, efficiently, and quickly, according to the baselines which are declared by the Department of Education, Science and Training.

It is a well-known phrase – and the title of numerous articles – that 'what gets measured gets managed'. If something cannot be – or for whatever reason is not – measured, then that thing cannot be, or simply is not, managed. The easier and the clearer the measure, the easier and the clearer the management and the management strategy. By and large, other things are simply left by the wayside. They do not count. I will return to this below.

A digression (but not really)

In 1975, Donald Kirkpatrick produced a model of measuring the effectiveness of workplace training, the Kirkpatrick Model (Kirkpatrick 1975). This consists of four levels:

Level 1: Reaction. What was the attendees' reaction to the training? Did the attendees like it? How did the trainees evaluate the effectiveness of the training?
Level 2: Learning. Did the trainees learn anything?
Level 3: Behaviour. Did the training change the behaviour of the attendees?
Level 4: Results. Does the changed behaviour have implications for business success?

In 1996, Jack Phillips suggested a fifth level (Phillips 1996):

Level 5: Return on investment (ROI). In terms of business, was the training worth the cost? What is the ROI? For this, Phillips suggested a formula designed to show the percent return on the costs involved for delivering a training program.

An amazing fact about all this is that in the world of education, as well as in the world of training programs provided for businesses and other organizations, there is very little done beyond Level 1 to evaluate any training. And this, despite the fact that the Kirkpatrick model is widely recognized and applauded. Student/attendee evaluations are distributed and collected; and that is pretty well that. With the relatively recent development of 'workplace training and assessment', with its identification of 'elements of competence', and 'performance criteria' and the like in the area of vocational training, at least that sector of the provision of training has made a serious effort at focusing on Level 2. But it is true that for nearly all education programs, the measure of their quality and their success – as well as the measure of the quality of the provider – is at Level 1 only.[6] Why is this? A reasonable suggestion for an answer is, 'because it's easy'. Attendee evaluations – 'tick a box', or 'evaluate this statement on a scale of 1–5' – are not difficult data to collect, the same questions can be asked of almost all types of training groups, and the results can be compared pretty well across the board of education and training. There has been only little work done, however, in terms of investigating any correlation between attendee satisfaction and any other important criteria for evaluating the effectiveness of training or education; and in particular, no systematic attempts to evaluate effectiveness at Levels 2, and particularly 3, 4, and 5. This is all the more amazing, given the amount of resources spent on training programs, at all levels.

So, what does this have to do with accountability? The state of affairs with the Kirkpatrick model is both an example and an analogy. It is an example in that it is an attempt to call trainers and training programs to account to measure their effectiveness in terms of the articulation of the things that matter. It is an analogy in that the current situation accepts whatever criteria it does accept because those criteria are the easiest to measure; they are the easiest to quantify. If the basis on which an evaluation is made is a set of quantifiable criteria which apply to a large range of activities, then this is very attractive. The evaluation itself can become mechanical, and there is no need – and no room – for the exercise of judgement in evaluating anything.

A serious difficulty with such evaluations is that in attempting to evaluate something (in this case, training), strong emphasis is placed on one facet of that thing – or better, on one result of the training (viz. attendee satisfaction) – to the exclusion of all others. It also – like other accountability systems – focuses attention *solely* on that facet. Someone once mentioned to me:

I like physical things. So, give me a rope-climbing course for 'team-building' or anything else, and of course I'll rate it highly. If we get to do the rope-climbing and other activities, then I'm happy. I don't even really think about anything else that might result from it.

So, there are important questions, largely left unanswered: For example:

- Are the criteria we are measuring really relevant to measuring what we are interested in measuring?
- Should we allow them to be the sole criteria – which they currently are?
- In any particular area, is it necessary – and is it possible – to have generic criteria?
- In some particular areas, is it necessary – and is it possible – to have quantifiable criteria?
- Can we legitimately do away with a judgemental element in the evaluation of these areas?

In identifying which activities or results are to count, an accountability system prescribes what activities to undertake. As mentioned earlier, accountability systems take stock over a short term. This, as well, serves as a prescription: If some activity cannot be done in ways that have countable outcomes over a short period of time, then, inasmuch as it falls outside the accountability regime, the activity itself does not count. It is, in this respect, a waste of time, and a waste of resources.

This is the way it is with accountability systems. But, with possibly some few exceptions, it simply is not possible to police quality into a product or activity, unless what we are concerned with is itself a purely mechanical, assembly-line process. As I have suggested, accountability systems can determine and monitor the norm. They can become invidious when they are used to define and evaluate excellence.

Responsibility

I want to go just a little further with this, in relation to business and organizational culture in general. We should not believe that accountability systems do everything. They are not all there is to ethical behaviour. They are not all there is to achievement – and certainly not all there is to high performance, or excellence. They are more geared toward, in fact, defining the ordinary. And they can act as an aid toward preventing corrupt conduct. This element is, of course, important. But, notice, it is not a high-end concern. It is not a concern about excellence. It is conceivable that some organization – or maybe even an entire society – is particularly concerned to weed out freeloaders. This organization really wants people to pull their own weight. We could imagine that in its statement of values or its mission statement, this point is highlighted – perhaps in the name of fairness or equity: 'No freeloaders here!' If, in fact, we look at organizations' values statements, we never – *not ever* – find reference to 'weeding out freeloaders' as a value. But we often find significant statements about promotion of excellence. By and large, it is a mis-fit to try, as organizations typically do, to put accountability systems in the same basket as whatever there is toward promoting excellence. These are different things. And the worry is that in the respects noted above, they can come into conflict with each other. Accountability systems display excellence in reporting within their terms. They do not show excellence in accomplishment. Accountability systems not only are different from excellence-producing systems; they also can work against promotion of excellence. I am not making a specific suggestion here about what other structures can be put into place in order to do the job of promoting excellence. Below, I will have something to say about recognition of responsibility, as different from accountability.

As a more focused example, it is undoubtedly true that universities – and departments and individual academics – have had a history of not being accountable for what they do, in the areas of both teaching and research:

> Stay out of my classroom. It is sacred territory.

And:

> In the name of academic freedom, I can research into any area I like, and I can do it in any way that I like, and I don't need anyone's permission or approval to do it. Actually, I've been *thinking* a lot lately, and I deserve research credit for exactly this.

The idea of making academics accountable for what they do is laudable, particularly if you believe that there have been numbers of freeloaders. We might, for instance, require some evaluation, or at least perception, of someone's teaching practice. And we might also require some evidence of research, probably on the order of evidence of publication. What has happened, however, has pretty well been as follows.

In the area of teaching. There are student evaluations (i.e. Kirkpatrick Model, Level 1, and nothing further). There has been a requirement to notify students of the assessment procedures and timetables involved in courses. And there is now more of a move to require production of formal lecture notes and other materials. These are items we can put into a list, and then tick boxes to indicate that they have been satisfied.

In the area of research. Progressing from viewing a particular researcher's activities as either 'on' or 'off' – academics either published things or they did not, and they either published a lot or they did not, and their work was well-regarded or not – an accountability regime has been established through DEST Guidelines, as described earlier. These guidelines specify what counts and what does not; and of those things which count, these guidelines provide a numerical value for each of them:

> Considering research for last year, you are 6 and Johnson is 8. Therefore, he is a better researcher than you are. We know this because each of the possible research activities receives a numerical value – or not. It is quantified.

As mentioned above, although the categories – and their numerical values – describe what counts for what, their effect is prescriptive. They are not merely keeping an account. They are prescribing what activities people should be engaging in:

> You didn't apply for any grant money last year. Successful grant applications are worth good points according to the DEST guidelines. If you were fiddling around writing an article that was worth '1' – or worse, it was worth '0.5' because you collaborated with someone else – that simply is not as good in terms of research as having received a grant. Oh, and wait: the journal in which you published the article isn't mentioned on the DEST list. No points.

Of course there is a rationale here. Some periodicals really are not of high quality. And some are not academic at all. It is also true that some self-proclaimed 'research activities' are not research activities at all. But any discussion or argument that we might have over this is reduced to numbers which sit beside the various categories on the DEST list. There is no room for discussion of particular research efforts, effectiveness, and quality beyond the list. Expert opinion either is not allowed, or has already been factored into creation of the list itself. The discussion is closed, and the values are set. There is no room for comment on any particular piece of work.

This, as with the situation for evaluation of teaching, is certainly an equaliser. It has created a uniform scale on which performance can be judged. And it provides a pretty finely grained comparative ability, as well: 'she is a 1.5 better researcher than he is – just look at the points'. In the name of accountability and uniformity, this has replaced qualitative judgement. It is very difficult to be a freeloader. This is a serious move. It is also very dangerous, as well as invidious.

Here is a parable: In the area in which I teach, students are marked, by and large, on written work that they submit: essays, short answers to questions, and the like. And, for the main, we operate on a system of continuous assessment. Each student receives a number of marks and a grade in the course of the semester. In Australia, these grades are named as follows: a mark of 85% or higher is named a 'High Distinction', 75%–84% is a 'Distinction', 65%–74% is a 'Credit', 50%–64% is a 'Pass', and 49% or below is a 'Fail'. In practice, when marking written work, a quality assessment comes first: 'this is Credit work'. And then a mark is assigned. 'For Credit work, this is the norm. Therefore, inasmuch as the Credit range operates from 65–74, I will assign this work 70. That was for the first piece of work. Let's assume that during the course of the semester, there were five pieces of work, each worth equal value, and I went through this process for each of them, coming up with the following marks: 70, 65, 55, 65, 60. At the end of the term, this student received a Pass, 63. Now let's suppose the student came to see me, asking about their mark, concerned to know why they had not reached a Credit level in the course, and looking for some explanation. It would not only be cruel and nasty, it would also miss the point if in response, I turned on my calculator, totalled up the marks, divided by 5, and said, 'Yep, it's 63 all right. That's what your marks average, and that's the way I figured the overall mark. That's why you got the mark you got'. Among other things, this would also be forgetting that the quality assessment came first; and then numbers were assigned. This student was asking about quality, and the answer came back in algorithmic terms only. It is more difficult to answer the question in terms other than arithmetic. It is more difficult to provide an explanation. But, anything else, although much easier, really misses the point.

As another parable I call to your attention again the story I offered earlier about accountants and auditing failure. In particular I am concerned with the current – ineffective – attempt to replace judgement and the responsibility for the exercise of good judgement with increases in formal rules and regulations. I want to gesture toward a couple of morals from these difficulties with accountability regimes. The first is to recognize precisely what their limits are, and that they can be misdirected and colossal failures at identifying excellence. Recognizing even that they have any limits at all would be a major step for a number of practices that have trumpeted the great and unqualified virtue of strong accountability systems. Judgement in a number of areas simply cannot be either replaced by or reduced to accountability systems. This is the moral for the macro level.

There is a more difficult, and perhaps personally costly, moral at the micro level. Suppose that a particular organization has introduced a strong accountability system, and that in this system with its *de facto* prescriptive nature – as I have explained – there are elements which are recognized as inadequate, inappropriate, or even wrong-headed by a particular section for application to its evaluating what it wants to evaluate in its own area of operation. Given that overall evaluation, excellence, and personal recognition are covered by the accountability system, it would be costly, but may be possible, for the particular section to buck the system. If it, by itself, is concerned for excellence, it might recognize that it can decide

– as an expert in the area – what is good and what is not. If it decided to do this, then, of course, it would have to recognize that there could be a terribly high price for the section itself to pay if it attempts to operate outside the prescribed accountability regime – even if this is for the purpose of achieving the stated goals that the accountability regime is installed to achieve: determining and distinguishing between what is good and what is not. This is not a real possibility for most areas of operation, where it could be simply suicidal to operate this way. But maybe it is a possibility for some. Even so, there would quite possibly be a big price to pay, in failing to treat the descriptive accountability system as prescriptive: for example, offering internal rewards, promotions, and so forth, based on what it has judged to be important, rather than on organization-wide accountability performance criteria. I realize that this is not a real option for many sections which sit under a larger organization, but it is for some. It should at least be recognized as a possibility.

In an article called '"Good Ethics is Good Business" – Revisited' (Cohen 1999), I argued that sometimes it simply is not the case that a business behaving ethically will be good for its profitability. Sometimes ethical behaviour is a cost against the bottom line. I argued that businesses that are, in fact, concerned to behave ethically should realize this point. Behaving ethically is sometimes a cost. It does not always go hand in hand with looking out for a business' self-interest, as defined in terms of profit. In our private lives, we by and large recognize this fact – that is that ethical behaviour sometimes does not go toward advancing our self-interest. As a matter of fact, the most typical cases in which a person asks the question of whether they should do the ethical thing are cases when a person is looking for a reason to forego their self-interest, or at least to not put their self-interest as the foremost consideration in deciding what to do. Business itself seems to have forgotten this simple fact about the environment and nature of most ethical deliberation; and wants to hear only, 'be ethical, because that will enhance the business' bottom line'. The dangerous corollary of this position is that if the behaviour is not good for business, then there is no reason to behave that way. So, if there is no prudential reason supporting ethical behaviour, then there is, in fact, no good reason for behaving ethically. However, we do really know that sometimes doing the right thing costs. Sometimes ethical considerations work as a constraint on considerations of prudence. Sometimes ethical considerations are simply different from concerns about advancing prudential interests. We should not forget this. We certainly should not merely assume that, of course, prudential and ethical interests go easily hand in hand.

Maybe – just maybe – there can be cases in which a part of an organization, or even more rarely a single individual within an organization, can see this as an analogy for how they should behave with regard to toeing the line with respect to accountability requirements. Sometimes someone just might know that judgement, rather than mechanically applied accountability requirements, might be the better way to achieve excellence. But, behaving in this way could certainly involve that section, or that individual, in paying a price to the organization. Maybe this is – and maybe it is more likely not – a good analogy with realizing that it is not always the case that good ethics is good business.

Judgement and baselines

As I have indicated earlier, the declaration of values can function to describe 'baselines' and 'closing off the discussion'. That is, the discussion about what is of value and what is not, and what procedure can be used to evaluate performance, can be closed once baselines are set. That is what baselines, or declared parameters, do: they constrain the discussion, they close it off with respect to exploration or argument or discussion in certain areas. Sometimes we should be wary of declared baselines. Often we are inclined to treat them as more rigid and as having more credibility than perhaps we should. In an article called 'Truisms in Business Ethics' (Cohen 1999), an essay about the acceptance of some claims not only as true, but as obviously true, which are not true at all, I spent a little time talking about announced baselines. Baselines are declared starting places, and declared to bound the discussion. They are presented as givens. For example:

> Because $97,000 of the $100,000 must be used for equipment, that leaves only $3,000 for paying the people who will be staffing the event.

This statement declares that the money will be partitioned in this way, and it does not invite – and actually discourages or prohibits – any suggestion that less than $97,000 might be spent on equipment, so that more than $3,000 could be spent on paying the staff. It has declared that '$97,000 on equipment' is a baseline – not up for discussion or debate. It declares that the only room for discussion is how we can possibly staff the event for no more than $3000. It declares that there is nothing else that can be discussed. Sometimes that might really be the case – but not always. In another university example:

> Because tutorial class sizes cannot rise above 18 students, we will all have to teach more classes.

The baseline is declared to be a certain maximum size for enrolment in tutorials. The discussion, then, is declared to be only about how we can manage to staff enough tutorials to accommodate this declared limit on enrolment. Well, maybe, given the circumstances, we *should* allow tutorial enrolment to be greater than 18. Maybe we could demand enough additional resources to hire another member of staff. Maybe without those extra resources, we should, in fact, allow tutorial enrolments to reach 45. Maybe a lot of things. But the initial statement declares a baseline. It defines the problem or difficulty in a particular manner; and represents that this is the only way to define it; and it limits the way the difficulty can be resolved. It presents a baseline; it sets the parameters. Sometimes there are satisfactory answers to questions like, 'Why should we see the problem that way?', and 'Why should we treat that as a baseline?'. But this is not always the case. Sometimes there is no satisfactory answer to that question; and still the question does not get asked, because we accept the baseline as declared, *simply because it has been declared to be a baseline*. Sometimes we simply accept them too quickly, and sometimes we even unwittingly accept them. That's the way it is with baselines. And sometimes, those presenting the baseline as a baseline are well aware of this feature of declaring a baseline to be a baseline, and can exploit it. Sometimes their presentation of it as such is inadvertent.

> Inasmuch as the DEST guidelines do not award any points at all for the particular activity that you are undertaking in the name of 'research', we in this Faculty simply cannot count it.

It is clear that without changing those guidelines, the Faculty will not receive funding based on that activity. But maybe this is a price a Faculty should be prepared to pay, if it thinks that the activity is worthwhile, or if it thinks judgement in evaluating the activity is called for, rather than a simple and straightforward tallying up of what does and what does not get counted according to the DEST formula. There are easily many examples of such declared baselines. My points are two about this:

1 We too easily accept, as though carved in granite, a declared baseline, when, in fact, sometimes the most appropriate reaction is to question and debate exactly that which has been declared to be outside the bounds of the discussion.
2 Sometimes in the face of such baselines, the response with the most integrity can be to act in the way you more firmly believe to be right, rather than accepting the baseline and the benefits that it holds out for compliance.

Responsibility and ethical empowerment[7]

I have suggested that, among other things, accountability systems provide a historical track, in that they identify who did what, and when they did it. Keeping tabs like this can reveal liability. Responsibility systems, on the other hand, are proactive. They provide an instruction that someone or some part of an organization is to 'take responsibility for' doing something. In this phrase, 'responsibility' itself is an ambiguous notion, and both of its senses apply here. On the one hand giving someone the responsibility to do something means that they are to do it, and to decide how to do it. On the other hand, someone's taking responsibility for doing something carries with it the requirement that they do it 'responsibly'. So, an instruction to take responsibility for something is an instruction to get something done, and to do it responsibly. Unlike accountability systems, a system of responsibility is a system of delegation, a system of authorization, or empowerment. It is a system which requires that people exercise judgement (see Figure 1).

Ethical empowerment, or authorization, is a top-down notion. It involves a delegation of authority for ethical decision-making. It authorizes, or empowers, members of the organization to exercise judgement in decision-making. Increasingly, organizations have recognized that they – and their managers and supervisors through the ranks – simply cannot afford to be 'risk averse'. They cannot afford for their people in managerial or supervisory roles to avoid making decisions in ethically charged situations. Organizations must recognize that the alternatives to ethical empowerment, that gives the employee authority to engage in ethical decision-making, are simply not very good:

- To try to eliminate the possibility of the occurrence of situations where judgement must be exercised is impossible. I have indicated earlier that

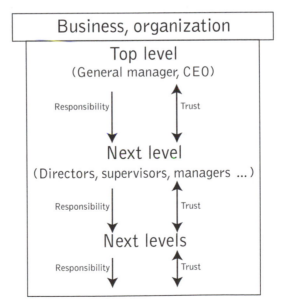

Figure 1   System of responsibility and empowerment

such attempts simply do not work, and can, in fact, make situations worse.

- To pass all ethically charged decisions up the line is a recipe for inefficiency.
- To simply avoid making decisions in ethically charged situations is a recipe for stagnation.
- To go ahead and do something, whatever you want, is cavalier, and almost certainly a recipe for disaster.

It is very dangerous to an organization not to invest in systems – e.g. training in ethical decision-making, clear job descriptions, ethical leadership training, robust codes of ethics – that equip managers to systematically exercise good judgement in such situations. To simply trust to common sense – or something like this – rather than realizing that the matter of ethical decision-making can be approached and dealt with specifically, seriously, and systematically is a common error. Charging managers with responsibility to make ethically defensible decisions is a matter of authorization, or empowerment. Appropriate responsibility, decision-making discretion can be delegated downward through the organization. Those receiving the responsibility are to recognize that they must make decisions and that they must exercise demonstrably good judgement in making them. Trust goes downward. From the top, those authorizing people below them must trust that those receiving the delegation are up to the task. Of course, this should not be simply a matter of luck – the person who receives the delegation must have the ability, skills, and resources to exercise it. It can be a matter of the right person for the job, providing the necessary resources, training, installing appropriate systems, etc. Of course, not everything is to be delegated; and delegation is not to everyone. Whatever provisions are made, it is a matter of trusting that the person who is empowered can do the task. Now – and this is at least as important – it is necessary that those who receive the delegation actually trust that the people who purportedly gave it to them actually meant what they said – that the delegation and the responsibility are real. We all know people who, when they say 'exercise your discretion' actually mean something like, 'you had better do this exactly as I would if I were in your position; otherwise, I'm going to come down on you like a ton of bricks'. This is not trust. This is not delegation. It is self-deception or fraud or some such thing. It is certainly not a recipe for authorizing ethical decision-making in ethically charged situations. It is, rather, a recipe for second-guessing and looking over one's shoulder. It is not empowerment at all. It is, rather, instilling fear and distrust. In an environment of ethical empowerment, responsibility is delegated downward, and trust must go in both directions. By and large, this is an important, probably indispensible, notion for an organization that is concerned to promote ethical performance.

Authorizing someone to engage in ethical decision-making does not mean being prepared to license, or support, whatever they decide – and it does not mean attempting to pass the buck. It means recognizing that specific prescriptions do not cover all cases, and allowing – or even insisting – that people can make decisions in those areas which will be supported, or at least not have untoward repercussions on them, if they can demonstrate that their decisions are 'reasonable'. A fair model of what I have in mind is as follows. It is mostly the case that when an appeal court hears a case, its job is not simply to decide whether the court of first instance made the correct or incorrect decision on the evidence. Rather, what is required in order for the appeal court to overturn the original verdict is a finding that the decision was 'unreasonable' on the evidence. An appeal court can well think – and even say – 'that verdict is not the one that we would have reached if we had been hearing the case in the first place; but nevertheless, we do not find the decision unreasonable, and hence we do not (cannot) overturn the verdict. The decision must be accepted'.[8]

Those who are authorized to make decisions should be able to expect that if they can offer justification which is appreciated as being reasonable, then they will not suffer. To that extent, the decision will be recognized as being licensed by the organization and the person making the decision will be supported, or at least not made to suffer. It is, of course, possible to retract authorization in particular areas; and there can be good reasons for doing this. Rules, regulations, codes of conduct, etc. are all mechanisms for doing this. But, if it is admitted, as it should be, that an environment of ethical empowerment is important and valuable, then reasons for diminishing empowerment should be made clear.

There is much more that can be said about creation and limitation of systems of ethical responsibility. The central point for here, however, is to distinguish accountability systems from responsibility systems, and to call attention to serious limitations and misconceptions of the former and the necessity of attention to the latter.

Notes

1 See, for instance, Clark and Dean (2001, 2002).
2 Michael Baume echoed this view in his 'You can't legislate for boardroom integrity' (Baume 2002).
3 Probably the two most widely used (and adapted) ethical decision-making models (and there are very many indeed) are the American Accounting Association Model (see, for instance, May 1990), and the Laura Nash Model (Nash 1981).
4 I offer this only as an example – as a striking example – of this point about the limits of the adequacy of accountability systems. My suggestion is that the point is not only generalizable to other organizations, but *obviously* generalizable to them.
5 See Higher Education Research Data Collection: Specifications for the Collection of 2004 Data, Higher Education Group, Department of Education,

Science and Training (February 2005). Available at www.dest.gov.au/highered/research/herdc.htm#specifications.

6 Of course a number of programs have elements of testing the attendees; examining them over the content of the course. Do not confuse this, however, with evaluating the success of the training. In holding trainers accountable, student evaluations are often collected. If we actually viewed whether or not trainees learned anything in the training as an indicator of the success of the training (i.e. Level 2), we would at least also ask trainers to provide data on something like the pass rates in their courses and percentages of grades awarded at all levels. We do not. We do use exams; but we basically do not use them as any part at all of an accountability system or as any part of the measurement of the effectiveness of the training. At most, they are used to evaluate the students; but not at all to evaluate the effectiveness of the training itself or the individual trainer.

7 Much of the following discussion is adapted from Grace and Cohen (2005), Chapter 10.

8 In *Anarchy, State, and Utopia*, Robert Nozick (1974: 90–108) makes basically the same point in arguing about the limits of one society having to accept the legal decisions of another being enforced against its own citizens on foreign soil, when it disagrees with them. If those decisions are appraised as being within the scope of what is 'fair' and 'reliable', even if not the same or as good as the society sees its own, then it should be obliged to accept the decisions.

Chapter 8

Management ethics and organizational networks

Robin Usher

Editors' introduction

Robin Usher argues, in this chapter, that ethical behaviour is not a matter of applying codes because ethics are immanent, always already embedded in and a part of specific practices. In this sense, there is no sense in the formula 'ethical practice = practice + ethics', where ethics comes into the frame from outside practice. Usher comments that it still remains common for ethics to be assumed to be equivalent to rules or moral codes, whether these are deontological, consequential or covenantal. However, ethics, rather than being seen through these frames must be seen as they are embedded in action and practices, he suggests. As Usher proposes, a means for doing this derives from the theoretical resources associated with Actor-Network Theory (ANT).

Usher issues a product advisory with respect to ANT. It is not, strictly speaking, a theory. Instead, it addresses how to study and understand things and events, as more of a method for describing things which is particularly useful for situations that are subject to rapid change with unclear boundaries. The elements of ANT are skilfully outlined. Then things start to get really interesting. ANT is applied to ethics at Enron – perhaps the most widely talked and written about case of business ethics gone wrong. Enron provides an incontrovertible, if perhaps extreme, example of a breakdown of organizational ethics and for Usher ANT provides an investigative strategy for unpacking complexity and for developing an understanding of how stability and order are negotiated and maintained through a social process of aligning interests and values.

In the actor networks that were constructed at Enron, philosophical frameworks, codes of ethics, statements of values, and moral rules, while not a guarantor of ethics, were all present. But Usher does not dismiss such things – for him they were all actors amongst other human and non-human actors in the networks that constituted the organization. None of these, however, could provide for the practices in which they were instantiated. By the lights of the situation, he suggests, as far as contemporary capitalism is concerned, it could be construed that Enron did 'the right thing' and its failure lay not in behaving unethically but in following the capitalist model too well. Given that contemporary capitalism is hardly ever the model of ethical behaviour, Usher closes on a sombre note by suggesting that the history of Enron might well repeat itself in the future.

Reduced to the basics, ethics is about 'doing the right thing'. However, and unfortunately, the 'right thing' is not always easy to discern. How is it to be known? Is it a matter of intuition? Possibly, but the trouble with intuition is that it's impossible to codify. How is one to decide what to do in situations where there appears to be more than one 'right thing' that could be done and where these various right things may be conflicting? What if doing the right thing leads to unintended yet unethical consequences? Is it a matter of having a code that can be applied to a situation and from which, one can then 'read off' the right thing to do?

In the world of liberal capitalist business, the codification of ethical behaviour has increasingly tended to become the norm. Every business, it is said, must have a code of ethics to govern behaviour and it is the duty of every employee from the highest down to understand and apply the code. If something goes wrong ethically, then it is argued the code must either be unclear, incomplete, not properly understood or inadequately applied. In this chapter, I shall mainly concentrate on this position and argue that it is highly problematic. In the same way that the traditional notion of theory being applied to practice has been challenged, so too I want to challenge the notion that ethics is applied to practice. Instead, I want to argue that ethical behaviour is not a matter of applying codes because ethics is immanent, it is *always already* in practices. With the use of this lens, we can begin to see the place and function of ethics in organizations in a very different way.

What's involved in understanding how ethics work – or do not work – in organizational settings? Ethics traditionally has been based on the stipulation of some sort of universal and final standpoint from which all else ethical is supposed to flow. My contention is that what's required is a way of understanding ethics differently from how it's usually understood, a different understanding from the dominant one that sees ethics as a set of rules or moral codes to be applied.

This dominant understanding has its roots in philosophical discourse. Ethics has traditionally been the playground of philosophers and their discourses have constructed, and 'externally imposed', a view of ethics precisely as a set of rules or moral codes, whether these be deontological, consequential or covenantal. These discursive constructions have generated normative and universal approaches that it could be argued are themselves unethical. For example, to approach ethics from a deontological perspective retains the impasse of a 'good-bad' dualism but without providing any answers about how ethics are to be construed in particular situations. It is precisely the normative prescriptions spun out of these philosophical discourses that have helped create a situation, I would argue, where there is now a plethora of codes of ethics for organizations but where too often organizational practices go their own, sometimes 'unethical', way and where these codes seem to be more a matter of window-dressing than of substance.

My argument then is that it is unhelpful to think of ethics in generalized or universalistic terms, of an ethics in general. These approaches decontextualize ethics and do not help us to understand properly the *embeddedness* of ethics, of the place of purpose and context, the processes whereby agents cope with the possibilities presented by particular situations. This alternative approach requires us to consider not universal prescriptions or codes but more productively to foreground the *practices* within which ethics is embedded – or in our case, the organizational practices through which ethics is 'performed' by agents dealing with the possibilities and constraints of particular situations within organizational settings.

ANT-ing organizations

In the same way as I challenge the notion of applying ethics so, too, I do not seek to *apply* Actor-Network Theory (ANT), nor to set out how organizations can become more ethical by doing this. Instead my aim is more modest. I shall draw on the conceptual resources provided by ANT to suggest how the place of ethics in organizations might be understood differently.

First, however, I need to emphasize that contrary to certain conventional social science canons, ANT does not provide generalized explanations. Nor is it a theory that is meant to be applied. As a theory, ANT is about how to study and understand things and events, so in a strong sense it's more a method for *describing* these and it is particularly useful for situations when they are subject to rapid change and when their boundaries are unclear. The understanding that may be gained arises from studying the complex negotiations and trade-offs performed by the actors. Apart from assuming the capacity of actors to negotiate with and enrol other actors, it is not legitimate to make any other assumptions about the object of study. ANT also assumes that people are sociologists in the sense that they are capable of doing their own work of interpretation and understanding and therefore do not require sociologists to come along and explain to them what they are *really* doing and how they could do it better.[1]

ANT[2] can be described in the following way:

Actor-network theory is concerned with studying the mechanics of power
as this occurs through the construction and maintenance of networks
made up of both human and non-human actors. It is concerned with
tracing the transformation of these heterogeneous networks ... that are
made up of people, organisations, agents, machines and many other
objects. It explores the ways that the networks of relations are composed,
how they emerge and come into being, how they are constructed and
maintained, how they compete with other networks, and how they are
made more durable over time. It examines how actors enlist other actors
into their world and how they bestow qualities, desires, visions and
motivations on these actors.

(Tatnall and Gilding 1999: 959)

At this point, I will just briefly highlight those things in the above
description that will figure significantly as this narrative unfolds. These
are that ANT is concerned with among other things: power, its use and
distribution, transformative processes, motivations, relations, and social
order and stability.

ANT understands an organization as a network of 'actors'[3] where the
network is constituted by the interactions of the actors composing it and
the actors are actors because they are networked.[4] Actor and network are
mutually constitutive, defining and redefining each other. An organization
is in effect therefore constituted by the networking or interaction of the
actors, where 'actors' can be animate or inanimate.[5] To put it another way,
organizations and agents are *effects* generated in patterned networks where
diverse entities whose resistance has been overcome have been brought
together, or in ANT-speak *mobilized* and *stabilized*.

ANT highlights practices as 'performances' of continuous relational
interplay. These are the *performative* characteristics of actor networks,
where actors are *performed* in and by their relations. Thus, for example,
a manager as an actor interacts with other actors in the network that is
the organization. Through these interactions, the manager is 'performed'
as a manager. A manager is a manager therefore not because of some
ascribed label or because of intrinsic qualities but because s/he is positioned
in a particular network of ordered interactions, does work through those
interactions, and with that positioning is accordingly identified as a manager.
As networks consist of actors, animate and inanimate who have different
and unequal possibilities for influencing other members of the network, the
specific power of an actor depends on their positioning within the network.
As Law (1999: 4) puts it, 'entities take their form and acquire their attributes
as a result of their relations with other entities, the actor is generated *in*
and *by* these relationships'. Actors achieve their form and attributes as a
consequence of their relations or interactions with other actors.[6]

This network of ordered interactions – or practices – is a sign that all the actors in an organization have, first, forged common definitions and meanings, second, that representations have been defined and, third, that all have been co-opted in the pursuit of personal and organizational objectives. This is referred to as *translation*[7] and it is the processes of translation that stabilize a network by aligning the interests and values of the actors.

An actor-network is configured by the enrolment of both animate and inanimate entities, through a series of negotiations and re-alignments whose purpose is redefinition. Here one set of actors seek to impose their definitions and representations onto others. To put it another way, it is about meaning generation in the cause of stability and social order. Within an actor network, the multiple and conflicting interests of various actors become translated and inscribed[8] into technical and social arrangements. Translation can be regarded as a means of obliging or persuading entities to go along a path whose direction is determined by another entity or entities. Through the processes of translation and *inscription*, actors' multiple and conflicting interests become aligned with each other and embedded into technologies that stabilize the actor-network, at least temporarily (Callon 1991). Once stabilized, an actor network becomes resistant, although not immune, to further translation. When actors feel no need to spend time opening and looking inside the 'black-boxes'[9] that the network has become but just accept these as given, the network can be said to have become durable and seemingly irreversible. What aids this process is an inherent dynamic in an actor-network to strive for stabilization since none of the entities comprising it would exist without that network in that form (Stalder 1997).

Inscription is perhaps the most important way in which an actor-network is 'translated'. Inscriptions can take the form of, among other things, documents, reports, academic papers, models, books, computer programs and formal discussions. All these can serve as the means whereby meanings are inscribed or 'written in' to the network such that they 'stand in' or speak for animate actors (Holmström and Robey 2002). Through inscription, actors embed their agendas into these socio/technical artifacts. As social relations become inscribed in material artifacts, they too assume the role of actors in the network.

Inscriptions can become stable and routinized, assuming a taken for granted existence and resisting assaults from competing translations.

They become 'frozen organizational discourse', resistant to change and irreversible.[10]

The success of a translation refers to the completeness with which actor interests are aligned, not to some objective criterion of whether the network is valuable. As Walsham (1997: 469) notes, successful networks of aligned interests are created 'through the enrolment of a sufficient body of allies, and the translation of their interests so that they are willing to participate in particular ways of thinking and acting which maintain the network'.

I mentioned earlier that networks could however become unstable. There are a number of possible factors that can bring this about; for example, the entry of new actors, the departure of existing actors, perturbations in translation through weakening of the obligatory point of passage,[11] or a shift in the alignment of interest and values. All this can cause the 'black-box' of networked actors to be opened and their contents reconsidered. As Callon (1986a) points out, a network relies for its stability and its continued existence on the maintenance of its 'simplifications', and these are always under constant challenge from increasing complexity.

ANT argues that actors are positioned by *intermediaries* that connect actors, in the sense of providing a 'language' that enables them to communicate with one another, thereby defining the network. An intermediary is 'anything that passes between actors in the course of relatively stable transactions' (Stalder 1997: 8).[12] For networks to operate successfully, the circulation of intermediaries needs to be coordinated. An optimal circulation of intermediaries strengthens the coordination of actors within the networks. This provides the push that I have noted earlier, for agreement or alignment on the part of the actors.

Turning now to look specifically at an organization, once the organization's actor-networks are 'translated', the interactions within the network are shaped by different organizational logics or *modes of ordering*. Law (1997) in a paper on actor-networks in a large publicly funded research facility isolated four organizational logics which he referred to as administrative, entrepreneurial, charismatic and vocational. In my own research on universities as actor-networks[13] there also appear to be a variety of such organizational logics which I refer to as bureaucratic, entrepreneurial and collegial. I agree with Law when he characterizes these logics both as modes of *ordering* or translation that maintain order and stability and at the same time as *moral* logics. They shape the identity and subjectivity of actors, their practices, what is, and is not, permitted and consequently how they deal with the constraints and possibilities of particular organizational situations. Thus, to return to our earlier example, a manager is 'performed' as a manager, positioned and 'subject-ified' through the different organizational logics or modes of ordering that frame the organization.

I would emphasize that I am not arguing that these logics are a set of rules that are *applied* to practice. They are definitely not rules, they have no independent, external existence because they are *embedded* in practices, they are themselves performed into being through practices – or networked interactions – whilst they themselves enable practices to be performed. This suggests an iterative process where it's impossible to say what is originating, what is cause and what is effect, what is general and what is specific.

I want now to highlight further some features of these organizational logics in order to start thinking differently about ethics in organizations. First, these logics frame the organizational arrangements and transactions within an organization. They also, as I have noted with my earlier example of the manager, participate in performing actors into being. One advantage that ANT has as a conceptual resource is that arrangements, transactions and identities whilst seen as stabilized are not however seen as given or fixed. Existing as performative modes of ordering, they are best understood as points of connection and lines of flow, always in the making where every ordering is always contested and contestable. With ANT, no version or account of an organization or an agent is ever either completely autonomous or completely final. Furthermore, this highlights the *work* that has to be done in the creation and stabilization of an actor-network. As Latour (2002) points out, being interconnected is not enough. That's the point of the 'actor' in actor-network. It's about the work that actors do, their performances, in relation to one another, and the changes that that work brings about.

There's no doubt, however, that the language of ANT can project a picture that appears very deterministic. As such, it would seem to excuse actors for any responsibility for what they do. However, the counter-argument would be that transactions always involve actors in making choices. Indeed, ANT assumes actors are radically indeterminate. Neither actors' personality nor the motivations behind their actions can ever be taken to be predetermined because ANT assumes that there are always multiple logics, invariably embodying elements of conflict. This is why 'doing the right thing' is not always readily and definitively discernible. Ordering is contingent, local and variable and, as noted above, is contestable and a site of contest. Since the possibilities of any particular situation are never fully clear and coherent, there are always choices to be made. Since they are agents, the responsibility of actors is always present. There is agency therefore even though it may be heterogeneous and incoherent.

Second, it is noticeable that in the examples given above there is no mode of ordering that can be dubbed 'ethical' per se. The reason for this is significant. ANT would argue that in any organization there is no mode of ordering which is uniquely and purely about ethics but rather every mode has an ethical dimension. Actors do not speak in pure ethics-speak and they don't take a set of ethical prescriptions and determine their actions in the light of those prescriptions. As I have argued, the ethics is *embedded*, albeit in a variety of different ways, in the organizational logics that have emerged through the processes of translation, the work done by actors in stabilizing the network. An actor-network embodies the characteristics of these logics so that the outcome is the result of a set of heterogeneous forces that affect and define the networked relational settings (Akrich 1992). To put it another way, practices are about the 'ought' as well as the 'is' and the 'how to'. ANT refers to *moral* logics because these logics *prescribe*[14] how people do and speak the 'ought' aspects of any situation. The actors embody the prescriptions so in any setting we can ask what the actors are doing to one another and what actors are making other actors do (Cordella and Shaikh 2003).

At the same time, the content and significance of the ethical dimension will vary. It will be different in, for example, a bureaucratic mode as against a collegial or entrepreneurial mode. All these modes of ordering will have embedded within them a 'doing of the right thing' but what that 'right thing' is will be different across the various modes as well as never being clear-cut within any particular mode. Hence 'doing the right thing' is never intuitively or prescriptively obvious. It's always a matter of negotiated performance within the patterned relationships that constitute the organization.

This notion of ordering logics which are embedded but which are also performative can provide different insights for thinking about ethics differently. To sum up, the conceptual resources provided by ANT allows us to understand ethics in terms of embeddedness, as situated within practices and therefore material, where ethical identities are forged relationally, configured and reconfigured within networks of encounter, and hybrid in the sense that the spaces of encounter are populated by both animate and inanimate actors.

Ethics and Enron

At this point, I want to take an ANT-framed analysis of Enron and its collapse as an example of the insights that ANT can provide in understanding organizational ethics. I have deliberately chosen Enron because few would argue that it provides an incontrovertible, if perhaps extreme, example of a breakdown of organizational ethics. I would argue that ANT's conceptual resources are particularly useful here for two reasons. First, it is an investigative strategy for unpacking complexity. Second, it helps to develop an understanding of how stability and order are negotiated and maintained through a social process of aligning interests and values. Enron provides a fascinating story of organizational complexity where stability and order were negotiated and maintained, perhaps at the expense of ethical behaviour, and it is in this sense that ANT may provide the key to understanding the place of ethics in that organization.

I start, however, by discussing the two types of conventional explanations of how the apparent breakdown of ethical behaviour happened at Enron. The first draws on what I call 'the rotten apple(s)' explanation – in the case of Enron, it is argued it was all down to the top men, Kenneth Lay, the Chairman of the Board, Jeffrey Skilling, the CEO, and Andrew Fastow, the Chief Financial Officer. Being themselves corrupt and greedy, they provided a model for unethical behaviour that flourished within, and permeated, the whole organization from top to bottom. Yet because of their positions of responsibility, it is they who must ultimately be held responsible.

I find this explanation highly problematic. Whilst not wanting to absolve Lay and the rest of responsibility, this easy demonization of the top executives should itself make us hesitate to accept this as a complete explanation of what went wrong ethically at Enron. By focusing attention on the so-called 'bad apples', it diverts attention away from explanations that highlight more systemic causes for the collapse. Furthermore, it wildly exaggerates the influence of top managers. ANT reminds us that the power of even the most powerful of managers is extended or distributed through the network of relations that constitute the organization, or to put it another way, managers are the *expression* of the organization. Latour (1986) argues that the notion that power is an attribute possessed by an actor is essentialist. The apparent 'possession' of power by an actor, for example, such as having the title 'CEO', or possessing some intrinsic quality such as 'intellectual capital' – of which more later – does not automatically confer an ability to bring about either stability or change unless other actors can be *persuaded* to perform the appropriate actions for this to occur – if in other words, a process of translation can be successfully completed.

The second type of explanation is more systemic, yet is still highly problematic. It argues that the problem with Enron lay in the failure of regulatory mechanisms, including codes of ethics, to insist upon and enforce ethical behaviour. Although Enron had a code of ethics, it was obviously not observed. Its Board failed to discharge its oversight duties. External regulators too such as the SEC did not carry out their oversight function. The auditors, Arthur Andersen, were also consultants for the company, a clear conflict of interest that prevented them from blowing the whistle over accounting irregularities and borderline financial practices. All this, it is argued, constituted a massive failure at every level to enforce clear codes of ethical behaviour. But the point here is that whilst all this may be the case, it also fails first, to take contextual factors into account and, second, to recognize that ethical behaviour is not defined and known simply by its intrinsic quality – and here it is important to distinguish between the unethical and the illegal. This kind of explanation, put simply, is a 'being wise after the event' type explanation. Why would, for example, have regulators initiated investigative action for a company that *Fortune* had rated the most innovative for five years running? Why, in a market-driven capitalist system geared to making profits would anyone have questioned the integrity and soundness of a company whose stock price had risen to $US 90 in ten years?

What I'm getting at here is that it's too easy with hindsight to construct Enron as the evil empire, particularly when its share price plummeted from that fabulous $90 to less than $1 in 2002. At the time, indeed, it could be argued that it was quite the opposite. Few were prepared to even contemplate, let alone articulate, that Enron was doing anything unethical.[15] Even after the company's downfall, when Enron stock was ascribed junk bond status and thousands had lost their jobs and their pensions,[16] many former employees had glowing things to say about the company, maintaining that they did not regret their time there. In the words of letters to the Press[17] by former employees:

> 'Enron had a pull for the best and the brightest. Entrepreneurship was always encouraged.'
> 'I feel a great sadness at the end of what for all its faults was a trail-blazing courageous and dynamic company.'
> 'Just because the company collapsed does not mean that everything it did and stood for was wrong.'
> 'It was an intoxicating atmosphere. If you loved business and loved being challenged and working with unique novel situations, it was the most wonderful place.'
> 'I was part of the greatest team that I have ever seen or heard of. We had unmatched talent and skill.'
> 'Enron was a tremendously exciting and vibrant place to work.'
> 'There have been so many negative comments about Enron that no one seems to remember the positive attributes. Enron was a great place to work; it equipped us to move into other jobs within society.'
> 'Our benefits and perks were a great way to show us how much we were appreciated and that our contributions to the company did not go un-noticed'.[18]
> 'It'd be great [a Bush win in the 2000 election]. I'd love to see Ken Lay as Secretary of Energy'.[19]

The rise and fall of Enron

I start the case study with a brief history to sketch in the context. Enron started out in 1985 as a small Houston based gas pipeline company. Its chance for expansion came with the deregulation of the energy market. In 1992, the Commodity Futures Trading Commission responded to an Enron request to help rewrite laws on energy futures, exempting these financial instruments from government oversight and fraud laws. From that time on, Enron evolved into a company that not only sold natural gas on the open market but virtually anything that could be sold online at a possible profit, in the process transforming itself from a gas pipeline operator into the world's largest energy trader. But as well as becoming the largest buyer and seller of natural gas and electricity in the US, Enron also traded numerous other commodities and provided risk management, project financing, and engineering services, pulp and paper products, petrochemicals and plastics, as well as esoteric products like clean air credits that could be purchased by utilities to meet emission limits. At one point Enron was doing business in broadband and even weather derivatives.

In effect, it became a giant middleman that worked like a hybrid of traditional commodity exchanges. But instead of simply bringing buyers and sellers together, Enron entered into contracts with both the seller and the buyer, making money on the difference between the selling price and the buying price and keeping the books closed, thus making it the only party that knew both prices – a clear source of profit for the company. Over time, increasingly varied and complex contracts were designed. Customers could insure themselves against all sorts of eventualities – such as a rise or fall in interest rates, a change in the weather, or a customer's inability to pay. By the end, the volume of such financial contracts far outstripped the volume of contracts to actually deliver commodities, and Enron came to be heavily dependent on what Jeffrey Skilling referred to as 'intellectual capital':

> Enron's 'intellectual capital' was Skilling's pride and joy. He recruited more than 250 newly minted MBAs each year from the nation's top business schools. Meteorologists and PhDs in math, physics and economics helped analyse and model the vast amounts of data that Enron used in its trading operations and to help manage the risk to which it was becoming increasingly exposed.[20]

By the time of the collapse, Enron had essentially become a futures trader, with the futures market a major source of company income. And very lucrative it was too – on paper at least. Enron's 1999 revenues of $40 billion made it the seventh largest corporation in the US and the sixteenth largest in the world.[21] Yet despite this seeming success, in late 2001 Enron filed for Chapter 11 bankruptcy protection and was forced to sell its primary energy trading unit. Its bankruptcy was the largest collapse in corporate history.

It's worth emphasizing that Enron's phenomenal growth occurred at a time when as financial institutions generated increasingly more exotic investment tools, a river of money became available and was looking for opportunities, no matter how risky these might be. This is a crucial aspect of the Enron story for its apparently phenomenal growth was based on the deliberate embrace of risk but in a context where investors were *also* embracing risk. It is not surprising therefore that Wall Street's links with Enron were complex, intimate, and above all, lucrative. In 2000 alone, Enron paid more than $250m in fees to banks, six of whom received more than $20m each. As one banker said:

> They [Enron] were the golden goose. Every once in a while in a heated market, there's someone who has the magic touch and everyone wants to do business with them. They were a deal shop.

The banks provided the solution to Enron's biggest financial problem; the large part of its asset portfolio that was not generating much cash. Enron did not want to finance underperforming assets, including foreign projects that had soured,[22] by raising straight debt in the bond market, because that would damage its credit rating and thereby jeopardize the company's key trading business. Instead, it began moving assets off balance sheet into partnerships, of which it eventually created some 3,500, with names such as Marlin, Firefly and Raptor. The assets were often sold at prices that Enron would never have achieved on the open market. Not only did these partnerships hide debt, but they also made Enron appear to be generating cash from operations rather than from its financing activities.[23] Furthermore, these financial structures had the merit of satisfying the letter, if not the spirit, of the law and of accounting standards.

Jeffrey Skilling turned to a bright young finance wizard, Andrew Fastow, to help him find capital for Enron's rapidly expanding trading empire. Fastow, who had worked for a bank on leveraged buyouts, was recruited to Enron in 1990 where he became CFO at age 36, receiving in 1999, *CFO Magazine*'s Excellence Award for Capital Structure Management. One structure put into place by Skilling and Fastow, was the partnerships that linked Enron business to investment in supposedly independent companies, thus keeping the debt off Enron's books. This, however, depended on a steady or rising stock price and an investment-grade credit rating that in the end, with the absence of real profits, could not be maintained.[24] Enron was probably unique in the volume of such deals and the amount of debt that it managed to move off balance sheet.[25] But while each individual deal may have been manageable, the sum of them posed an enormous and, in the end, unmanageable risk for Enron.[26]

Enron's financial clout was matched by its political influence; indeed it has been argued that these were interlinked. Between 1989 and 2001, Enron contributed nearly $US 6 million to political parties and candidates, with more than two-thirds going to the Republicans. More than $2 million of that money came during the 1999–2000 election cycle alone, when the company became one of the biggest contributors to President Bush's campaign for the White House. More than 250 members of the US Congress across all parties received political contributions and at least 14 high-ranking officials in the first Bush administration owned stock in the company.[27]

Most significant for our purpose this history tells a lot about the way Enron's culture developed. For Jeffrey Skilling, the CEO, pipelines were 'boring'. He proceeded to change the company in his own image – one which leveraged its 'intellectual capital', or as his critics now maintain, made the company smart and confident, arrogant and flashy.[28] Jeffrey Skilling had this to say about risk: 'The key is to take on risk that you can manage better than your competitors'.

He brought together a fast moving band of self-described 'pioneers' where taking risks was seen as the royal road to profits and whose modus operandi was summed up in the words of former traders : 'we like risk because you make money by taking risks. We take profits now and worry about the details later'.

Press commentary and analysis of what happened at Enron reinforce this. The company was characterized by:

'A growth at any cost culture that drowned caution and over-rode checks and balances'

'A relentless push for creativity and competitiveness'

'A tendency to get impatient with rules ... the relentless demand to create new ways to make money spawned an environment where raising questions about a deal ... was considered an indication that you "didn't get it"'.[29]

'He [Jeffrey Skilling] pushed Enron to change constantly in a quest for the next new thing ... a different venture that would be its [Enron's] next big score'.[30]

It seems clear in retrospect that Enron, in the cause of embracing risk, tried to do too much, too fast, without the safeguard of substantial real returns. For example, its $US 1.2 billion investment in fibre-optic capacity and trading facilities was shortly followed by a crash in the broadband market. In other commodity markets, it could never generate the profits that it generated from energy trading.

ANT-ing Enron

At this point, using the conceptual resources provided by ANT, I want to stay with Enron and see how these resources might provide us with a way of understanding the place of ethics in the sorry saga of that company. My starting point is to note the main characteristics of an actor-network, which can be summarized as *embeddedness*, *relationality*, *materiality* and *hybridity*. Understanding the place of ethics therefore requires understanding the network of practices prevalent at Enron since it was within these that ethics was embedded.

Following the analysis earlier, I would argue that whilst there were a number of different ordering logics at Enron, one would seem to have predominated. This could be characterized as an 'entrepreneurial' logic although it took such an extreme form that perhaps 'macho' might be a more apt descriptor. The comments below illustrate what I mean by this:

'You've got to shoot first.' (Kenneth Lay)

'The company was always looking to dominate new markets.'

'Executives were chosen on the basis of would they fit in as a ruthless trader ... "we weren't looking for softies."'

'The princes were the dealmakers or "developers", in-house entrepreneurs who launched businesses and structured deals so they could claim huge profits for the company and bonuses for themselves.'
'They [the traders] thought they had nothing else they needed to learn.'
'You'd have to become ruthless and aggressive before they would say "good boy, you're one of us now"'.[31]
'[There was] a forced ranking system [called] "rank and yank" that weeded out the poor performers – a committee of executives rated employees on a numerical scale to determine promotions, bonuses and firings. The bottom 10 per cent of employees were then fired. "It was as competitive internally as it was externally"' (former Enron executive).

All this points to a number of things. It's clear that in the light of its ultimate collapse, the actor-networks that constituted Enron became dysfunctional. But how did this happen? First, key senior executives such as Skilling, Fastow and Kenneth Lay became the focal actors; in ANT-speak they became the 'obligatory passage point' (OPP), the actors through whom other actors had to pass, in the process making their values and interests indispensable:

'The key management failure was curbing dissent.'
'[Jeffrey] Skilling didn't act in a vacuum. He had a hands-off chairman, compliant board, impotent accountants, lawyers and auditors.'
'Inside Enron, a wide circle of executives saw what was wrong and didn't stop it. Most never thought to try … Enron's tale of success was so compelling that people who had ethical doubts just doubted themselves'.[32]

The above is a good example of Callon's point that entities become strong, acquiring greater strength and credibility by gathering a mass of 'silent others' (Callon 1987). In the case of Enron, these 'silent others' not only included the management and many of the lower level employees but also the banks, Wall Street, accountants, attorneys, regulators and so on. As we noted earlier, many former employees found the experience of working for the company stimulating, exciting and rewarding. However, whilst accepting that silence was not a function of repression, it was however a function of the success of inscription where the agent of inscription at Enron was the *deal*. The dominant social relationships at Enron became inscribed into the deal and the various instrumentalities that secured deals, themselves becoming actors in the network that was Enron. Since the deals were so productive in terms of cash bonuses and stock options there was an understandable reluctance to rock the boat. Deals made Enron a black box and the higher the costs of opening the black box, the more likely it was to remain closed.

As we have seen, translation is the way in which an actor-network is stabilized. Interests, values and identities become aligned, ordered and stabilized. Motivation is central to this process and occurs by influencing actors' current evaluations of reality and instilling notions of more desirable states and how to reach them (Callon 1986b). The motivation at Enron evaluated reality as an environment where the potential for unrestricted deal-making was virtually infinite. With Skilling as the OPP setting the tone and the pace,[33] all other interests and values became subservient to the making of deals from which paper profits could be amassed, stock prices artificially inflated, and all identities other than those of the tough fast moving trader marginalized.

The dominance of this macho entrepreneurial logic created a situation therefore where 'doing the right thing' meant pulling off trading deals and setting up financial structures in order to maximize paper profits and thence the stock price:

'The company had an obsession about its stock price.'
'It was doing deals for the sake of doing deals.'

At the time of the California electricity crisis in 2000–1, when the state legislature was considering imposing caps on electricity wholesale prices, Kenneth Lay told them: 'In the final analysis, it doesn't matter what you crazy people in California do, because I got smart guys who can always figure out how to make money'.[34]

The interests of California's consumers subject to rolling electricity blackouts over nearly a year played no part in Enron's considerations.

Earlier I discussed the role of an intermediary as the communicative 'currency' of an actor-network, the 'language' through which actors share and 'trade' meanings. I want to argue now that at Enron the intermediary was *risk*. As we have noted earlier, the language of risk literally predominated. The tone was set by Jeffrey Skilling,[35] the primary OPP, for whom the taking of risk powered by the 'intellectual capital' of those he hired in his own image became a mantra. Risk might at first glance seem to be too immaterial to function as an intermediary. At Enron, however it assumed a concrete materiality and was reinforced by its close link with money, with which, as we have seen, Enron seemed to be awash even whilst its hunger for it never seemed to be satisfied.

As I noted earlier, ANT does not conceptualize actors as purely human entities. Non-human entities can also be actors; this includes machines such as computers and texts such as codes of ethics. An actor is an actor through interacting, and doing work, in a network; the nature of its being is irrelevant. Composed of human and non-human entities, actor-networks can be said therefore to be characterized by their hybridity. This again has a number of implications. First, we are now in a position to rethink the role of a code of ethics. Rather than being a set of rules or prescriptions which are then applied to practice, the code can now be better understood as itself an actor in the networks which perform the organization. How it is used and the potency it has will vary within each mode of ordering and which mode has the most powerful performativity. In any event, a code of ethics is neither irrelevant nor foundational but rather something embedded within organizational logics with varying degrees of potency. In the case of Enron, it is clear that the code whilst it existed as a material artefact had little or no work to do.

Second, a variety of non-human entities played a critical part in the actor-networks of Enron. These entities could even include Arthur Andersen's infamous paper-shredder.[36] More seriously perhaps, is the part played by the financial instruments such as the partnerships which enabled it to move debt off the balance sheet and the accounting procedures including for example, the now notorious 'mark-to-market' accounting that enabled Enron to report as revenue the total value of a deal over its projected lifetime. Without such an accounting instrument Enron would not have been able to report such fabulous profits. Even something like the internet has to be taken into account as a crucial actor that enabled Enron to become the largest online energy trader and eventually the largest e-commerce website in the world. It was this growth, coinciding with the dotcom boom fuelled by the growth of the internet, which pushed Enron's share price to fantastic levels but at the same time, the lack of profits – kept secret by the company – was a critical contributor to its final downfall.

This links to another point. The actor-network that was Enron was also constituted by connected networks beyond, yet also materially, part of Enron. These included not just the internet but, as we have noted earlier, banks, accountants, Wall Street, and ultimately global capitalism, itself an actor-network. Whilst all these networks beyond Enron reinforced the durability of itself as an actor-network, they at the same time, added to its complexity – a complexity which it could be argued countered the 'simplifications' necessary for its stability. Whatever else, this complexity increased the potential for unethical behaviour.

What can we say therefore about the place of ethics at Enron? First, we can see that ethical identities and behaviour at Enron were a matter of relationality. Whilst the morality or otherwise of executives such as Skilling and Fastow are not irrelevant in other contexts of understanding, it is the nature of the relations and how these relations worked throughout the whole organization that is more significant in understanding how ethics was performed at Enron. Relationality has to be understood as material in the sense that it was not really about what people at Enron *were* but more about what they *did*, which as we have seen was about making deals, ranking and yanking, moving funds into partnerships and engaging in 'aggressive accounting'. Thus we have a macho dominant ordering logic, inscription through the deal and risk without safeguards as the intermediary, all of this within wider actor-networks that rewarded this kind of behaviour.

In the same way as money can cease to be simply a medium of inscription and can become an end in itself, so too deal-making at Enron became a 'frozen organizational discourse' where deals came to be made for the sake of making deals. This happened because deals became not just a means of personal enrichment and profit for the company but also the mark of status and dominant positioning within the organization. They became in effect the currency of power and influence at Enron.

Furthermore, the more risky the deal the better.[37] It was the *quality* of the deal that counted, with quality measured by the degree of risk involved. Not only that, but the best risk was considered to be the one without safeguards. This pursuit of the risk-enriched deal can be seen in Enron's role in the California energy crisis of 2000–1. Leaked documents written by Enron's own lawyers seem to indicate that the company manipulated the crisis through its energy trading arm.[38] Here Enron's arrogance had become such that it was prepared to take on the wealthiest entity in the US, in the process setting up the beginning of the end for itself.

In this culture the line between ethical and unethical behaviour became completely blurred – not surprisingly, given that the management culture was one of pushing boundaries. The pursuit of risk through the deal and other instrumentalities ultimately led from an entrepreneurial logic, a dynamic required by contemporary capitalism,[39] into a logic where Enron 'performed' itself as a criminal, as well as an unethical, entity.

Without conclusions

'Being ethical can advance my career? You know, it's crazy enough, it might just work!'

It's not ethics until it hurts.[40]

I have tried to lay out in very broad terms a theorization that could be productive in understanding differently the place of ethics in organizations. In this way of understanding, ethics are embedded in the practices of organizations. Philosophical frameworks, codes of ethics, statements of values, moral rules, all take their place as actors, amongst other actors, human and non-human, in the actor-networks that constitute, or 'perform' the organization. But whether these embedded ethics are 'right' morally is another matter altogether. All one can say is that ethical behaviour is a feature of the complex order/disorder and stability/instability that 'performs' a functioning actor-network.

What I have not done, and indeed cannot do, is put forward recommendations about how organizations might do better ethically. As I noted earlier,

ANT does not enable this. It is in this sense that this story must be one without conclusions.

Certainly as far as contemporary capitalism is concerned it could be argued that Enron did 'do the right thing' and its failure lay not in behaving unethically but in over-reaching itself. This may seem cynical but equally, a case could be made that contemporary capitalism is hardly ever the model of ethical behaviour. Many would say that it is an environment that actually encourages corporate misbehaviour. As long as managers think they can get away with unethical behaviour the economically rational response will be to engage in it. This is what many would say accounts for what happened at Enron – except of course, the managers did not think they were behaving unethically. They thought they were making money just as everyone else was in those days. And of course Enron was not the isolated case. We have also had WorldCom, Tyco and in Australia HIH. No doubt, there will be others in the future.

However, Enron has been and gone. While lessons can and have been learnt from its collapse,[41] it is doubtful the events that led to its collapse could have been prevented even with stronger laws and a more robust code of ethics. And of course, even if these do exist and are enforced with the utmost rigour, there is always a downside in the stifling of the entrepreneurial dynamic without which contemporary capitalism would cease to be viable.

Notes

1 Bruno Latour (2002) asks the question: 'What makes you think that a study is always supposed to teach things to the people being studied?'. See www.ensmp. fr/~latour/articles/article/090.html.

2 For more on ANT, see John Law (1992) 'Notes on the Theory of the Actor-Network: Ordering, Strategy and Heterogeneity', Centre for Science Studies, Lancaster University. Available at www.comp.lancs.ac.uk/sociology.

3 According to Latour (1992: 241) actors are 'entities that do things'. This switches the emphasis from what entities are to what they do. Law (1999) adds that entities take their form and acquire their attributes as a result of their relationship with other entities.

4 A network is defined as 'a group of unspecified relations among entities of which the nature itself is undetermined' (Callon 1993: 263).

5 An actor-network can therefore be defined as 'a heterogeneous network of aligned interests'.

6 To talk of 'actors' itself poses an issue of inappropriate homogenization. ANT therefore understands an actor as not simply a 'point object' but as itself an association of heterogeneous elements.

7 Translation is the creation of an actor network. Translation refers to all the negotiations, intrigues, calculations, acts of persuasion thanks to which an actor (or force) takes, or causes to be conferred upon itself, authority to speak or act on behalf of another actor (or force). Translation always has a direction (Stalder 1997), http://felix.openflows.org/html/Network_Theory.html.

8 A translation must have a medium of translation or a medium into which it is inscribed. Inscription is the mechanism by which translations are 'embodied in

texts, machines, skills, which become their support, their more or less faithful executive' (Callon 1991: 143).

 9 A 'black box' is defined as 'that which no longer needs to be considered, those things whose contents have become a matter of indifference' (Latour 1981: 285). Anything that is now so stable that only inputs and outputs matter.

10 The irreversibility of an inscription depends to which it is impossible to get back to a situation where the translation was only one amongst a number of alternatives (Callon 1991).

11 An obligatory point of passage (or OPP) refers to what has to occur in order for all actors to satisfy the interests attributed to them by the focal actor. The latter defines the OPP through which other actors must pass and by which the focal actor becomes indispensable, http:carbon.cudenver.edu/~mryder/itc_data/ant_dff.html.

12 An intermediary is 'anything that passes between actors in the course of relatively stable transactions. It can be, among other things, a text, a product, a service or money' (Bijker and Law 1992: 25).

13 See Usher, R. (2002) 'Theorising the Research Environment through Actor-Network Theory', Conference on Quality in Postgraduate Research, Adelaide, April 2002.

14 In ANT a prescription is defined as 'what a device allows or forbids from the actors – humans and non-humans – that it anticipates; it is the morality of a setting both negative (what it prescribes) and positive (what it permits)' (Akrich and Latour 1992).

15 Even the whistle-blower, Sherron Watkins, could not be said to have been motivated entirely by ethical considerations. 'Watkins was not Enron's Mother Teresa. Ambitious like her peers, she worried about her future after an unsuccessful stint at Enron's failing broadband venture', see www.washingtonpost.com, 'Dream job turns into a nightmare', July 2002.

16 It is estimated that The crash of Enron's share price wiped out more than $US 60 billion of stock market investment, most in mutual funds and retirement accounts, see www.washingtonpost.com, 'Hidden debts, deals scuttle last chance', August 2002.

17 Houston Chronicle online, www.HoustonChronicle.com, 'Enron letters', February 2002.

18 In 2000 Enron paid out $US 750 million in cash bonuses. This amount was almost the same as the company's profits for that year.

19 From 'Enron traders caught on tape', June 2004, www.cbsnews.com/stories/2004/06/01/eveningnews.

20 See www.washington.post.com.

21 Enron at that point had 25,000 employees in 30 countries.

22 Including Wessex Water in the UK and the power project at Dabhol in India. In the latter Enron was criticized for its human rights record – for more see www.consortiumnews.com/2001/123001a.html.

23 In 1999, Enron invested in a risky Internet start-up called Rhythm NetConnections. The latter's stock price rose so dramatically that the investment was worth $US 300 million. Although Enron could not sell the stock immediately it counted the paper gain as profit. See www.washingtonpost.com, 'Visionary's dream led to risky business', July 2002.

24 For more on this see www.businessweek.com/magazine/content/01_51/b3762001.htm.

25 This has come to be known as 'Enronomics'!

26 See Financial Times online. 'Enron: the collapse', 18 November 2004, www.ft.com/enron.

27 Reported in www.cbsnews.com/htdocs/enron.

28 www.washingtonpost.com, 'Visionary's dream led to risky business', July 2002.

29 Houston Chronicle online, 'The pride and fall of Enron', October 2002, www.HoustonChronicle.com.

30 www.washingtonpost.com, 'Dream job turns into nightmare', July 2002.

31 Houston Chronicle online, 'Enron's implosion was anything but sudden', June 2004, www.HoustonChronicle.com.

32 www.washingtonpost.com, 'Hidden debts, deals scuttle last chance', August 2001.

33 Skilling's management style has been described as 'loose-tight'. He pushed executives to be creative in pursuing the big deal. 'Loose' meant taking risks. 'Tight' meant close control over critical parts such as online trading.

34 See http://en.wikipedia.org/wiki/California_electricity_crisis.

35 '[Skilling] pushed Enron to change constantly in a quest for the next new thing. Each annual report emphasized a different venture that would be its next big score', 'Dream job turns into a nightmare', July 2002, www.washingtonpost.com.

36 Arthur Andersen filled more than 18 large trunks and 30 boxes with shredded Enron documents. www.washingtonpost.com, 'Losses, conflicts threaten survival', July 2002.

37 'Stupid or not, Enron did it [make partnerships deals] and kept doing more like it, making riskier and riskier bets. Enron's top executives, who fancied themselves the best and the brightest, the most sophisticated connoisseurs of business risk, finally took on more than they could handle', 'Visionary's dream led to risky business, July 2002, www.washingtonpost.com.

38 It is alleged that a number of scams, all given colourful names, were used by Enron traders. 'Death Star' involved Enron being paid for moving energy to relieve congestion without actually moving any energy or relieving any congestion. 'Ricochet' allowed Enron to send power out of California and then resell it back into the state to avoid price caps that applied only to transactions within California. See 'Papers show that Enron manipulated California crisis', May 7, 2002, *Washington Post*, reported in www.commondreams.org and 'Enron is manipulating the California market' 05/08/02 in www.discussanything.com/forums.

39 According to Robert F. Bruner, professor of business at the University of Virginia: 'Enron was a product of its times. It became addicted to growth, and when real growth stopped took greater and greater risks to create the appearance of growth, 'Hidden debts, deals scuttle last chance', July 2002, www.washingtonpost.com.

40 IDG.net IS Survival Guide www.infoworld.com.

41 The US Congress in 2002 passed the Sarbanes-Oxley Act. Under Section 406 of the Act, companies are required to demonstrate a strong system of ethical procedures in all aspects of their operations and at all levels.

Chapter 9

Management ethics
and consumers

George Ritzer

Editors' introduction

George Ritzer is justly famed for a body of work that has opened consumption to as serious consideration, sociologically, as production has long enjoyed. In this chapter he switches focus to the ethical connection between the two worlds, seen in terms of the relations between figures such as the manager, employees and consumers. Typically, the ethics taken to govern these relations are those of mistrust: as he says, managers – and consumers – generally operate on the basis of such modern ethics as 'profit maximization' and 'buyer beware'. It is an ethic premised on exploitation as the norm; exploitation of employees in the expropriation of their labour power and exploitation of markets, and by extension, of consumers.

   Such ethics of exploitation are resolutely modern, yet today we live in times which have been post-modernized, theoretically. The plausibility of singular grand narratives is neither convincing theoretically nor practically. Thus, modern business ethics are indefensible in light of the postmodern critique and stand in contradiction to postmodern ethics. These ethics, after the work of Bauman's reading of Levinas, are generally considered to be founded on an ethic of being for the other, especially the other that is open to vulnerabilities such as exploitation. Thus, in this chapter, Ritzer seeks to position the modern manager as the subject of his analysis, and to suggest that such subjects should be willing to call their modern ethics into question. While this might strike those who are successful exploiters as a bizarre proposition, it might not seem so strange to those for whom the ethic of exploitation has failed; the corrupt, the chancers, the managers whose calculated gamble went belly up, whose public relations spin spun out of control, whose products proved fatal or at least injurious to health or damaging to society. For those alert to these pitfalls of normal business an ethic of being for the other, of genuinely being for the other – and not just a public relations campaign with that as the theme – could inadvertently contribute to the achievement of other organizational goals such as profit and reputation. That is Ritzer's proposition, which he explores in the following essay: that postmodern ethics provide a basis for the practice of a far more ethical business.

While postmodern social theory has now largely passed into – very recent – history, its effects linger in many places and ways. For example, it is nearly impossible to do social theory today in light of postmodern critiques of the grand narrative and totalizations, as well as ideas such as decentering and deconstruction. It is even more difficult to retain an ethical stance in social theory – and elsewhere – especially a modern sense of ethics, in light of postmodern revelations and critiques of such horrors as the Holocaust (Bauman 1989) and the Gulag Archipelago (Solzhenitsyn 1973) committed in the name of modern ethics. Thus, the mass murder of Jews and others in Nazi Germany was committed in the name of an ethic of racial purity. More recently, George W. Bush had the US military undertake a disastrous invasion of Iraq in support of an ethic of democracy.

Zygmunt Bauman (1993: 21) has defined a modern ethical code as 'a coherent set of precepts that ought to be obeyed by any moral person'. Such broad, if not all-encompassing, ethical codes seem naive and even ill-intentioned in light of the modern offenses committed in their name. Thus, Bauman – and many others – have turned away from such modern ethical codes. However, while many have given up on ethics altogether, Bauman – relying heavily on Levinas – has sought to develop a new, postmodern ethics. While we, in his view, can no longer rely on a modern ethical code, we can depend on our own subjectivity to help us make ethical judgements. Here, Bauman argues that as individuals we need to be *for* the other, especially others who are weaker than ourselves. What is good or evil in the relationship between a person and another is not determined by some larger ethical code, but needs to be worked out by the individual who, in Bauman's view, has an ethical responsibility to be for the other.

It is in this context that I would like to discuss the ethics, particularly managerial ethics, that are suggested by my work on consumption (Ritzer 2001), fast food restaurants and McDonaldization (Ritzer 2004a), credit cards (Ritzer 1995), the cathedrals of consumption (Ritzer 1999), and, more generally, the global proliferation of 'nothing' (Ritzer 2004b). I am particularly interested here in the problems traceable to these phenomena such as 'hyperconsumption', the 'temptation to imprudence' and 'loss amidst monumental abundance' – of 'nothing'.

The other in this case is the individual consumer,[1] especially the consumer of fast food and other franchised products, the credit card user – and abuser – the 'shopper' in any of the many cathedrals of consumption, and more generally the purchaser of nothing. However, our focus here is not on these others and their problems, but rather the need for someone – in this case management – in each of these domains to be for the other, the consumer. While we will focus here on the need to be for the consumer, it is also possible for management to be for still others in these contexts, especially those who work in them, particularly in low-status, low-paying, dead-end 'McJobs' (Royle 2000).

Obviously, a postmodern being for the other is a radical suggestion since managers – and consumers – generally operate on the basis of such modern ethics as 'profit maximization' and 'buyer beware'. That is, management is expected to look out for its own interests – and those of its employers – especially the profitability of its operations. It is supposed to maximize profitability which means that it is supposed to get all it can from consumers – and employees. It is the consumers' responsibility, in turn, to do what they can to be aware of what management is seeking to do and to limit the impact on them, especially what they pay for given products and services.

However, it is just such modern ethics that are called into question by postmodern thinking. After all, many consumer problems, including those mentioned above, are traceable to such modern ethics as buyer beware and profit maximization. Thus, these modern business ethics are indefensible on two grounds. First, they are modern ethics that are impossible to sustain in light of the postmodern critique. Second, they stand in contradiction to the postmodern ethic of being for the other, mentioned above, by not only not helping consumers but actually causing them great problems. Few managers and owners are going to be willing to call their modern ethics into question, but that is exactly what this chapter will ask them to do.

Interestingly, it could be argued that being for the other makes good business sense and would prove profitable to the companies that adopt such an ethic. That is, a number of companies suffer public relations disasters and economic losses because of their modern ethics of buyer beware and profit maximization. Public outcries over excessive charges, products that are harmful to the consumer's health and well-being, and the outrageously high pay of executives have led to huge problems for some companies. An ethic of being for the other, of *genuinely* being for the other – and not just a public relations campaign with that as the theme – could be a public relations bonanza that leads to increased business and higher profits.

An examination of some of the basic realities of the industries of concern here makes it clear that it is very difficult, to put it mildly, to find any evidence that management is currently for the other. That is, instead of being for the consumer, these industries are leading consumers into all sorts of behaviour that are having an adverse impact on them in many different ways:

- As documentarian Morgan Spurlock – among many others – has recently shown in 'Super Size Me',[2] the encouragement of excessive consumption of fast food – in his case McDonald's offerings – is dangerous to one's health.

- The aggressive marketing of credit cards to virtually everyone, but especially young people in college and even high school, is creating a *temptation to imprudence* (Ritzer 1995) among them – many adults are already quite imprudent when it comes to credit card debt – and is leading large numbers into a lifetime pattern of excessive spending and deficit financing.
- The *cathedrals of consumption* – shopping malls, mega-malls (e.g., Mall of America), superstores, and so on – are playing their role in a society increasingly characterized by *hyperconsumption* where people consume more than they want, should and can afford on the basis of their savings and current income. Consumers are led to place great stock in goods and services that almost always disappoint once obtained (Campbell 1987) and/or lead to ever-escalating expectations that in most cases cannot, in the long run, be satisfied.
- The global proliferation of consumer goods – most of which fit the definition of *nothing* (centrally conceived, controlled and lacking in distinctive content) – have set the stage for consumer dissatisfaction with the 'emptiness' of those products. Furthermore ever-escalating quantities of nothing are driving out those products we can think of as something – locally conceived, controlled, rich in distinctive content – with the result that consumers are faced with a sense of loss – of something – within the monumental abundance – of nothing.

If we deal with only these few domains and the set of problems delineated within each, we are in a position to address what an ethical management position might be on each of them.

We will approach this in two ways. First, we will adopt a modern point of view and discuss what a collective ethic that is for the consumer might look like and what it would lead to in terms of the issues mentioned above. However, this would be just another modern ethic from Bauman's perspective suffering from most, if not all, of the problems produced by all modern ethics. Thus, in the next section of the chapter we will discuss what a truly postmodern ethic of being for the other might look like in the case of management. As we will see, this is not a collective ethic, but rather one that focuses on the individual, in this case the individual manager, and the need for such an individual to be for the other, the consumer. Finally, we will turn to the issue whether there is any way that such a postmodern individual ethic can co-exist in the contemporary world with a modern collective ethic that has no interest in the well-being of the other.

As implied above, both a new modern ethic or a postmodern ethic would involve a radical reconceptualization of the role of management vis-à-vis consumers. Traditionally, management in capitalistic organizations focuses on profit maximization derived, in large part, from exploitation of *both* workers *and* consumers. In the early days of capitalism, the focus was on the exploitation of workers. Gradually during the twentieth century, the realization grew that consumers should no longer be left alone to muddle their way through the marketplace. Consumers had to be controlled and ultimately exploited[3] through advertising (Ewen 1976), marketing, the structuring of consumption sites, and so forth. The consumer came to be seen as fair game and there were few restraints – except for those enacted by the government, usually as a result of public uproars over the abuse of consumers – on what managers could do to maximize consumption and therefore sales and profits. Consumers were left to their own devices – save for the occasional Ralph Nader, Eric Schlosser, or Morgan Spurlock – and it was their responsibility to be sure that they did not fall prey to exploitative management practices.

While putting the responsibility for protection on the consumer sounds good in this neoliberal era, it is ultimately unfair since management has many more tools at its disposal than does the consumer. Take, for example, the work of the 'retail anthropologist' Paco Underhill (1999), and the insights he offers as a consultant – most settings employ their own in-house experts, as well – to those who own and manage consumption settings. For example, knowing that consumers almost always turn to the right when entering a shopping site means that that site can be structured to take advantage of that fact through, for example, product placement at the point at which customers make their customary right turn. And, management is far more organized to deal with the consumer, than vice versa. Indeed, consumers are virtually without organization of any kind and they certainly cannot afford to hire someone like Paco Underhill to help them.

We are led in a very different direction if we take seriously Bauman's idea of being for the other, the consumer. We begin with a modern approach which looks at management as a whole guided by a collective ethic of being for the consumer.

A modern ethic of being for the other

Rather than discuss such a modern ethic in general, let us look at some of the specifics of what it would mean for management as a collectivity to be for the other – the consumer – in each of the instances discussed above.

Fast food restaurants and other McDonaldized settings

Consumers experience a broad array of problems in the fast food restaurant that are traceable, at least in part, to the set of principles associated with McDonaldization (Ritzer 2004a) that inform it and many other sectors of society.

We can begin with the health problems associated with eating fast food to excess as detailed, most recently, in 'Super Size Me'. Of course, in discussing this, one immediately comes up against the ethic of buyer beware that contends that consumers are responsible for making themselves aware of the health effects of such food and therefore for not eating it to excess. The modern ethics of profit maximization and buyer beware mean that management in the fast food industry need do nothing to inhibit the excess intake of such food; indeed, the goal remains to get people to consume more and more of it. This whole issue was pointed up, among many other places, in those unfortunate lawsuits claiming that eating McDonald's food made consumers fat. The suits were tossed out on the grounds that consumers had the responsibility for knowing that much of fast food is fattening and for guarding against growing obese. While it is certainly the case that consumers should be aware of these and related facts, they often are not. In any case, the ethic of being for the other espoused in this section means that management in the fast food industry needs to do more about the health issue.

In fact, recent history indicates that management in the fast food industry has reluctantly been forced to go beyond buyer beware into accepting some responsibility for the health of the consumer. One example is the listing and public display of ingredients and levels of fat, cholesterol, salt and so on in various products. Then there is the increased offering of healthier alternatives to its traditional fare such as salads – albeit often with salad dressing that is loaded with fat and cholesterol. Finally, there is the recent example of McDonald's decision to eliminate 'super sizing' a variety of its products. Super sizing has the unfortunate consequence of adding super levels of all sorts of things that have, as Spurlock shows, disastrous consequences for people's health.

While there is precedent for fast food management taking responsibility for the well-being of its customers, it is clear that this has not gone nearly far enough – and is not likely to go further without public and government pressure. So what else could management in the fast food industry do, short of shuttering their restaurants or turning them into centers of veganism? Models can be found in the liquor and cigarette industries – although they, too, were forced to act – which lead to the following suggestions for a collective being for the other in this industry:

- Cease advertising to children, especially on cartoon programs aimed at them, often with toy promotions or movie tie-ins, where the goal is to lure them into a lifetime fast food habit.
- Get fast food restaurants out of locales that cater to children and young people, especially on college campuses and in and around high schools and grade schools.
- Put warning labels – I argued for this as early as 1993 in the first edition of *The McDonaldization of Society* (like those on cigarette packs) – on the windows of fast food restaurants, as well as on the packaging for major offenders – Big Macs, large fries, thick shakes, and especially

'value meals' that combine them all in super sizes – making the health hazards of such food abundantly clear to consumers.

- Have the fast food chains emulate the cigarette companies with campaigns aimed at warning the public of the health risks associated with their food.

A great attraction of taking actions like those listed above is that instead of being constantly criticized for amoral, if not immoral, actions, the fast food industry would be doing the right thing, at least from the point of view of the ethic of being for the other. This would be a public relations bonanza that might well lead to an increase in business, hopefully for healthier offerings. Furthermore, as things are, the fast food industry is likely to be *forced* into such actions in the not-too-distant future. Rather than waiting for that dreaded day, the industry would be far better off getting out front on this issue.

Turning to McDonaldized franchises in general, the major ethical problem stems from the dehumanization of these settings. That is, their basic characteristics – for example, their orientation toward efficiency and replacement of human workers with non-human technologies – tend to make them less human, or even non-human, settings as far as consumers are concerned. Being for the consumer in this case would involve an active effort not only to halt the trend toward dehumanization, but to engage in positive efforts to re-humanize these settings. For example, instead of deskilling franchise workers by, for example, introducing non-human technologies that control their actions or even perform many – or even all – of them, the idea would be to *re*skill and *re*empower those who work in franchises. This would allow customers to deal with more fully human employees rather than those who are increasingly robot-like. More specifically, employees should be allowed to develop their techniques of relating to consumers rather than relying, for example, on the scripting of their thoughts, words and actions. Changes like these would make it clear that franchise management is for the customer as well as the worker.

As before, the humanization of McDonaldized settings might well turn out to be a good business decision. For example, costly employee turnover might be reduced and less alienated workers might be far more productive. Humanization might also lead to an increase in business as customers decide that they want some human interaction with their purchase of blue jeans, T-shirts, or Big Macs.

Credit cards

A collective being for the other – in this case the credit card user – would mean several things for the management of the credit card industry, most generally a concern for the increasing indebtedness of the most coveted customer in the credit card industry – the 'revolver'. Revolvers do not, often can not, pay their bills in full each month and therefore must pay exorbitant interest rates that also make it difficult for them to pay off the principal in a timely manner, if ever. While it is in the interest of the credit card companies to reward those who do not pay their balances in full – e.g. by increasing their credit limit as an existing limit is approached – or even to lure people into such behaviour, it is generally *not* in the interest of the consumer to rotate balances and to pay the accompanying interest. Such indebtedness certainly allows them to consume various things that they might not otherwise be able to afford, but they often remain in debt long after the things they purchased have ceased to be of utility or interest and after the services they procure are half – if not entirely – forgotten.

A collective being for the other – 'revolvers' in this case – means discouraging, or at least *not* encouraging, their indebtedness. For example, a time limit – say six months – might be placed on repaying principal amounts – as well as accrued interest – much as charge cards like American Express insist that each bill be paid in full in a month. Such a course of action would be very costly to credit card companies in terms of lost interest payments and they would need to find a way of making up for the loss. My suggestion is that those who pay their bills in full each month be made to pay for the credit they receive – often for up to a month – and now get for free. In fact, under the current system, the free credit period enjoyed by these 'convenience users' is subsidized by the revolvers and their high and continuing interest payments. Having convenience users pay, at least in part, for their credit would ease the burden currently being placed on revolvers.

Another 'other' who should be of concern to the management of credit card companies is the young credit card user. The credit card companies have long targeted college – and to a lesser extent high school students – not only for their immediate business, but more importantly for their long-term involvement with credit cards and a life of debt. In this, they have been aided by many universities that allow the credit card companies to solicit students on campus, often associated with the opening of the semester or a major sporting event on campus, and with giveaways of T-shirts and the like. Furthermore, many universities have, in effect, gone into the credit card business in the co-branding of cards with major credit card firms. Even high schools have been in bed with the credit card companies by, for example, relying on course materials created by these companies in order to teach students about the 'responsible' use of credit cards.

Before turning to what management of credit card companies should do in this area, it seems clear that the main responsibility of universities and high schools is to their students and *not* to the credit card companies – and other commercial ventures – no matter how much income they derive from their association with those firms. Of course, educational institutions have been driven into this unfortunate situation, and many others, by government cutbacks in the funding of education. However, it is questionable, to say the least, for educational systems to deal with their economic problems by creating the conditions that will undoubtedly cause economic problems for their students, not only while they are in school, but for much, if not all, of their lives. Thus, in their case, being for the other means that educational institutions must divest themselves of their associations with the credit card business. Furthermore, they should develop their own materials and courses to better prepare students for dealing with credit cards and debt.

Of course, the same logic leads to the view that the credit card companies must cease their efforts to recruit students. More specifically, they must get off college campuses and cease contributing to high school curricula.

More generally, being for the other means that the management of credit card firms must desist from their aggressive recruitment of credit card users. Many people will undoubtedly find their way into credit use and debt without being cajoled by these firms, but the credit card companies are just too aggressive about this and make it too easy and attractive for people to use their products. Furthermore, once they have 'hooked' users, they are all too eager to offer more cards and to raise the credit limits on existing cards so that customers can plunge even more deeply into debt. Concern for the other would lead the management of credit card companies to limit, or eliminate, programs designed to lure people into obtaining and using credit cards.

A warning label, like those on cigarette packages, and suggested above for fast food restaurants, would also make sense for a credit card industry truly interested in the welfare of the other. The wording on every credit card might read something like the following:

> Credit cards may be hazardous to your financial well-being. They have been shown to lead people to spend more than is prudent and to lead a significant number of users in the direction of excessive interest payments and years of indebtedness from which many find it difficult to extract themselves.

Cathedrals of consumption

The cathedrals of consumption are closely related to the phenomena discussed above. That is, fast food restaurants and franchises more generally are themselves cathedrals of consumption and also often exist in larger cathedrals such as shopping malls and mega-malls. Furthermore, virtually all cathedrals of consumption would find it difficult, or impossible, to function without the use of credit cards – most obviously, online malls and shops could not exist without them. However, there is a whole other set of problems associated with the cathedrals of consumption, which also include superstores, discounters, theme parks, cruise ships and casino-hotels. All of the cathedrals of consumption are oriented to, and designed for, luring consumers to them and once they are in them, to engage in extraordinarily high levels of consumption; hyper-consumption. Being for the other here would mean that the management of cathedrals of consumption would at least warn consumers about the problems and dangers associated with hyper-consumption.

Of course, those who run cathedrals of consumption are likely to react to this suggestion by arguing that consumers should be allowed to consume at any level they wish. While this is difficult to argue against, we do know that there are all sorts of costs associated with hyper-consumption – most notably debt and the inevitable dissatisfaction that stems from a life focused on ever-escalating levels of consumption. Consumers need to be made aware of such problems and it is the responsibility of the management of the cathedrals of consumption that is for the other to make these and other problems clear to consumers.

While the above is controversial and few, if any, managers of cathedrals of consumption are likely to take such actions, far less controversial – although no more likely to be undertaken by the cathedrals of consumption – would be the idea that management must desist from, or at least make clear and public, its use of a variety of hidden devices designed to lead people to buy more than they need or want. Cathedrals of consumption are likely to employ consultants like Paco Underhill – and/or in-house experts – whose expertise lies in the area of creating mechanisms and conditions that lead consumers in the direction of hyper-consumption. For example, the previously discussed fact that customers usually turn to the right on entering such sites leads to the placement of products and structures to the right designed to exploit and take advantage of that fact. Then there is the huge shopping bag offered to customers on entering the stores of US clothing retailer Old Navy – and now other settings – that seems, on the surface, to be a kindly effort to be helpful. In fact, it is proffered because management knows that consumers can only hold so many garments in their arms; much more can be stuffed into those oversized bags. With such bags in hand, consumers are likely to buy more than they otherwise would. To add insult to injury, they are asked at checkout whether they would like to buy the very thing – the bag – that led to higher expenditures. This is akin to an executioner asking one about to be hanged if he would like to buy the rope to be used in the hanging! I doubt that Bauman would consider such an invitation being for the other.

Particularly egregious examples of this are to be found in casino hotels. For example, Las Vegas casinos abound with signs claiming that slot machines return, say, 95 per cent or even 97 per cent of everything bet on them. Gamblers are led by this to believe that the odds of winning are overwhelmingly in their favour and that they are highly likely to emerge winners. In fact, when they play slot machines, especially if they play for any length of time, the vast majority will almost surely lose. It is because of that fact that an increasing amount of floor space in virtually every casino is occupied by slot machines. Another is that the gambler does all the work – pushing buttons, pulling arms, gathering up the occasional coins that they win on any given play – with the result that few employees are needed and they are mainly there to be sure that the slots keep spinning ... and retaining the gamblers' money. Gamblers do all the work in a game they will almost inevitably lose. Once again, insult is added to injury.

Those who run cathedrals of consumption *for* the other would *not* have consultants like Paco Underhill and in-house experts and they would *not* put in place the kinds of structures designed to take advantage of knowledge of consumer behaviour – and would remove those that are already in place. While those who run such settings say they are merely giving consumers what they want, they are doing far more than that. In fact, they are taking advantage of their knowledge of consumer behaviour to get them to want – and more importantly to buy – much more than they want. Such additional sales may be good for the cathedrals of consumption, their sales, their profit margins, and the careers of managers, but they may not be so good for consumers who are led in the direction of hyper-consumption and in many cases debt to pay for all those goods and services.

Instead of touting things like deceptive winning percentages, casino management that is for the gambler would go a long way toward reducing excessive, even compulsive gambling by posting the actual odds of winning at various casino games. Alternately, they could make clear the actual house advantage on each type of game. A few years ago, a veteran Las Vegas taxi driver told me that less than 1 per cent of those he drove to the airport on their way home were leaving town winners – and that is probably an overestimate because there are those without enough money left to take a taxi. A posting of real odds on each casino's website and entrance, as well as on billboards at McCarran airport, would go a long way toward giving gamblers a much more accurate sense of their chances. Such postings would truly be for the gambler/consumer. Ironically, many gamblers will not be put off by such signs and the casino can feel assured that those who continue to gamble and lose have been better informed of the odds against them.

The purveyors of nothing

Most of the phenomena discussed thus far fit the definition of *nothing* – social forms that are centrally conceived, controlled and lacking in distinctive content (Ritzer 2004b). Were the purveyors of nothing for the other, they would portray what they have to offer as what it is – nothing. In fact, of course, they do exactly the opposite and make what they have to offer seem to be quite *something* – social forms that are locally conceived, controlled and rich in distinctive content. The pervasiveness of nothing, as well as efforts to make it seem like something, is well-illustrated by fast food restaurants, franchises, the other cathedrals of consumption, as well as the credit card industry.

It is important to remember that despite the wording, 'nothing' is not necessarily problematic or bad – just as 'something' is not inevitably positive. For example, pharmaceuticals – say, medications like Lipitor or Nexium – fit the definition of nothing, but for many people they are life savers. Nevertheless, if nothing itself is not necessarily a problem, the rampant proliferation of nothing around the world is. At one level, since all of the phenomena discussed above can be described as nothing, the problems mentioned in the context of the discussion of each of these phenomena are also problems posed by nothing. However, there are additional, more general, problems associated with the proliferation of nothing itself.

At the most general level, we are discussing the loss experienced by the other, the consumer, in a world increasingly characterized, even defined, by nothing. There are great profits associated with the production and distribution, especially globally, of nothing – infinitely greater profits than to be derived from the global distribution and sale of something. Thus, it is in the interest of manufacturers – and distributors – to reduce all that can be to nothing, or at least moved in the direction of the nothing end of the continuum, thereby increasing potential sales and profits. Large numbers of others – consumers – from all over the world are obviously eager consumers of nothing in its infinite varieties, but they also experience a loss – the loss of something. Nothing is, by definition, empty – of distinctive content – at its core, but, as we have seen, while it can be seen as a problem for the other, nothing is not necessarily problematic. However, what is problematic is the fact that nothing is proliferating wildly, often at the expense of something, so that, in the end, it is that something that is lost even amidst the monumental abundance of nothing.

Lest we think this is merely a problem for the less well-to-do, it is clear that the relationship between economics and nothing is far from simple or clear-cut. For example, while they are certainly more likely to be able to afford and experience something, the rich are increasingly inundated with, and attracted to, nothing, albeit expensive forms of nothing – Gucci bags, Rolex watches, Four Seasons hotels. Then there is the fact that the very poor in the world do not even have enough resources to afford nothing. In fact, their poverty 'dooms' them to something – e.g. home-cooked meals from scratch, native entertainment, and the like. It is those in and around the middle class who are most likely to live largely, if not almost exclusively, in a world of nothing.

Concern for the other would lead management in manufacturing, distribution and retailing to temper the rush to nothing and to find ways of supplying – and profiting from – something. Furthermore, the proliferation of nothing leads people – especially the youth – to lose a sense of something and the joys – and sorrows – to be derived from it. Of course, that sense is never completely lost – at least, not as yet – with the result that even those who find themselves deeply immersed in the world of nothing have a nagging sense of loss – a loss of something. Thus, concern for the other would lead those in a position to decide to work actively for the maintenance of something, clearly in a way that would be profitable to them.

A postmodern ethic of being for the other

The argument made in the preceding section is a modern one in which the case is made for the replacement of one modern collective ethic – profit maximization, buyer beware – by another – being for the other. While he would be for the idea of being for the other, Bauman would reject the idea of yet another modern collective ethic. All modern ethics seem desirable to those who create and support them and the above is no exception. Even the final solution to the Jewish problem was seen as desirable by those who created it, but as we all know it had disastrous effects, even for its supporters and implementers. Similarly, capitalist ethics of profit maximization and buyer beware are seen as desirable by capitalists not only for themselves, but society as a whole. However, we also know that capitalism has a wide range of negative effects, including many of those outlined above.

From Bauman's perspective, all modern collective ethics are undesirable. Furthermore, they are all coercive over individuals and Bauman objects to them on that basis as well. Thus, we need a postmodern ethic and that is one in which *individual* managers, *as individuals*, are *for the other*, the consumer in this case. They are not for the other because they are forced to be, but because they are led to be by their very nature as human beings; to be human is to be for the other. And the other need not, indeed should not, demand that an actor be for them. It is incumbent on a human being *qua* human to be for the other. And this being for the other occurs in face-to-face interaction between an actor and the other. One must be for the other in the company of the other. Thus it is not part of some general policy, nor is creating such a general policy enough.

What is required is for individual managers – be they in fast food restaurants, credit card companies, cathedrals of consumption, or other settings – to be for the other in their everyday actions. This can occur in concert with a collective ethic of being for the other like the one described in the preceding section, but that is not likely since such a collective ethic is neither ever likely to come to pass and in any case is not desirable from a postmodern perspective. This means that the individual ethic of being for the other must occur in the context of a collective ethic that is diametrically opposed to it.

This, of course, puts great, if not overwhelming, pressure on the individual manager. It would require individual managers to tell individual customers to *not* eat Big Macs, *not* rotate their credit balances, *not* play slot machines, and so on. They would need to do this in the face of a collective ethic that urges, no requires, that they push customers to maximize the number of Big Macs they eat, to go heavily into debt to the credit card companies, and to play the slot machines around the clock. Given this contradiction, the power clearly lies with the employing organization, the larger capitalist system, and the collective ethic of profit maximization/buyer beware. Thus, managers who follow a postmodern ethic of individually being for the consumer are at the minimum likely to see their careers suffer and more likely to lose their jobs.

This points up a real failing in Bauman's ideas. A postmodern ethic of the type he suggests is only viable in face-to-face relationships outside of most organizational contexts – the exceptions would be organizations that are collectively for the other, but such organizations are rarities and are all-but-nonexistent in the business context being discussed here. In virtually all organizational settings (e.g. a concentration camp, a capitalist business) a manager who is for the other (e.g. the inmate, the consumer) is, to put it mildly, likely to suffer grave consequences.

This seems to leave little room for a postmodern ethic among managers in contemporary businesses. The only obvious answer is a schizophrenic one involving the adherence to a modern ethic at work, and a postmodern ethic outside of the work context. This would mean, for example, that the same manager who during the day pushes credit card debt on unwary customers, advises them at night or on weekends in some free counselling centre on how to get out of debt and to refuse offers of greater credit – that might even be offered by him during the day – and therefore debt, in the future. This is a near-impossible situation that few could tolerate for very long, but it seems the only alternative for an individual manager who wishes to adopt a postmodern ethic within a workplace dominated by a modern collective one. The likelihood is that managers who are drawn to a postmodern ethic of being for the other are apt to leave quickly for other contexts – private business, a non-profit organization – where such an ethic is predominant or at least is not as much at odds with the collective ethic.

Of capitalists and consumers

Even to me, all of the above sounds high-minded and totally unrealistic. Of course, a discussion of these matters from an ethical point of view – even one involving a postmodern ethic – is bound to sound this way.

To capitalists, all of this is likely to sound quite naive. In their ethical system, they are merely doing what capitalists are supposed to do – produce and sell most profitably what consumers are willing to purchase. Thus, they see themselves as being guided, if not determined, by the dictates of the capitalist system and its consumers – and therefore, in their view, they are for the other, albeit in a collective sense. While there is certainly some truth to this, it ignores the fact that capitalists are agents, often quite powerful agents, who are not merely shaped by external forces, but are active creators and shapers of those forces. It is the capitalists who, for example, understand the great profits to be made from nothing, the need to distribute nothing globally, the need to convince consumers of nothing's worth, and the requirement of attempting to drive competing forms of nothing from the marketplace. Ultimately, capitalists are, by definition, modernists who are interested in themselves and their own welfare, and *not* the other.

Take Starbucks and its coffee (Schultz 1997). Admittedly, Starbucks sells reasonably high quality coffee, often quite better than the coffee that was being served in settings that it drove out of business, but that coffee – and the coffee shops – clearly meets the definition of nothing. Indeed, at its most basic, Starbucks is selling flavoured water. Early on, Starbucks realized that there were great profits to be earned from selling that particular form of nothing. In a few short years, of course, it has become a ubiquitous site not only in the US, but in many other countries – it seems to be *the* most common site in London's Soho, Piccadilly and Fleet street areas. Perhaps most importantly, it has developed a strategy of opening outlets in such great concentrations in certain areas that it drives the competition out – and inhibits other competitors from moving in – especially the small local coffee shop that can be thought of as something. To the degree that this strategy is successful, coffee consumers come to lose sight of the something-ness of local coffee shops and their offerings.

Thus, I reject the idea that capitalists, like those behind Starbucks, are innocents merely responding to the dictates of the capitalist system and consumers. In fact, they are actively shaping *both* by, among other things, systematically driving out competitors, especially those who offer something. If they were for the consumer, and true supporters of a capitalist system, they would want to sustain competitors, not destroy them. Furthermore, they would not charge such extraordinarily high prices for their flavoured hot water.

All of this must also sound naive to most consumers who not only clearly want the various forms of nothing, but are often fanatic devotees – e.g., the many devotees of Guess, Starbucks and McDonald's. While this is certainly true on the surface, I believe this ignores certain realities. First, I hypothesize that many consumers experience a nagging sense of loss – of something – amidst the abundance of nothing. Second, consumers generally ignore the billions spent on marketing, advertising and branding designed to get them to covet the various forms of nothing. Third, they are unaware of the role played, sometimes quite conscious and direct, by the forces behind the proliferation of nothing in the loss of something. Thus, many of the reasons behind the desire for nothing, and the lack of existence of alternatives to it, are traceable to these forces. In these and other ways consumers are unaware of the reasons they are drawn to nothing. If they were more aware of these things, they might be less drawn to nothing and more likely to seek out and protect the remaining forms of something.

More generally, consumers also tend to buy into a modern ethic that it is the task of capitalists to maximize profits and it is their responsibility to be wary of the capitalists. They do not expect capitalists and their managers to be for them and, indeed, would be shocked if they were, even if it was only after hours and the managers were doing volunteer work to help consumers.

The joys (and sorrows) of all this

It should be made clear that all of the phenomena discussed and critiqued in these pages offer much to the other, the consumer, who is quite pleased with most, if not all, of them. Many people have access to more consumables – some of them quite spectacular. The vast majority would be quite unconcerned with the ethical issues being discussed here. They would not understand the call for those in charge of production and consumption to act on their behalf. In fact, they probably think that they already do. Among the uncomprehending would be Richard North whose notion of 'ethical [pro-] capitalism' is virtually the opposite of the ethical view being espoused here. To him, and many others, the credit card and fast food industries, the owners of the cathedrals of consumption, and the global purveyors of nothing are doing much good; a great service to society and the world (see www. richarddnorth.com/10_propositions/ethical_capitalism.htm). In spite of such views, it is clear that there are great problems associated with consumption and it is necessary to discuss them from an ethical point of view.

I hold out no illusions about the arguments being made here. Most of those in charge of consumption are going to be uncomprehending, if not incredulous. The position taken here would require a paradigm shift on the part of management from self-interest and buyer beware to a concern for the consumer as other. It is a shift that few are going to make on their own, or even under duress.

Yet, we do have examples – cigarettes, alcohol – where management has been led on its own, or more likely forced by public opinion and external pressure, to a concern for the other. While most of this has in the past resulted from outside pressure, if not government legislation, it is possible, even advisable, for management to get out front on such issues rather than waiting for adverse publicity leading to public outcry and government legislation. For example, it seems only a matter of time before the government will be forced to take some action to deal with the adverse health consequences of fast food, or the efforts of credit card companies to lure people, especially young people, into debt. Such issues are already public relations disasters for some industries and some of the companies involved. Rather than be hammered for years to come over these and similar issues, and then be forced into submission, wouldn't it be better that they take action now on their own accord? An ethic of being for the other, modern or postmodern, would allow management to be more proactive on these and related issues, to avoid the negative publicity – and negative effects on the other – and, just maybe, to be even more profitable in the long-run because of public appreciation of their forward-looking action and the belief, likely for the first time, that management is genuinely looking out for their – the others' – interests.

At a more personally self-interested level, all of those involved in capitalist businesses–owners, managers, and lower-level employees – are also consumers. Indeed, most of us are both employees in, and consumers of, these businesses. Thus in being for the consumer, we are in a very real sense for ourselves.[4] This is true in both a very practical sense – we help ourselves to avoid going into excess debt or eating that which is likely to kill us – and also in the higher sense that we are behaving in an ethical manner. In that way, we have the best of both worlds since we serve our self interests – and those of the other – *and* we can feel good in the knowledge that we are behaving ethically.

Notes

1   My focus, as is Bauman's, is on the 'normal' consumer, but Bauman (1997: 14) is also concerned, as am I (see Ritzer 2001: 233–5), with the 'flawed', 'dangerous', or 'obscene' consumer, one who refuses to play the consumer game or who plays the game differently.

2   While this documentary is to be welcomed for the way it has raised public consciousness about the health dangers of fast food, it is in other ways quite scurrilous, for example, nobody recommends that one eat *nothing* but McDonald's fast food for a month.

3   The problem of consumer exploitation, at least in comparison to the exploitation of workers, poses considerable difficulties. It is easy to explain how workers are exploited, e.g. in Marxian theory they are paid far less than they produce, but much more difficult to explain how consumers are exploited, especially since consumers generally consume voluntarily while workers must work, often in the specific settings in which they are employed.

4   I would like to thank Bu Zhong for making this point clear to me.

Chapter 10

Conclusions

Possible ethics and ethical possibilities

Stewart R. Clegg and Carl Rhodes

We started this book with a concern with the meaning and practice of ethics in an era where corporate power, organizational complexity and managerial responsibility are all taking on new and expanded forms. We wanted to relate these issues to a question of what ethics ground organizing in today's institutional environment and what is the meaning of ethics for the practice of management and the organization of work and business today? It is such a question that is addressed by the contributors to the volume as they have reflected on some of problems and possibilities of ethics and managing.

In concluding, we will not summarize or reflect on each chapter: this would merely repeat what we and the contributors have said already. Instead, we consider some possibilities for ethics, and the study of ethics, engendered by this work and our reflection on the process of its production. To do so, we turn back to some intellectual issues raised by C. Wright Mills at an important turning point in contemporary social science. In his 1959 book, Mills inaugurated the idea of *The sociological imagination*. Concerned with the scientization of the social 'sciences', he stood opposed to all forms of social inquiry that plundered the world through 'smash and grab' raids with a questionnaire, and that rendered important social issues obscure and trivial. Mills' was a critique of rule-following methodological preoccupations at the expense of a sociological imagination that could connect private issues with public troubles. Such a situation was created, he claimed, by a social ethos requiring that for knowledge to be reliable and secure it must be developed using the procedures imagined in the laboratory. He felt that the development of the social sciences as a set of formalized techniques administered by experts had led to a dubious science, one in which those issues critically relevant to the public were neither understood nor attended to.

Mills retained a measure of optimism, despite his trenchant critique of a scholarly direction that did, if anything, intensify since his death in 1962. His optimism came from his faith in the 'sociological imagination', a term he used in relation to a 'quality of mind that will help [people] to use information and to develop reason in order achieve lucid summations of what is going on in the world and of what may be happening within themselves' (Mills 1959: 11). Such an imagination attends to the social relations between history and biography as well as between the political and the psychological. Most importantly, for Mills, the issue that the sociological imagination was to address was one where the domination of individualism as a social ethos meant that people were unaware of the connection between social and historical realities, and the often troubled experiences of their own lives. Mills' hope was that the holder of the sociological imagination would be able to understand society and history in relation to his or her own personal and inner life. In possession of this imagination the individual would be able to reconsider their past, to understand better the potential of their own life, and to remain astonished by the possibilities of the future.

Mills argued that this quality of mind was of critical importance in an era where the swiftness and vastness of social change was so great that no individual was outside its impact. He perceived these changes to be 'pervasive transformations of the very "nature" of man [sic]' (Mills 1959: 20). Mills described his era as one characterized by indifference, apathy and anxiety, where change had eroded traditional values without them having been fully replaced. The state of affairs was one where the ambiguity attendant on this structural gap was coupled with a feeling that the problems people faced remained poorly understood or formulated, let alone addressed. For Mills, the promise of the sociological imagination was primarily an issue for morality. As the fires of modernity were dying down, Mills bewailed a society where the ascendance of individuality as a prized social value had dulled the moral senses of those very individuals who held the value. The result, he felt, was a *moral stasis* characterized by the loss of established emotional and rational ways of being, yet ones whose replacements remained ambiguous.

Almost half a century after Mills outlined the promise of the sociological imagination, the requirement for it seems no less pressing. Rather than having equilibrated, social change has continued as an unabating series of upheavals resulting in a context where the moral ambiguities of the past, rather than being resolved, are replaced, time and time again, with newly ambiguous moralities. If, as Zygmunt Bauman argues, 'being moral means being bound to makes choices under conditions of acute and painful uncertainty' (in Bauman and Tester 2001: 46), then the ambiguity and volatility of our era suggest that morality is increasingly complex and challenging. This is an ethical crisis where the magnitude of human power has increased such that people's actions can have greater and more far reaching consequences than ever before, yet where no singular, accepted or authoritative set of ethical rules or principles are in place to 'solve' the crisis (Bauman 1993). For Bauman, the postmodern ethical condition that results is one in which 'we yearn for guidance we can trust and rely upon, so that some of the haunting responsibility for our choices could be lifted from our shoulders. But the authorities we may entrust are all contested, and none seems to be powerful enough to give us the degree of reassurance we seek' (Bauman 1993: 21).

As we described in our introductory chapter, part of the overall formulation of this book was to assemble a team of scholars, thinkers and writers from different academic disciplines and parts of the world so that each could consider the ethics of organizing in today's globalizing society. What we very much wanted to avoid, however, was to think of the people involved as a group of ethics 'experts' or 'authorities'. Instead, we put together an inter-disciplinary team that could bring some new thinking and insight into a consideration of ethics. We sought for the book to eschew the 'lazy safety of specialization' (Mills 1959: 28) that so often typifies the knowledge of professionalized business ethics and the practice of professional business ethicists. If, as it has been suggested, the instrumental rationalization of business ethics is antithetical to any considered or reflective notion of ethics (Parker 1998), then new ways of imagining that practice appear essential. Such imagining would question a techno-rational approach to the calculation of ethics, and instead integrate a form of affective imagination that might consider ethics in relation to the full weight of its socio-historical potency and its impact on persons.

What we have tried to do with this volume is to engender discussions of ethics and organizations that employ some sociological imagination without being confined to the technical and self-referential specialization either of sociology or of business ethics more narrowly. The book has been presented, both in and between the various chapters, from a variety of social scientific and philosophical disciplines, perspectives and approaches. Drawing connections between management practices and the organizational discourses that create – and are created by – them, is a matter of examining management and ethics in relation to its specificity, perspectivality and variety. That such conversations can be created is, we suggest, an important part of both what we have tried to exemplify and of the possible futures to which the study of management ethics might be directed. Such a project seeks to develop new and innovative ways of considering ethics and management so as to provide forms of knowledge informing thinking, practice, and thinking about practice. Such work has not been defined as the domain of ethical experts; instead we have sought to infuse a highly specialist discussion through the imagination to which we aspire, avoiding the development of authoritative ethical frameworks and replacing them with considered reflections on what is going on in the world. As Martin Parker suggests '[l]osing the certainties of ethical frameworks might actually sensitize us to ethical issues in a more helpful way' (Parker 1998: 294).

Our point of reflection in relation to management and ethics outside certainty draws on Derrida's thesis that considerations of the ethical must go beyond 'the programmable application or unfolding of a calculable process' (Derrida 1992: 24). The point to be made is that ethical deliberations do not 'involve perfect and clear knowledge and absence of [...] decision-making difficulties, but are themselves emergent in and even defined by the experience of double-binds' (Jones 2004: 53). As Derrida theorizes, ethics requires a necessary undecidability – a non-rational process of having to consider and deliberate over the various options and possibilities of action that are possible, and to take responsibility for choosing between them without recourse to action-defining codes. Choice means no rule, norm or model can guarantee ethicality. Rather than being rational and calculable, such a conception of ethics sees the choices that we make as being such that 'the instant of decision is madness' (Derrida 1992: 26) because moral choice must always interrupt the cognitive and rational deliberation which precedes it. Ethics passes through what Derrida calls the 'ordeal of the undecidable' because it is 'foreign to the order of the calculable and the rule' (Derrida 1992: 24).

If we follow the line of thought introduced above, what is required of social science is not rule- and model-based ethical normativism but rather the capacity to enhance thinking about ethics and the formulation of choice. The democratization of ethics increases moral sensitivity and reflection without foreclosing morality through the singularity of a rule. Where democracy is premised on individual freedom and choice within the context of a civil society, then the freedom and responsibility inherent in the undecidable is 'the condition of possibility of a democratic politics worthy of its name' (Jones 2004: 52). Such democracy requires that we are able to think through, conscientiously, the ethical concerns and conditions that are imbued in the power-laden organizational world in which we live. We should climb down from the comfortable judgmental high ground of moral conviction and certitude so as to engage fully in the uncertainties of the world and of the complex experience of living in it. Ethical democracy as a form of organizing 'calls for its own critique and ... admits the fundamental revisability, and openness to challenge, of its own self-understanding' (Fritsch 2002: 579). The completion of such an imaginative project of critique, responsibility, freedom and choice can never nor should ever be claimed to be achieved. If anything, what can be hoped for, to use a phrase from Derrida (1994), is a management ethics-to-come that holds an 'absolutely undetermined messianic hope at its heart [...] of an alterity that cannot be anticipated' (Derrida 1994: 64). Such an imagined ethics can only be an event subject to the unpredictability of the future – a condition similar to what Mills called 'astonishment' and what Derrida calls 'the unanticipated'. The position where such an ethics might be located is between the hope of the to-come and the knowledge made possible by imagination.

Mills referred to the sociological imagination as a *promise* – a promise to embrace the political task of social analysis to understand social historical structures and render them 'of direct relevance to urgent public issues and insistent human troubles' (Mills 1959: 28). Indeed, in ending this contributed book, while we may retain the hope of having contributed to such an analysis, we can only conclude that such a promise needs to be kept and to keep on being kept. Ethical questions are at the core of what modern organizations offer the world, in their modes of organizing. Indeed, it is essential that the ethical promise not be deemed completed in any specificity because it would entail the acceptance of a fatalistically pre-determined ethics; an eschatological ultimate destiny for ethics that would be one without choice and responsibility. Of course, should such things be avoided there would be no ethics at all. It is this irony that might indeed be able to keep an imaginative notion of ethics alive. Not a utopian dream of the resolution of all problems and an end to history but the ethical requirement of the necessarily incomplete pursuit of the keeping of a promise.

In place of nostalgia for moral certainty, it is perhaps the case that something like the sociological imagination is the measure with which we should manage the ethical challenges of postmodernity. Such an imagination would not 'expropriate the individual's right to moral choice' (Bauman 1993: 45), but rather provide a form of knowledge that would better enable that choice to be made. It is our hope that, in some humble way, this book might have contributed to such a form of knowledge and done something to exemplify the intellectual imagination at its best, through the promise of what C. Wright Mills proposed.

References

Agamben, G. (1993) *The Coming Community* (*Theory Out of Bounds*, Vol. 1), Minneapolis, MN: University of Minnesota Press.

Akrich, M. (1992) 'The de-scription of technical objects', in W. Bijker and J. Law (eds), *Shaping Technology, Building Society: Studies in Sociotechnical Change*, Cambridge, MA: MIT Press.

Akrich, M. and B.B. Latour (1992) 'A summary of a convenient vocabulary for the semiotics of human and nonhuman assemblies', in W. Bijker and J. Law (eds), *Shaping Technology, Building Society: Studies in Sociotechnical Change*, Cambridge, MA: MIT Press.

Aldridge, A. (1998) 'Reproducing the value of professional expertise in post-traditional culture: financial advice and the creation of the client', *Cultural Values*, 2 (4): 445–62.

Alford, J. and O'Neill, D. (eds) (1994) *The Contract State: Public Management and the Kennett Government*, Geelong: Deakin University Press.

Amin, S. (2003) *Más allá del capitalismo senil: por un siglo XXI no norteamericano*, Buenos Aires: Paidós.

Anscombe, E. (1958) 'Modern moral philosophy', *Philosophy*, 33: 1–19.

ATTAC (2002) 'Otra Europa es posible', in ATTAC (ed.), *Contra la dictadura de los mercados: alternativas a la mundialización neoliberal*, Barcelona: Icaria, pp. 147–56.

Attali, J. (1989) *Historia de la propiedad*, Barcelona: Planeta.

Babb, S. (2004) *Managing Mexico: Economists from Nationalism to Neoliberalism*, Princeton, NJ: Princeton University Press.

Bakan, J. (2004) *The Corporation. The Pathological Pursuit of Profit and Power*, New York: Free Press.

Balibar, E. (2004) *We, the People of Europe? Reflections on Transnational Citizenship*, Princeton, NJ: Princeton University Press.

Banerjee, S.B. (2000) 'Whose land is it anyway? National interest, indigenous stakeholders and colonial discourses: the case of the Jabiluka uranium mine', *Organization and Environment*, 13: 3–38.

Banerjee, S.B. (2001) 'Corporate citizenship and indigenous stakeholders: exploring a new dynamic of organizational-stakeholder relationships', *Journal of Corporate Citizenship*, 1: 39–55.

Banerjee, S.B. (2003) 'Who sustains whose development? Sustainable development and the reinvention of nature', *Organization Studies*, 24: 143–80.

Banerjee, S.B. and Linstead, S. (2001) 'Globalization, multiculturalism and other fictions: colonialism for the new millennium?', *Organization*, 8: 683–722.

Barnard, C.I. (1938) *The Functions of the Executive*, Harvard, MA: Harvard University Press.

Bauman, Z. (1989) *Modernity and the Holocaust*, Oxford: Blackwell.

Bauman, Z. (1991) *Modernity and the Holocaust*, Ithaca, NY: Cornell University Press.

Bauman, Z. (1993) *Postmodern Ethics*, Oxford: Blackwell

Bauman, Z. (1997) *Postmodernity and its Discontents*, Cambridge: Polity Press.

Bauman, Z. (1998) *Globalization: The Human Consequences*, New York: Columbia University Press.

Bauman, Z. (2002) *Society under Siege*, Oxford: Polity Press.

Bauman, Z. and Tester, K. (2001) *Conversations With Zygmunt Bauman*, Cambridge: Polity Press.

Baume, M. (2002), 'You can't legislate for boardroom integrity', *Australian Financial Review*, 4 November: 55.

Beck, U. and Beck-Gernsheim, E. (2002) *Individualization: Institutionalized Individualism and its Social and Political Consequences*, London: Sage.

Beck, U., Giddens, A. and Lash, S. (1994) *Reflexive Modernisation: Politics, Tradition and Aesthetics in the Modern Social Order*, Cambridge: Polity Press.

Bello, W. (2001) *The Future in the Balance: Essays on Globalization and Resistance*, Oakland: Food First Books.

Bendix, R. (1952) 'Compliant behaviour and individual personality', *American Journal of Sociology*, 58: 292–303.

Bergesen, A. and Fernández, R. (1999) ¿Quién posee las 500 empresas líderes mencionadas por *Fortune*?, in J. Saxe-Fernández (ed.) *Globalización: crítica a un paradigma*, Mexico: UNAM/Plaza and Janés, pp. 247–87.

Berle Jr., A.A. and Means, G.C. (1968) *The Modern Corporation and Private Property*, New York: Harcourt, Brace and World.

Bijker, W. and J. Law (1992) *Shaping Technology/Building Society*, Cambridge, MA: MIT Press.

Birch, D. (2001) 'Corporate citizenship: rethinking business beyond corporate social responsibility', in J. Andriof and M. McIntosh (eds) *Perspectives on corporate citizenship*, Sheffield: Greenleaf Publishing, pp. 53–64.

Bourdieu, P. (1984) *Distinction: A Social Critique of the Judgement of Taste*, London: Routledge and Kegan Paul.

Bovens, M. (1998) *The Quest for Responsibility: Accountability and Citizenship in Complex Organisations*, Cambridge: Cambridge University Press.

Bowman, S.R. (1996) *The Modern Corporation and American Political Thought: Law, Power, and Ideology*, University Park, PA: Penn State University Press.

Braithwaite, J. (1998) 'Institutionalizing distrust, enculturating trust', in V. Braithwaite and M. Levi (eds) *Trust and Governance*, New York: Russell Sage, pp. 343–75.

Brechin, A. and Swain, J. (1988) 'Professional/client relationships: creating a "working alliance" with people with learning difficulties', *Disability and Society*, 3: 213–26.

Brotherton, J.M. (2004) 'Internet is indeed useful source for patients with cancer', *British Medical Journal*, 10 April 2004, 328 (7444): 898.

Brunsson, N. (1989) *The Organization of Hypocrisy: Talk, Decisions and Actions in Organizations*, Chichester: John Wiley.

Burnham, J. (1960) *The Managerial Revolution*, Bloomington, IN: Indiana University Press.

Cacciari, M. (1998) *Der archipel Europa*, Cologne: Dumont.

Callon, M. (1986a) 'The sociology of an actor-network: the case of the electric vehicle', in M. Callon, J. Law and A. Rip (eds), *Mapping the Dynamics of Science and Technology*, London: Macmillan.

Callon, M. (1986b) 'Some elements of a sociology of translation: domestication of the scallops and the fishermen of St. Brieuc Bay', in J. Law (ed.) *Power, action and belief*, London: Routledge and Kegan Paul.

Callon, M. (1987) 'Society in the making: the study of technology as a tool for sociological analysis', in W. Bijker, T. Hughes and T. Pinch (eds), *The Social Construction of Technological Systems*, Cambridge, MA: MIT Press.

Callon, M. (1991) Techno-economic network and irreversibility, in J. Law (ed.) *A sociology of monsters: Essays on power, technology and domination*, London: Routledge.

Callon, M. (1993) 'Variety and irreversibility in networks of technique conception and adoption', in D. Foray and C. Freeman (eds), *Technology and the Wealth of Nations*, London: Pinter.

Campbell, C. (1987) *Romantic Ethic and the Spirit of Modern Consumerism*, Oxford: Blackwell.

Cantell, T. and Pedersen, P.P. (1993) 'Modernity, postmodernity and ethics: an interview with Zygmunt Bauman', *Telos*, Fall.

Capgemini/Merrill Lynch (2004) *World Wealth Report 2004*, New York: Capgemini/Merrill Lynch.

Capra, F. (1989) *Uncommon Wisdom: Conversations with Remarkable People*, New York: Bantam Books.

Carlin, J. (1966) *Lawyers' Ethics: Survey of the New York City Bar*, New York: Russell Sage Foundation.

Carroll, A.B. (1979) 'A three-dimensional conceptual model of corporate social performance', *Academy of Management Review*, 4: 497–505.

Cash, C.D. (2005) 'Suicide risk management: foreseeing future problems', *Behavioral Health Management*, March/April 2005: 21.

Cassirer, E. (1967) *The question of J. J. Rousseau*, Bloomington, IN: Indiana University Press.

Cavanagh, J. and Mander, J. (eds) (2004) *Alternatives to Economic Globalization: A Better World is Possible*, San Francisco, CA: Berrett-Koehler.

Chossudovsky, M. (2003) *The Globalization of Poverty and the New World Order*, Pincourt: Global Outlook.

Clark, F. and Dean, G. (2001) 'Corporate collapse analysed', in *Collapse Incorporated: Tales, Safeguards and Responsibilities of Corporate Australia*, Sydney: CCH Australia, pp. 71–98.

Clark, F. and Dean, G. (2002) 'Legislators and regulators have failed to get the principles right', *Australian Financial Review*, 7 November: 71.

Clegg, S. (2003) 'Managing organization futures in a changing world of power/knowledge', in H. Tsoukas and C. Knudsen (eds) *The Oxford Handbook of*

Organization Theory: Meta-theoretical Perspectives, New York: Oxford University Press, pp. 536–67.

Cohen, S. (1999) '"Good ethics is good business" – revisited', *Business and Professional Ethics Journal*, 18 (2): 57–68.

Cohen, S. (2004) *The Nature of Moral Reasoning: The Framework and Activities of Ethical Deliberation, Argument, and Decision-Making*, Sydney: Oxford University Press.

Condren, C. (1998) 'Sidney Godolphin and the Free Rider', *Business and Professional Ethics Journal*, 17 (4): 5–19.

Cordella, A. and M. Shaikh (2003) 'Actor network theory and after: what's new for IS research?', *European Conference on Information Systems*, online, available at http://is.lse.ac.uk/homepages/shaikh/ANT%20ECIS%20FINAL%20VERSION%2031%20March.pdf.

Cortés, F., Hernández, D., Hernández, E., Székely, M. and Vera, H. (2002) *Evolución y características de la pobreza en México en la última década del siglo XX*, Mexico: SEDESOL, online, available at www.e-local.gob.mx/wb2/ELOCAL/ELOC_Evolucion_y_caracteristicas_de_la_pobreza_en_.

Cunningham, L. (1999) 'Corporate governance roundtable', *Cornell Law Review*, 84: 1289–95.

Cushman, M., Venters, Y., Cornford, T. and Mitev, N. (2002) 'Understanding sustainability as knowledge practice', *British Academy of Management Conference: Fast-Tracking Performance through Partnerships*, 9–11 September 2002, London.

Dahl, R.A. (1973) 'Governing the giant corporation', in R.J. Nader and M.J. Green (eds), *Corporate Power in America*, New York: Grossman Publishers.

Dawkins, K. (1997) *Gene Wars: The Politics of Biotechnology*, New York: Seven Stories Press.

de la Garza, M.T. (2002) *Política de la memoria: Una mirada sobre Occidente desde el margen*, Barcelona: Anthropos/UIA.

Demmers, J., Hogenboom, B. and Fernández, A.E. (eds) (2001) *Miraculous Metamorphoses: The Neoliberalization of Latin American Populism*, London: Zed Books.

Derber, C. (1998) *Corporation Nation*, New York: St Martin's Griffin.

Derrida, J. (1992) 'Force of law: the mystical foundation of authority', in D. Cornell, M. Rosenfeld and D.G. Carlson (eds), *Deconstruction and the Possibility of Justice*, London: Routledge, pp. 3–67.

Derrida, J. (1994) *Specters of Marx: The State of the Debt, the Work of Mourning, and the New International*, New York: Routledge.

Derrida, J. (1995) *The Gift of Death*, Chicago, IL: Chicago University Press.

Desmond, J. (1998) 'Marketing and moral indifference', in M. Parker (ed.), *Ethics and Organization*, London: Sage, pp. 173–96.

Devisch, I. (2003) *Wij. Jean-Luc Nancy en het vraagstuk van de gemeenschap in de hedendaagse wijsbegeerte*, Leuven, Belgium: Peeters.

Dewandre, N. (2002) *Critique de la raison dialectique*, Paris: Seuil.

Dewey, J. (1926) 'The historic background of corporate legal personality', *Yale Law Journal*, 35: 655–73.

Dow Jones (2000) *Dow Jones Sustainability Index*, online, available at www.dowjones.com/djsgi/index/concept.html, accessed, 1 April 2004.

Drucker, P. (1981) 'What is "business ethics"?', *The Public Interest*, 63: 18–36.

du Gay, P. (2000) *In Praise of Bureaucracy: Weber, Organization, Ethics*, London: Sage.

Duggar, W.M. (1989). *Corporate Hegemony*, Westport, CT: Greenwood Publishing.

Dussel, E. (1995) *Invention of the Americas: Eclipse of 'the Other' and the Myth of Modernity*, New York: Continuum International Publishing Group.

Dussel, E. (1997) 'Modernidad, globalización y exclusión', in H. Dieterich (ed.) *Globalización, exclusión y democracia en América Latina*, Mexico: Joaquín Mortiz, pp. 75–98.

Dussel, E. (2002) 'World-system and "trans"-modernity', *Nepantla: Views from the South*, 3: 221–44.

Dutt, R. (1970) *India Today*, New Delhi: Navjivan Press.

Dylan, B. (1963) With God on our side, *The Times They are A-changing*, CBS Records.

Elias, N. (1983) *The Court Society*, Oxford: Basil Blackwell.

Elias, N. (1991) *The Society of Individuals*, Oxford: Basil Blackwell.

Elias, N. (1996) *The Germans: Studies of Power Struggles and the Development of Habitus in the 19th and 20th Centuries*, Cambridge: Polity Press.

Elias, N. (2000/1939) *The Civilizing Process*, Oxford: Basil Blackwell.

Elliott, P. (1972) *The Sociology of the Professions*, London: Macmillan.

Enron (2002) *Corporate Responsibility Annual Report*, online, available at www.enron.com/corp/pressroom/responsibility/CRANNUAL.pdf, accessed 1 August 2003.

Entine, J. (1995) 'Rain-forest chic', *Toronto Globe and Mail Report on Business*, October: 41–52.

Etzioni, A. (1964) *Modern Organizations*, Englewood Cliffs, NJ: Prentice-Hall.

Ewen, S. (1976) *Captains of Consciousness: Advertising and the Social Roots of the Consumer Culture*, New York: McGraw-Hill.

Fineman, S. (1998) 'The natural environment, organization and ethics', in M. Parker (ed.) *Ethics and Organizations*, London: Sage, pp. 238–52.

Fish, S. (1999) *The Trouble with Principle*, Cambridge, MA: Harvard University Press.

Florescano, E. (1994) *Memory, Myth, and Time in Mexico: From the Aztecs to Independence*, Austin, TX: University of Texas Press.

Florescano, E. (2000) *Memoria mexicana*, Mexico: Fondo de Cultura Económica.

Flores-Olea, V. and Mariña, A. (2004) *Crítica de la globalidad: Dominación y liberación en nuestro tiempo*, Mexico: Fondo de Cultura Económica.

Flynn, R. (2002) 'Clinical governance and governmentality', *Health, Risk and Society*, 4: 155–73.

Forrester, V. (1999) *The Economic Horror*, Oxford: Blackwell.

Foucault, M. (1997) *Ethics, Subjectivity and Truth*, New York: The New Press.

Foucault, M. (2000) 'The subject and power', in M. Foucault (edited by J. D. Faubion) *Power. Essential Works of Foucault, 1954–1984, Vol. III*, New York: The New Press, pp. 326–48.

Foucault, M. (2003) 'The birth of biopolitics', in P. Rabinow and N. Rose (eds), *The Essential Foucault*, New York: The New Press, pp. 202–7.

Foxley, A. (1983) *Latin American Experiments in Neoconservative Economics*, Berkeley, CA: University of California Press.

Frank, T. (2001) *One Market under God: Extreme Capitalism, Market Populism and the End of Economic Democracy*, New York: Anchor Books.

Friedman, M. (1962) *Capitalism and Freedom*, Chicago, IL: The University of Chicago Press.

Friedman, M. and Friedman, R. (1990) *Free to Choose. A Personal Statement*, New York: Harcourt.

Fritsch, M. (2002) 'Derrida's democracy to come', *Constellations*, 9: 574–97.

Frooman, J. (1999) 'Stakeholder influence strategies', *Academy of Management Review*, 24: 191–205.

Fuentes, C. (1997) *Por un progreso incluyente*, Mexico: IEESA.

Galeano, E. (1998) *Open veins of Latin America: Five Centuries of the Pillage of a Continent*, New York: Monthly Review Press.

Gallant, M.H., Beaulieu, M.C. and Carnevale, F.A. (2002) 'Partnership: an analysis of the concept within the nurse–client relationship', *Journal of Advanced Nursing*, 40: 149–57.

Gamble, A. (1996) *Hayek: The Iron Cage of Liberty*, Hong Kong: Westview Press.

George, S. and Sabelli, F. (1994) *Faith and Credit: The World Bank's Secular Empire*, Boulder, CO: Westview Press.

Gibbons, M., Limoges, C. and Nowotny, H. (1994) *The New Production of Knowledge*, London: Sage.

Giddens, A. (1992) *The Transformation of Intimacy: Sexuality, Love and Eroticism in Modern Societies*, Cambridge: Polity Press.

Ginzburg, C. (1980) *The Cheese and the Worms: The Cosmos of a Sixteenth-century Miller*, London: Routledge and Kegan Paul.

Glasbeek, H. (2002) *Wealth by Stealth: Corporate Crime, Corporate Law, and the Perversion of Democracy*, Toronto: Between the Lines.

Goffman, E. (1959) *The Presentation of Self in Everyday Life*, New York: Anchor Books.

González, R. (2003) 'Ruinoso, privatizar empresas; costó el triple rescatarlas: Los fracasos de particulares han costado al país 109 mil 214 mdd', *La Jornada*, Mexico, July 25.

González, R. (2004a) 'El rescate bancario, tan oneroso como los ataques de EU a Irak', *La Jornada*, Mexico, July 28.

González, R. (2004b) 'Las remesas de EU mantienen el consumo interno en México', *La Jornada*, Mexico, February 4.

Grace, D. and Cohen, S. (2005) *Business Ethics: Problems and Cases*, 3rd edn, Melbourne: Oxford University Press.

Grantham, R. and Rickett, C. (1998) 'The bootmaker's legacy to company law doctrine', in C.E.F. Rickett and R.B. Grantham (eds), *Corporate Personality in the Twentieth Century*, Oxford: Hart Publishing.

Gray, J. (2000) *False Dawn: The Delusions of Global Capitalism*, New York: The New Press.

Grice, S. and M. Humphries (1997) 'Critical management studies in postmodernity: oxymorons in outer space?', *Journal of Organization Change Management*, 10: 412–25.

Grugulis, I., Vincent, S. and Hebson, G. (2002) *The Future of Professional Work? The Rise of the 'Network Form' and the Decline of Discretion*, Working paper no. 24, ESRC Future of work Programme, University of Salford, Salford.

Guillén, H. (1997) *La contrarrevolución neoliberal en México*, Mexico: Era.

Gurevitch, Z. (2000) Plurality in dialogue: A comment on Bakhtin, *Sociology*, 34: 243–63.

Hardt, M. and A. Negri (2004) *Multitude: War and Democracy in the Age of Empire*, New York: Penguin Press.

Harvard Law Review (1989) *Incorporating the Republic: The Corporation in Antebellum Political Culture, 1883–1903*, Harvard, MA: Harvard Law Review.

Harvey, D. (2003) *The New Imperialism*, Oxford: Oxford University Press.

Hawken, P. (1995) *The Ecology of Commerce: A Declaration of Sustainability*, London: Phoenix.

Hawley, S. (2000) 'Exporting corruption: privatization, multinationals and bribery', *Briefing*, 19: 1–24.

Hayek, F.A. (1978) *Constitution of Liberty*, Chicago, IL: University of Chicago Press.

Hayek, F.A. (1990a) *Law, Legislation and Liberty, Vol. 1. Rules and Order*, Chicago, IL: University of Chicago Press.

Hayek, F.A. (1990b) *Law, Legislation and Liberty, Vol. 2. The Mirage of Social Justice*, Chicago, IL: University of Chicago Press.

Hendry, J. (2001) 'After Durkheim: an agenda for the sociology of business ethics', *Journal of Business Ethics*, 34: 209–18.

Hertz, N. (2001) *The Silent Takeover: Global Capitalism and the Death of Democracy*, London: Arrow.

Hessen, R. (1979) *In Defense of the Corporation*, Stanford, CA: Hoover Institution Press.

Hirschman, A.O. (1977) *The Passions and the Interests: Political Arguments for Capitalism before its Triumph*, Princeton, NJ: Princeton University Press.

Holmes, S. (1994) 'Liberalism for a world of ethnic passions and decaying states', *Social Research*, 61: 598–609.

Holmes, S. (1995) *Passions and Constraint: On the Theory of Liberal Democracy*, Chicago, IL: University of Chicago Press.

Holmström, J. and D. Robey (2002) *Inscribing Organizational Change with Information Technology: An Actor Network Theory Approach*, online, available at www.idi.ntnu.no/~ericm/ant.FINAL.htm.

Horton, J. and Mendus, S. (1994) 'Alasdair MacIntyre: after virtue and after', in J. Horton and S. Mendus (eds), *After MacIntyre: Critical Perspectives on the Work of Alasdair MacIntyre*, Cambridge: Polity Press, pp. 1–15.

Huffington, A. (2003) *Pigs at the Trough. How Corporate Greed and Political Corruption are Undermining America*, New York: Crown Publishers.

Huntington, S.P. (1997) *Clash of Civilizations and the Remaking of World Order*, New York: Simon and Schuster.

Ibarra-Colado, E. (1998) 'Neoliberalismo, educación superior y ciencia en México', in E. Ibarra-Colado (ed.), *La universidad ante el espejo de la excelencia*, Mexico: Universidad Autónoma Metropolitana-Iztapalapa, pp. 117–82.

Ibarra-Colado, E. (2002) 'Organizational paradoxes and business ethics: in search of new modes of existence', in S. Clegg (ed.), *Management and Organization Paradoxes*, Amsterdam: John Benjamins, pp. 165–84.

Ibarra-Colado, E. (2005) 'Origen de la *empresarialización* de la universidad: el pasado de la gestión de los negocios en el presente del manejo de la universidad', *Revista de la Educación Superior*, 34: 13–37.

Ibarra-Colado, E. (2006) 'Organization studies and epistemic coloniality in Latin America: thinking otherness from the margins', *Organization*, 13: (forthcoming).

Ireland, P. (1999) 'Company law and the myth of shareholder ownership', *Modern Law Review*, 62: 32.

Iterson, A. van, Mastenbroek, W., Newton, T. and Smith, D. (eds) (2002) *The Civilized Organization: Norbert Elias and the Future of Organization Studies*, Amsterdam: John Benjamins.

Jackall, R. (1988) *Moral mazes: The World of Corporate Managers*, New York: Oxford University Press.

Jackson, T. (2000) 'Management ethics and corporate policy: a cross-cultural comparison', *Journal of Management Studies*, 37: 349–69.

Jacoby, S.M. (1997) *Modern manors: Welfare Capitalism since the New Deal*, Princeton, NJ: Princeton University Press.

Johnson, P. and Smith, K. (1999) 'Contextualizing business ethics: anomie and social life', *Human Relations*, 52: 1351–75.

Johnson, T. (1972) *Professions and Power*, London: Macmillan.

Jones, C. (2004) 'Jacques Derrida', in S. Linstead (ed.), *Organization Theory and Postmodern Thought*, London: Sage, pp. 34–63.

Jones, C., Parker, M. and ten Bos, R. (2005) *For Business Ethics*, London, Routledge.

Jones, M. (2003) 'Beyond discretion: re-casting professionalism in social work', in L. Briskman and M. Muetzelfeldt (eds), *Moving Beyond Managerialism in Human Services*, Melbourne: RMIT Publishing.

Jones, M. (2004) 'Supervision, learning and transformative processes', in N. Gould and M. Baldwin (eds), *Social Work, Critical Reflection and the Learning Organisation*, Aldershot: Ashgate.

Kaulingfreks, R. and ten Bos, R. (2005) 'Are organizations bicycles? On hosophobia and neognosticism in organizational thought', *Culture and Organization*, 11: 83–96.

Kerbaj, R. (2005) 'Forget the doctor: now the internet makes house calls', *Australian Financial Review*, 9–10 April 2005: 27.

Kingwell, M. (2003) *Practical Judgments. Essays in Culture, Politics, and Interpretation*, Toronto: Toronto University Press.

Kirkpatrick, D.L. (1975) *Techniques for Evaluating Training Programs*, Alexandria, VA: ASTD.

Knights, D. (1992) 'Changing spaces: the disruptive impact of a new epistemological location for the study of management', *Academy of Management Review*, 17: 514–36.

Korten, D. (1995) *When Corporations Rule the World*, Bloomfield, CT: Kumarian Press.

Korten, D.C. (1999) *The Post-corporate World: Life after Capitalism*, San Francisco, CA: Berrett-Koehler.

Kristof, K.M. (2003) 'Study ties biggest CEO raises to largest layoffs', *Los Angeles Times*, 26 August, B4.

Kroll, L. and Goldman, L. (2005) 'The world's billionaires', *Forbes.com*, online, available at www.forbes.com/2005/03/09/bill05land.html.

Krugman, P. (2003) *The Great Unraveling: Losing our Way in the New Century*, New York: W. W. Norton and Company.

Küng, H. (1998) *Global Ethic for Global Politics and Economics*, New York: Oxford University Press.

Kymlicka, W. (2002) *Contemporary Political Philosophy*, 2nd edn, Oxford: Oxford University Press.

Latour, B. (1986) *The Pasteurisation of France*, Cambridge, MA: Harvard University Press.

Latour, B. (1991) *Technology is Society Made Durable*, London: Routledge.

Latour, B. (1992) 'The sociology of a few mundane artefacts', in W. Bijker and J. Law (eds), *Shaping Technology/Building Society*, Cambridge, MA: MIT Press.

Latour, B. (2002) *A Prologue in the Form of a Dialogue Between a Student and his (somewhat) Socratic Professor*, online, available at www.ensmp.fr/~latour/articles/article/090.html.

Law, J. (1997) *The Manager and his Powers*, Lancaster: Lancaster University, Centre for Science Studies, online, available at www.comp.lancs.ac.uk/sociology.

Law, J. (1999) 'Actor network theory and after', *Sociological Review*, Special Issue, J. Law and J. Hassard: 1–14.

Letiche, H. (1998) 'Business ethics: (in-)justice and (anti-)law – reflections on Derrida, Bauman and Lipovetsky', in M. Parker (ed.), *Ethics and Organizations*, London: Sage, pp. 122–49.

Levy, A.B. (1998) *Private Corporations and their Control*, London: Routledge.

Linossier, P. (2000) 'The view from inside: managing competition and market constraints', paper presented at the conference: *Playing the market game? Governance models in child and youth welfare: International experiences – perspectives for Germany*, University of Bielefeld, 9–11 March 2000.

Lozano, W. (2005) 'La izquierda latinoamericana en el poder: interrogantes sobre un proceso en marcha', *Nueva Sociedad*, 197: 129–45.

Lubit, R. (2001) 'Tacit knowledge and knowledge management: the keys to sustainable competitive advantage', *Organizational Dynamics*, 29: 164–79.

Lyotard, J.-F. (1979) *The Postmodern Condition: A Report on Knowledge*, Manchester: Manchester University Press.

MacIntyre, A. (1981) *After Virtue: A Study in Moral Theory*, Notre Dame, IN: University of Notre Dame Press.

MacIntyre, A. (1988) *Whose Justice? Which Rationality?* London: Duckworth.

MacLeod, D. (2004) *Downsizing the State: Privatization and the Limits of Neoliberal Reform in Mexico*, Philadelphia, PA: Pennsylvania State University Press.

Mantziaris, C. (1999) 'The dual view theory of the corporation and the Aboriginal corporation', *Federal Law Review*, 27: 283–321.

Marcos (EZLN's Subcomandante insurgente) (2004) 'El ridículo en horario triple A', *La Jornada*, Mexico, October 28.

Margolis, J. and Walsh, J. (2003) 'Misery loves companies: rethinking social initiatives by business', *Administrative Science Quarterly*, 48: 268–305.

Marichal, C. (2003) La deuda externa, in I. Bizberg and L. Meyer (eds) *Una historia contemporánea de México: Transformaciones y permanencias, Tomo 1*, Mexico: Océano, pp. 451–91.

Martín, V. (2003) *La era de la perplejidad. Una reflexión en torno a postmodernidad y empresa*, Alicante: Universidad de Alicante.

Maturana, H. (1990) *Emociones y lenguaje en educación y política*, Santiago de Chile: HACHETTE/CED.

May, W. W. (ed.) (1990) *Ethics in the Accounting Curriculum: Cases and Readings*, Sarasota, FL: American Accounting Association.

McElroy, M.W. (2002a) 'Ethics, innovation and the open enterprise', *Knowledge Management*, 6(1), 2 September.

McElroy, M.W. (2002b) *The New Knowledge Management: Complexity, Learning and Sustainable Innovation*, Boston, MA: KMCI Press, Butterworth-Heinemann.

Méndez, E. (2004a) 'Contribuyentes ya han pagado $483 mil 785 millones por deuda del rescate', *La Jornada*, Mexico, July 28.

Méndez, V. (2004b) *El filósofo y el mercader. Filosofía, derecho y economía en la obra de Adam Smith*, Mexico: Fondo de Cultura Económica.

Meyer H.-D. (2003) 'Between theory and experience: the dialogical nature of managerial knowledge – implications for the preparation of education leaders', *Journal of Educational Administration*, 41: 455–70.

Mezirow, J. (1985) 'A critical theory of self-directed learning', in S. Brookfield (ed.), *Self-directed Learning: From Theory to Practice*, San Francisco, CA: Jossey Bass.

Mezirow, J. (1991) *Transformative Dimensions of Adult Learning*, San Francisco, CA: Jossey Bass.

Mezirow, J. (2000) *Learning as Transformation*, San Francisco, CA: Jossey Bass.

Micklethwait, J. and Wooldridge, A. (2003) *Company: A Short History of a Revolutionary Idea*, New York: Modern Library.

Mignolo, W. (1999) *Local Histories/Global Designs: Coloniality, Subaltern Knowledges, and Border Thinking*, Princeton, NJ: Princeton University Press.

Mignolo, W. (2001) Introducción, in W. Mignolo (ed.), *Capitalismo y geopolítica del conocimiento: el eurocentrismo y la filosofía de la liberación en el debate intelectual contemporáneo*, Buenos Aires: Ediciones del Signo, pp. 9–53.

Mills, C.W. (1959/1970) *The Sociological Imagination*, Harmondsworth: Penguin.

Mises, L. von (1979) *Liberalism, a Socio-Economic Exposition*, New York: New York University Press.

Mitchell, N.J. (1989) *The Generous Corporation: A Political Analysis of Economic Power*, New Haven, CT: Yale University Press.

Monsiváis, C. (2002) La globalización y sus definiciones, in R. Corral and A. Rojas (eds), *México en la aldea global*, Mexico: Universidad Autónoma Metropolitana-Iztapalapa, pp. 13–28.

Morin, E. and Kern, A.B. (1998) *Homeland Earth: A Manifesto for the New Millennium*, New York: Hampton Press.

Mueller, F. (1994) 'Societal effect, organization effect and globalization', *Organization Studies*, 15: 407–23.

Muetzelfeldt, M. (2003) 'Market rationality, organisational rationality and professional rationality: experiences from the "Contract State"', in L. Briskman and M. Muetzelfeldt (eds), *Moving beyond Managerialism in Human Services*, Melbourne: RMIT Publishing.

Mulgan, R. (2005) *Outsourcing and Public Service Values: The Australian Experience*, Policy and Governance Program Discussion Paper 05-5, Asia Pacific School of Economics and Government, The Australian National University, Canberra, online, available at http://apseg.anu.edu.au/degrees/pogo/discussion_papers/PDP05-5.pdf, accessed 11 September 2005.

Munro, R. (1998) 'Ethics and accounting: the dual technologies of self', in M. Parker, (ed.), *Ethics and Organization*, London: Sage, pp. 197–220.

Murillo, J.A. (2002) 'La banca en México, privatización, crisis y reordenamiento', *VII Meeting of the Central Banks Research Network of the Americas*, Guatemala, Banco Central de Guatemala/CEMLA, online, available at www.cemla.org/RED-07-documentos.htm.

Murphy, J.B. (1993) *The Moral Economy of Labor. Aristotelian Themes in Economic Theory*, London: Yale University Press.

Nader, R., Green. M. and Seligman, J. (1976) *Taming the Giant Corporation*, New York: W.W. Norton.

Nancy, J.L. (1988) *L'expérience de la liberté*, Paris: Galilée.

Nancy, J.L. (1991) *The Inoperative Community*, Minneapolis, MN: University of Minnesota Press.

Nancy, J.L. (1996) *Être singulier pluriel*, Paris: Galilée.

Nancy, J.L. (1997) 'The insufficiency of "values" and the necessity of "sense"', *Cultural Values*, 1: 127–31.

Nancy, J.L. (2002) *De indringer*, Amsterdam: Boom.

Nancy, J.L. (2003) *A Finite Thinking*, Stanford, CA: Stanford University Press.

Närhi, K. (2004) *The Eco-social Approach to Social Work and the Challenges to the Expertise of Social Work*, Academy Dissertation, Faculty of Social Sciences, University of Jyväskylä: Jyväskylä.

Nash, L. (1981) 'Ethics without the sermon', *Harvard Business Review*, 59 (Nov.–Dec.): 79–90.

Nijhof, A., Cludts, S., Fisscher, O. and Laan, A. (2003) 'Measuring the implementation of codes of conduct: an assessment method based on a process approach of the responsible organization', *Journal of Business Ethics*, 45: 65–78.

O'Gorman, E. (1972) *The Invention of America: An Inquiry into the Historical Nature of the New World and the Meaning of its History*, Westport, CT: Greenwood.

Ong, A. (1987) *Spirits of Resistance and Capitalist Discipline: Factory Women in Malaysia*, Albany, NY: State University of New York Press.

Otero, G. (ed.) (1996) *Neoliberalism Revisited: Economic Restructuring and Mexico's Political Future*, London: Harper Collins.

Otero, G. (ed.) (2002) *Mexico in Transition: Neoliberal Globalism, the State and Civil Society*, London: Zed Books.

Paramio, L. (2003) *Perspectivas de la izquierda en América Latina*, Real Instituto Elcano de Estudios Internacionales y Estratégicos, Working Paper 6, online, available at www.realinstitutoelcano.org/documentos/37/37.pdf.

Parker, M. (2002) *Against Management*, Cambridge: Polity Press.

Parker, M. (ed.) (1998) *Ethics and Organizations*, London: Sage.

Perrow, C. (2002) *Organizing America: Wealth, Power and the Origins of Corporate Capitalism*, Princeton, NJ: Princeton University Press.

Perrow, C. (1991) 'A society of organizations', *Theory and Society*, 20: 725–62.

Phillip-Morris (2002) *Listening, Learning and Changing: The Path to Corporate Responsibility at Philip Morris Companies*, online, available at www.philipmorris.com/pressroom/executive_speeches/speech_nicoli_fresno.asp, accessed 1 August 2003.

Phillips, J.J. (1996) *Accountability in Human Resource Management*, Houston, TX: Gulf Publishing.

Phillips, L. (ed.) (1998) *The Third Wave of Modernization in Latin America: Cultural Perspectives on Neoliberalism*, Wilmington: Scholarly Resources.

Picciotto, S. and Campbell, D. (eds) (2002) *New Directions in Regulatory Theory*, Oxford: Blackwell.

Pickering, M.A. (1968) 'The company as a separate legal entity', *Modern Law Review* 31: 481.

Ramírez, M.D. (1995) 'The political economy of privatization in Mexico, 1983–92', *Organization*, 2: 87–116.

Rancière, J. (2003) *Short Voyages to the Land of the People*, Stanford, CA: Stanford University Press.

Rawls, J. (1971) *A Theory of Justice*, Oxford: Oxford University Press.

Regan, M.C. (1998) 'Corporate speech and civic virtue', in *Debating Democracy's Discontent: Essays on American Politics, Law and Public Philosophy*, Oxford: Oxford University Press.

Rifkin, J. (1999) *The Biotech Century: How Genetic Commerce will Change the World*, London: Phoenix.

Ritzer, G. (1995) *Expressing America: A Critique of the Global Credit Card Society*, London: Sage Publications.

Ritzer, G. (1998) *The McDonaldization Thesis: Explorations and Extensions*, London: Sage.

Ritzer, G. (1999) *Enchanting a Disenchanted World*, Thousand Oaks, CA: Pine Forge Press.

Ritzer, G. (2001) *Explorations in the Sociology of Consumption*, London: Sage.

Ritzer, G. (2004a) *The McDonaldization of Society: Revised New Century Edition*, Thousand Oaks, CA: Pine Forge Press.

Ritzer, G. (2004b) *The Globalization of Nothing*. Thousand Oaks, CA: Pine Forge Press.

Rizzi, B. (1985) *Bureaucratization of the World*, New York: Simon and Schuster.

Roberts, J. (2003) 'The manufacture of corporate social responsibility: constructing corporate sensibility', *Organization*, 10: 249–65.

Roy, W.G. (1997) *Socializing Capital: The Rise of the Large Industrial Corporation in America*, Princeton, NJ: Princeton University Press.

Royle, T. (2000) *Working for McDonald's in Europe: The Unequal Struggle?*, London: Routledge.

Sampson, A. (1995) *Company Man: The Rise and Fall of Corporate Life*, London: Times Business/Random House.

Sandel, M. (1982) *Liberalism and the Limits of Justice*, Cambridge: Cambridge University Press.

Santillán, R.J. (2001) 'The Mexican banking sector: recent past and current situation', Monterrey: EGADE-ITESM, online, available at http://cetai.hec.ca/ny/cases/Mexican_B_Sys2001.pdf.

Sarukhán, J. and Whyte, A. (eds) (2005) *Millennium Ecosystem Assessment Synthesis Report*, Malaysia: Millennium Ecosystem Assessment.

Scharpf, F.W. (1993) 'Coordination in hierarchies and networks', in F.W. Scharpf (ed.), *Games in Hierarchies and Networks, Analytical and Empirical Approaches*, Frankfurt am Main: Campus Verlag; Boulder, CO: Westview Press.

Schultz, H. and Jones, D. (1997) *Pour your Heart into it: How Starbucks Built a Company one Cup at a Time*, New York: Hyperion.

Selznick, P. (1992) *The Moral Commonwealth: Social Theory and the Promise of Community*, Berkeley, CA: University of California Press.

SEP (2003) *Informe nacional sobre la educación superior en México*, Mexico: SESIC/IESALC/UNESCO.

Sevares, J. (2003) *El capitalismo criminal. Gobiernos, bancos y empresas en las redes del delito global*, Buenos Aires: Norma.

Shapiro, S.P. (1987) 'The social control of impersonal trust', *American Journal of Sociology*, 93: 623–58.

Shiva, V. (2001) *Protect or Plunder: Understanding Intellectual Property Rights*, London: Zed Books.

Singer, P. (2002) *One World: The Ethics of Globalization*, New Haven, CT: Yale University Press.

Sloterdijjk, P. (1995) *Europa, mocht het ooit wakker worden*, Amsterdam: De Arbeiders Pers.

Sloterdijk, P. (1999) *Sphären I: Blasen*, Frankfurt am Main: Suhrkamp.

Sloterdijk, P. (2004) *Sphären III: Schaum*, Frankfurt am Main: Suhrkamp.

Smart, G. (1999) 'Storytelling in a central bank', *Journal of Business and Technical Communication*, 13: 249–74.

Smith, A. (2000) *Theory of Moral Sentiments*, New York: Prometheus Books.

Snell, R.S. (2000) 'Studying moral ethos using an adapted Kohlbergian model', *Organization Studies*, 21: 267–95.

Solomon, R. (1992) 'Corporate roles, personal virtues: an Aristotelian approach to business ethics', *Business Ethics Quarterly*, 2: 317–39.

Solomon, R. (1993) *Ethics and Excellence: Cooperation and Integrity in Business*, Oxford: Oxford University Press.

Solomon, R. (2004) 'Aristotle, ethics, and business organizations', *Organization Studies*, 25: 1021–43.

Solzhenitsyn, A.I. (1973) *The Gulag Archipelago 1918–1956: An Experiment in Literary Investigation*, New York: Harper and Row.

Stalder, F. (1997) *Actor-network Theory and Communication Networks: Towards Convergence*, online, available at http://felix.openflows.org/html/Network_Theory.html.

Stark, A. (1993) 'What's the matter with business ethics?', *Harvard Business Review* May–June: 38–48.

Stokes, J. and Clegg, S.R. (2002) 'Once upon a time in a bureaucracy', *Organization*, 9: 225–48.

Strauss, G. (2003) 'CEOs still sitting on piles of pay', *USA Today*, August 25, C3.

Swain, J. and Walker, C. (2003) 'Parent–professional power relations: parent and professional perspectives', *Disability and Society*, 18: 547–60

Tatnall, A. and Gilding, A. (1999) *Actor-network Theory and Information Systems Research*, 10th Australasian Conference on Information Systems.

Tatz, C. (1982) *Aborigines and Uranium and Other Essays*, Victoria: Heinemann Educational Australia.

Taylor, C. (1989) *Sources of the Self: The Making of Modern Identity*, Cambridge: Cambridge University Press.

ten Bos, R. (1997) 'Business ethics and Bauman ethics', *Organization Studies*, 18: 997–1014.

ten Bos, R. and R. Kaulingfreks (2002) 'Interfaces', *Theory, Culture and Society*, 19: 139–51.

Thompson, D.F. (2005) *Restoring Responsibility: Ethics in Government, Business, and Healthcare*, Cambridge: Cambridge University Press.

Tönnies, A. (2001) *Community and Civil Society*, Cambridge: Cambridge University Press.

Treviño, L.K. and G.R. Weaver (1999) 'The stakeholder research tradition: converging theorists – not convergent theory', *Academy of Management Review*, 24: 222–7.

Tugendhat, E. (1993) *Vorlesungen über Ethik*, Frankfurt am Main: Suhrkamp.

Underhill, P. (1999) *Why we Buy: The Science of Shopping*, New York: Simon and Schuster.

van Doorn, J.A.A. (1956) *Sociologie van de Organisatie*, Leiden: H.E. Stenfert Kroese.

van Iterson, A., Mastenbroek, W., Newton, T. and Smith, D. (eds) (2002) *The Civilized Organization: Norbert Elias and the Future of Organization Studies*, Amsterdam: John Benjamins.

van Krieken, R. (1996) 'Proto-governmentalization and the historical formation of organizational subjectivity', *Economy and Society*, 25: 195–221.

van Krieken, R. (1998) *Norbert Elias*, London: Routledge.

van Krieken, R. (1999) 'The barbarism of civilization: cultural genocide and the "stolen generations"', *British Journal of Sociology*, 50: 297–315.

van Krieken, R. (1989) 'Social discipline and state formation: Weber and Oestreich on the historical sociology of subjectivity', *Amsterdams Sociologisch Tijdschrift*, 17: 3–28.

van Vree, W. (1999) *Meetings, Manners and Civilization: The Development of Modern Meeting Behaviour*, London: Leicester University Press.

Vodovnik, Z. (ed.) (2004) *Ya basta!: Ten Years of the Zapatista Uprising. Writings of Subcomandante Insurgente Marcos*, Edinburgh: AK Press.

Volpi, J. (2004) *La guerra y las palabras. Una historia intelectual de 1994*, Mexico: Era.

Waddock, S. (2001) 'Integrity and mindfulness: foundations of corporate citizenship', in J. Andriof and M. McIntosh (eds), *Perspectives on corporate citizenship*, Sheffield: Greenleaf Publishing, pp. 26–38.

Walsham, G. (1997) 'Actor-network theory and IS research: current status and future prospects', in A. Lee, J. Liebenau and J. DeGross (eds), *Information Systems and Qualitative Research*, New York: Chapman and Hall.

Watson, D. (2003) *Death Sentence: The Decay of Public Language*, Milsons Point, NSW: Knopf.

Watson, D. (2004) *Watson's Dictionary of Weasel Words, Contemporary Cliches, Cant and Management Jargon*, Milsons Point, NSW: Knopf.

WCED (World Commission for Economic Development) (1987) *Our Common Future*, New York: Oxford University Press.

Weber, M. (1930) *The Protestant Ethic and the Spirit of Capitalism*, London: Allen and Unwin.

Weber, M. (1948) 'Politics as a vocation', in H.H. Gerth and C. Wright Mills (eds), *From Max Weber: Essays in Sociology*, London: Routledge and Kegan Paul, pp. 77–128.

Weber, M. (1976) *The Protestant Ethic and The Spirit of Capitalism*, London: Allen and Unwin.

Weber, M. (1978) *Economy and Society*, Berkeley, CA: University of California Press.

Whyte, W.H. (1960) *The Organization Man*, Harmondsworth: Penguin Books.

Wilber, K. (1997) 'An integral theory of consciousness', *Journal of Consciousness Studies*, 4: 71–92.

Willmott, H. (1995) 'What has been happening in organization theory and does it matter?', *Personnel Review*, 24: 33–53.

Windsor, D. (2001) 'Corporate citizenship: evolution and interpretation', in J. Andriof and M. McIntosh (eds), *Perspectives on Corporate Citizenship*, Sheffield: Greenleaf Publishing, pp. 39–52.

Winn, P. (ed.) (2004) *Victims of the Chilean Miracle: Workers and Neoliberalism in the Pinochet Era, 1973–2002*, Durham, NC: Duke University Press.

Wood, D. (1991) 'Corporate social performance revisited', *Academy of Management Review*, 16: 691–718.

World Bank (2004) *Poverty in Mexico: An Assessment of Conditions, Trends and Government Strategy*, Washington, DC: The International Bank for Reconstruction and Development/The World Bank.

Wouters, C. (1986) 'Formalization and informalization: changing tension balances in civilizing processes', *Theory, Culture and Society*, 3: 1–18.

Wouters, C. (1999) 'Changing patterns of social controls and self-controls: on the rise of crime since the 1950s and the sociogenesis of a "third nature"', *British Journal of Criminology*, 39: 416–32.

Yack, B. (1999) 'Community and conflict in Aristotle's political philosophy', in R. Bartlett and S. Collins (eds), *Action and Contemplation: Studies in the Moral and Political Thought of Aristotle*, Albany, NY: State University of New York Press, pp. 273–92.

Zapatista (1998) *Documentary Film*, Cambridge, MA: Big Noise Films.

Zea, L. (1996) *Fin de siglo XX ¿Centuria Perdida?*, Mexico: Fondo de Cultura Económica.

Zeraffa, M. (1976) *Fictions: The Novel and Social Reality*, Harmondsworth: Penguin.

Zermeño, S. (2005) *La desmodernidad mexicana y las alternativas a la violencia y a la exclusión en nuestros días*, Mexico: Océano.

Ziebland, S., Chapple, A., Dumelow, C., Evans, J., Prinjha, S. and Rozmovits, L. (2004) 'How the internet affects patients' experience of cancer: a qualitative study', *British Medical Journal*, 6 March 2004, 328 (7439): 564.

Ziegler, J. (2003) *Los nuevos amos del mundo*, Madrid: Destino.

Zimmerman, D.H. (1971) 'The practicalities of rule-use', in J.D. Douglas (ed.), *Understanding Everyday Life: Toward the Reconstruction of Sociological Knowledge*, London: Routledge and Kegan Paul.

Žižek, S. (2005a) 'Beyond discourse analysis', in *Interrogating the Real*, London: Continuum, pp. 271–84.

Index